*With the Master*

# HOLDING FAST TO THE TRUTH

A WOMEN'S BIBLE STUDY
ON 2 TIMOTHY

SUSAN J. HECK

316Publishing.com

Printed in Korea
28 27 26 25 24 / 1 2 3 4 5

ISBN: 978-1-63664-318-2

***To James and Erin Coates*** who held fast to the truth of God's Word, amidst persecution and suffering. May we learn from their example that it is better to suffer for doing what is right than to suffer for doing what is wrong.

Susan Heck's Bible study on 2 Timothy is nothing short of transformative. Excellently composed, it engages both new and seasoned believers with deep verse-by-verse insights. With clarity and profound truth, Susan explores critical topics such as assurance of salvation, overcoming the fear of man, and the importance of spiritual disciplines. Her teachings on motherhood and submission—grounded in a life faithfully lived out—inspire and equip women to embrace the full blessed life God intends. This study is a treasure trove for any woman looking to deepen her faith and walk in obedience to God's call.

**Bre Wood,** Homemaker, Pastor's Wife
Co-host of "Date Night with the Woods" Podcast

With steadfast conviction to the Word of God, Susan Heck has become one of the foremost women of our day for teaching and discipling women in the Scriptures. By God's grace, Susan has been a wonderful Bible teacher at Grace Community Church of Tulsa for many years, discipling women not only through her weekly ministries at the church but also through her books and speaking opportunities around the world. It is a privilege to commend to you the ministry of Susan Heck and specifically this resource on 2 Timothy, which is merely an outflow from her ministry among the ladies of our local church. As her pastor, I highly recommend this resource for you or your women's ministry.

**Matt Turkington,** Pastor
Grace Community Church of Tulsa Oklahoma

Susan clearly believes in the power of the Word of God to change and mold people into the image of Christ. It is also clear that Susan believes in the authority of the Word of God as our sole rule for living. These beliefs come out in this excellent study on 2 Timothy. Susan is unashamedly biblical as she carefully explains each text to help the reader understand what the author (Paul) meant when he wrote it, and then as she skillfully applies each text to the reader in a manner that is challenging, encouraging, and convicting. Not only does Susan do an excellent and careful job of this, but the questions at the end of each chapter will help solidify the biblical information and the ways of applying it to the reader. I highly recommend this study for women.

**Jon Kile**, Pastor
Faith Community Church of Vacaville California

If you're looking for a women's Bible teacher who is faithful to the Scriptures and offers practical applications for everyday life, look no further than Susan Heck. Her work on 2 Timothy is exceptional, reflecting a deep commitment to biblical truth and a compassionate, nurturing approach often laced with humor. Susan is a reliable mentor, model, and guide for countless women, and her teachings indeed bless the body of Christ.

**Tony Wood,** Teaching Pastor
Mission Bible Church of Orange County California

Susan Heck is just the right person to reflect on Paul's final words to his disciple Timothy. Like Paul, she is a lifelong student of the Word and a steadfast disciple-maker pouring out her life for the gospel. As a seasoned woman of God, her study is both careful and warm-hearted, both substantial and practical. It will feed your faith, nourish your hope, and strengthen your spiritual resolve. I love that no matter the trends, Susan always seeks to go with the Word instead of going with the flow. Most importantly, I have seen her life up close for more than 25 years, and her life matches her words.

**David "Gunner" Gundersen**, Pastor
BridgePoint Bible Church of Houston Texas

In a time where many churches are severely lacking in expository teaching of God's Word, Susan is a gift to the church and specifically to the ministry of Christian women. Her study of God's Word, and the clarity with which she writes and teaches, is evident on each page of her book. She carefully exposes the meaning of each verse in the proper context in which it was written and draws the heart of the reader to apply the deep truths of the Scripture. As a fellow pastor's wife, director of Women's Ministry, and friend of Susan, I am grateful to have resources like this to recommend to women without any hesitation concerning error in her life and doctrine. Susan applies the truths that she so effectively teaches and I am confident that women who read this book will know and love Christ more after spending time in this excellent study through the book of 2 Timothy.

**Tiffany Kile**, Pastor's Wife
Director of Women's Ministry, Faith Community Church
of Vacaville California

# TABLE OF CONTENTS

# Introduction: The Person of Christ and the Promise of Life

*2 Timothy 1:1–2*

ACCORDING to a recent study, only 37% of Americans attend church, and the statistics indicate that the percentage is decreasing with every passing year. We can only speculate as to why this is. Perhaps the busyness of life has drowned out any thoughts of God or eternity. Maybe it's the excuse often given that there are too many hypocrites in the church. It could be the continual defaming of God's name by Christian leaders who have fallen morally or doctrinally. It might be that the church has become a place where we are entertained instead of educated, a place where we amuse ourselves instead of adoring God.

As concerned as I am about the vacating of the church by Americans, there is a concern I have that is much greater: the departure from the Word of God by so many who are still left in the church. There is a famine for the Word of the Lord in our land, and it is *not* because we lack plenty of Bibles to read from; it is because there are few shepherds willing to read and teach the Bible to their parishioners. I thought it ironic that the very day I wrote this chapter, my husband received a birthday card from one of our parishioners, which read: "Praying for many more years of hearing you teach expositionally because you are the only one doing it and you do it so well." Have the pastors of our day forgotten their charge to preach the Word and to hold fast to sound teaching? Have they forgotten that they are to pass the baton of truth down to the next generation of men who will be called by God to shepherd the flock? We are living in an age in which we can plainly see the truth of Jesus' words in Luke 18:8b (LSB): "when the Son of Man comes, will He find that faith on the earth?"

My dear friend, we must reclaim the call to hold fast to the Word of God. And I know of no other book in the Word of God that will stir us up to this aim more than Paul's second letter to Timothy. You cannot read this short epistle without hearing Paul's heart, as he pours out strong and impassioned words to his son in the faith. John R. Stott put it well,

> The church of our day urgently needs to heed the message of this second letter of Paul to Timothy. For all around us we see Christians and churches relaxing their grasp of the gospel, fumbling it, in danger of letting it drop from their hands altogether. A new generation of young Timothys is needed, who will guard the sacred deposit of the gospel, who are determined to proclaim it and are prepared to suffer for it, and who will pass it on pure and uncorrupted to the generation which in due course will rise up to follow them.[1]

This letter to Timothy, Paul's dear son in the faith, is warm and tender. Several years ago, when I was speaking at a conference, a young woman quoted from memory this entire letter to us, one chapter before each of my four sessions. I was so moved by the passion and heartfelt manner in which she recited it, that I could picture in my mind Paul's love for his son Timothy and the concern Paul had that his spiritual son would hold fast to the truth. It is nearly impossible to read Paul's letter and not be moved by it. One man says of it,

> This letter is personal throughout. Tender, yet with the tenderness of a strong, heroic heart. It is far from being sentimental. Timothy may have read and reread it with tears blurring his eyes, but every line braced him with power to make him valiant to contend in the noble contest, to receive at his own death the crown laid up also for him.[2]

Before we examine the first two verses of this book, which was inspired by God, let's consider some information that will be helpful to us in understanding 2 Timothy as a whole. Let's ask and answer some vital questions about this epistle. First, let's ask: *Who wrote this epistle?* We know that Paul wrote this letter because we clearly see him asserting

1 John R. W. Stott, *The Message of 2 Timothy* (Downers Grove: InterVarsity Press. 1973), 22.

2 R. C. H. Lenski, *The Interpretation of St. Paul's Epistles to the Colossians, to the Thessalonians, to Timothy, to Titus, and Philemon* (Minneapolis: Augsburg Fortress, 2008), 739.

his authorship in verse 1. This letter is one of the 13 New Testament books Paul wrote (or 14, if you think he wrote Hebrews).

A second question we should ask is: *To whom was this letter written?* We can see from verse 2 that Paul wrote this letter to Timothy. At the time of this letter's writing, Timothy was still in Ephesus, but it was Paul's desire that Timothy come to him. In 2 Timothy 4:21a, Paul wrote, "Do your utmost to come before winter." And before that, Paul wrote, in 2 Timothy 4:9-11, "Be diligent to come to me quickly; for Demas has forsaken me, having loved this present world, and has departed for Thessalonica—Crescens for Galatia, Titus for Dalmatia. Only Luke is with me. Get Mark and bring him with you, for he is useful to me for ministry." We see from these verses that not only was it Paul's desire for Timothy to come to him, but also that Luke was with Paul at the time. In addition to understanding this letter was written to Timothy, we can conclude that it was intended for the benefit of the church at Ephesus, where Timothy was the pastor. And, by extension, we can also conclude that it was intended for the universal church of God—of which you and I are a part.

Two more questions we should ask of this letter include: *Where was Paul when he wrote 2 Timothy?* And *When did Paul write 2 Timothy?* Paul was in his final imprisonment when he wrote this letter, and the year was about 66 or 67 A.D. He expected to be put to death soon, as evidenced by what he said in 4:6-8:

> For I am already being poured out as a drink offering, and the time of my departure is at hand. I have fought the good fight, I have finished the race, I have kept the faith. Finally, there is laid up for me the crown of righteousness, which the Lord, the righteous Judge, will give to me on that Day, and not to me only but also to all who have loved His appearing.

In fact, only a few short months after writing this letter, Paul would be beheaded by Nero. It is interesting to note that Nero committed suicide not long after he had Paul beheaded. Nero was a wicked ruler and was responsible for the killing of many Christians. He was so evil that even his own people considered him a wicked ruler and eventually rebelled against him. Given that these are the final words Paul wrote, it should be of great interest to us to consider what was in the heart of this apostle, one sent by God and inspired by the Holy Spirit to write these very words.

A fifth and final question we should ask about this epistle is: *Why did Paul write this letter?* The reason Paul wrote this letter was to encourage Timothy to hold fast to the truth. This is the theme of 2 Timothy: Hold fast to the truth! We can easily see this theme running throughout the letter. For example, in chapter one, verses 13-14, we read:

> Hold fast the pattern of sound words which you have heard from me, in faith and love which are in Christ Jesus. That good thing which was committed to you, keep by the Holy Spirit who dwells in us.

In chapter two, verse 15, Paul writes,

> Be diligent to present yourself approved to God, a worker who does not need to be ashamed, rightly dividing the word of truth.

In chapter three, Paul admonishes Timothy again, in verses 14-17,

> But you must continue in the things which you have learned and been assured of, knowing from whom you have learned them, and that from childhood you have known the Holy Scriptures, which are able to make you wise for salvation through faith which is in Christ Jesus. All Scripture is given by inspiration of God, and is profitable for doctrine, for reproof, for correction, for instruction in righteousness, that the man of God may be complete, thoroughly equipped for every good work.

And from chapter four, Paul's heart can be heard again as he writes in verses 2-5,

> Preach the word! Be ready in season and out of season. Convince, rebuke, exhort, with all longsuffering and teaching. For the time

> will come when they will not endure sound doctrine, but according to their own desires, because they have itching ears, they will heap up for themselves teachers; and they will turn their ears away from the truth, and be turned aside to fables. But you be watchful in all things, endure afflictions, do the work of an evangelist, fulfill your ministry.

Oh, dear one, if there is a message that needs to be heeded today, it is the message of 2 Timothy: *Hold fast to the truth!* Let's consider the first two verses of this epistle together.

> Paul, an apostle of Jesus Christ by the will of God, according to the promise of life which is in Christ Jesus, To Timothy, a beloved son: Grace, mercy, and peace from God the Father and Christ Jesus our Lord.

Our outline for this chapter will include: *The Persons Mentioned in this Letter* (vv 1a, 2a); *The Promise Mentioned in this Letter* (v 1b); and *The Peace Mentioned in this Letter* (v 2b).

## The Persons Mentioned in this Letter *2 Timothy 1:1-2*

> Paul, an apostle of Jesus Christ by the will of God, (2 Timothy 1:1a)

The first person we see mentioned in this letter is *Paul*. Who is he? We know from this verse that he is *an apostle*, which means he is an ambassador of the gospel. Paul mentions this in Romans 11:13 (LSB), where he writes, "But I am speaking to you who are Gentiles. Inasmuch then as I am an apostle of Gentiles, I magnify my ministry." We also have the account in Acts of God saving Paul on the road to Damascus, and in Acts 9:15-16 (LSB) we read, "But the Lord said to him, 'Go, for he is a chosen instrument of Mine, to bear My name before the Gentiles and kings and the sons of Israel; for I will show him how much he must suffer for My name.'" We must keep in mind that part of being a messenger of the gospel is suffering. We must be willing to endure suffering with Him if we would desire to reign with Him, as Paul explains to us in 2 Timothy 2:12.

Paul makes it clear that he is not just an apostle, but an apostle *of Jesus Christ*. *Jesus Christ* is the Messiah, the One who was anointed by God. *Jesus* is the second person mentioned in this introduction. But there is a third person mentioned, and that is *God*. Paul makes it clear that he's an apostle of Jesus Christ, but this was *by the will of God*. God made a determinative choice to make Paul an apostle, which is what the word *will* means. It is similar to what we see in Jeremiah 1:5 (LSB), where God told Jeremiah, "Before I formed you in the innermost parts I knew you, and before you came out from the womb I set you apart; I have given you as a prophet to the nations."

## The Promise Mentioned in this Letter *2 Timothy 1:1*

> according to the promise of life which is in Christ Jesus, (2 Timothy 1:1b)

Paul explains that his apostleship is *according to the promise of life*. The word *promise* means a divine assurance of good, and the word *life* refers to eternal life. The gospel, my friend, is a promise by God of a life that is guaranteed and kept safe by God. Keep in mind that, in this greeting to Timothy, Paul is rehearsing the fact that he was called to be an apostle to preach the gospel, and he is tying that apostleship to this *promise of life*. He mentions this same reality to the church at Ephesus in Ephesians 3:6-7 (LSB),

> that the Gentiles are fellow heirs and fellow members of the body, and fellow partakers of the promise in Christ Jesus through the gospel, of which I was made a minister, according to the gift of God's grace which was given to me according to the working of His power.

Sometimes we get the odd idea that we are called to carry out some grand plan of our own, but as daughters of the King, our mission (like Paul's) is to carry forth the gospel, the truth, the promise of life to all who believe.

It's worth noting here that Paul brings up this promise of life in his opening words to Timothy. Paul knows that his death is awaiting him, something he is clear about in 4:6-8, where he says that the time appointed for his departure has come (especially note verse 8). He knows that to depart from this world meant he would be present with Christ. No doubt, his spiritual son Timothy would be sorrowful at the thought of losing his mentor, but Paul comforts his son in the faith with the hope of the promise of life eternal. This promise of life eternal isn't only for Paul as he faces death, but it is for Timothy as he faces life without Paul, a life of holding fast to the truth amidst opposition. Timothy needs to remember that this eternal life *is* only *in Christ Jesus*. He is the only way, the only truth, the only life. There is no eternal life apart from Him.

We've noted a few of the persons Paul has mentioned in his opening address: Jesus, God, and Paul. The promise Paul has mentioned is life eternal. Now, in verse 2, Paul mentions another person in the opening to his letter.

## The Persons Mentioned in this Letter *2 Timothy 1:1-2*

> To Timothy, a beloved son: (2 Timothy 1:2a)

Here, we see yet another person Paul mentions, and this time it is *Timothy*. Who is Timothy? It is assumed by most scholars that Paul and Barnabas met Timothy while they were on their first missionary journey, and that he was converted at that time. Timothy was chosen by Paul to accompany him while Paul was on his second missionary journey, probably because others had spoken well of Timothy (Acts 16:2). Acts 16:1-4 reveals to us that Timothy was one of Paul's co-laborers. And, according to 2 Timothy 1:3-5 and 3:14-15, Timothy's mother and grandmother had a tremendous spiritual influence on him. (That should be an encouragement to you and me as we invest in the lives of our children and grandchildren. Who knows? We might be influencing a Timothy!) In Paul epistles, Timothy is mentioned 18 times. He was prone to frequent stomach problems and struggled with fear and timidity. But, this, too, should greatly encourage us; God uses ordinary men and women to accomplish His purposes. Despite the celebrity culture rampant in the church today, there are no super-Christians.

Here, in verse 2 of Paul's introductory words to Timothy, Paul calls Timothy *a beloved son*. The words mean dearly-loved son, and it's interesting to note that Paul uses the Greek word *teknon* here, which refers to a child one produces. However, we know that Paul was not related to Timothy; rather, Paul looked at Timothy as a son. That's how it is in the family of God. Often, our Christian family becomes closer to us than our physical family. Jesus felt this way too. Consider what He says in Matthew 12:46-50 (LSB),

> While He was still speaking to the crowds, behold, His mother and brothers were standing outside, seeking to speak to Him. Now someone said to Him, "Behold, Your mother and Your brothers are standing outside seeking to speak to You." But Jesus answered the one who was telling Him and said, "Who is My mother and who are My brothers?" And stretching out His hand toward His disciples, He said, "Behold My mother and My brothers! For whoever does the will of My Father who is in heaven, he is My brother and sister and mother."

In another place, Jesus even tells us that if we lose our physical family in this life, we will gain a hundredfold more. Mark 10:28-30 (LSB) reads,

> Peter began to say to Him, "Behold, we have left everything and followed You." Jesus said, "Truly I say to you, there is no one who has left house or brothers or sisters or mother or father or children or farms, for My sake and for the gospel's sake, except one who will receive one hundred times as much now in the present age—houses and brothers and sisters and mothers and children and farms, along with persecutions—and in the age to come, eternal life."

This letter to Timothy is full of tenderness. No doubt, Paul wanted Timothy to be assured of Paul's love, especially knowing that he would likely soon be gone. Paul also wanted to pass down the spiritual baton to Timothy, something that becomes clear in the second chapter of this letter. At this point, Paul had been preaching the gospel for some 30 years, and he wanted to make sure someone who was faithful would take that baton and continue to teach others.

As we think about the persons mentioned in these first two verses, Paul, Jesus, God, and Timothy, we must note that Jesus is primarily on Paul's mind as he faces his death. Three times Paul mentions Jesus' name in these two short verses. Paul's hope was in Christ alone and Paul knew that to be absent from his body would mean to be present with the Lord (2 Corinthians 5:8). In his unconverted state, Paul had not only witnessed the stoning of Stephen but had given approval to it as well (Acts 7) and knew that what had passed from Stephen's lips at his death would be true for Paul as well. Acts 7:54-8:1a (LSB) reminds us of this,

> Now when they heard this, they became furious in their hearts, and they began gnashing their teeth at him. But being full of the Holy Spirit, he gazed intently into heaven and saw the glory of God, and Jesus standing at the right hand of God; and he said, "Behold, I see the heavens opened up and the Son of Man standing at the right hand of God." But crying out with a loud voice, they covered their ears and rushed at him with one accord. And when they had driven him out of the city, they began stoning him; and the witnesses laid aside their garments at the feet of a young man named Saul. They went on stoning Stephen as he was calling out and saying, "Lord Jesus, receive my spirit!" Then falling on his knees, he cried out with a loud voice, "Lord, do not hold this sin against them!" And having said this, he fell asleep. Now Saul was in hearty agreement with putting him to death.

Fixing one's eyes on Jesus is imperative in life, especially when we are facing the end.

## The Peace Mentioned in this Letter *2 Timothy 1:2*

> Grace, mercy, and peace from God the Father and Christ Jesus our Lord. (2 Timothy 1:2b)

Next, we find the triad greeting of *grace, mercy and peace* that marks all of Paul's pastoral letters. *Grace* is a spiritually divine influence upon the heart which grants forgiveness; an undeserved favor. *Mercy* is compassion which delivers us from the misery of our sin. *Peace* is that quietness and rest of the soul which is the result of having received grace and mercy. Peace is not a feeling but, rather, a condition of one's soul. At the time of 2 Timothy's writing, this triad of grace, mercy, and peace would be much needed for our brother Paul. He calls himself the chief of sinners and was a murderer of Christians before the Lord saved him. As Paul faces his final days, his past may haunt him, but he must remember that God's *grace* has granted forgiveness to even this chief of sinners. Paul also wrestled with his sin; in Romans 7, he recounts the good he wants to do, yet doesn't do, and the evil he doesn't want to do, yet too often does. As he faces his final days, his fight against sin may haunt him, but he must remember God's *mercy* has delivered even him from the misery of his sin. Paul recounts often the false brethren of his day who were continually undermining his ministry; the thorn in his side he begged God to take away; the numerous persecutions that mark so many of his letters. As he faces his final days, he must not allow himself to dwell on those things from his past and their potential for spiritual unrest, but he must allow the *peace* of God to rule his soul, even in the face of death. But notice, my friend, these three things—grace, mercy, and peace—come *from God the Father and Christ Jesus our Lord. God the Father* means one who is in supreme authority and yet is our parent. He is our Abba Father, our Papa Daddy, as Paul mentions in Romans 8:14-15 (LSB), "For as many as are being led by the Spirit of God, these are sons of God. For you have not received a spirit of slavery leading to fear again, but you have received the Spirit of adoption as sons by whom we cry out, 'Abba! Father!'"

But you and I are also promised these things from Christ Jesus our Lord. Peace was promised by Jesus in the upper room before He went to the cross: "Peace I leave with you; My peace I give to you; not as the world gives do I give to you. Do not let your heart be troubled, nor let it be fearful." (John 14:27, LSB).

Notice that Paul is clear to Timothy, to the church at Ephesus, and to all Christians, that Jesus Christ is *Lord*. In fact, Paul says *our Lord*. Jesus is supreme in authority over our lives. Before we go on, I would be negligent if I did not explain this further. Since so many today are not holding fast to the truth, and especially the truth of the Lordship of Christ, I want to be clear on what the term Lord means. Lord is a word which means master or owner. Many in our day love the fact that Jesus is their Savior, but to acknowledge that He is their Lord and Master is not so wonderful to them. Yet, in the New Testament, the term Savior is mentioned only 24 times, while the term Lord is used more than 600 times in regard to Jesus. Acts 16:31b (LSB) is clear: "Believe in the Lord Jesus, and you will be saved." This means that when an individual becomes a believer, a Christian, he takes on a new Lord. That person is no longer the master of his or her own life but is now yielded to a new master: the Lord Jesus Christ. This, my friend, is truly liberating! I no longer am a slave to my own fleshly desires, but I am a slave to His desires, and I delight to do His will. I have been made dead to my old life and have been raised to a new life, a life in Christ Jesus my Lord. This means I repent of my sins; I turn away from them; I choose to walk in obedience to His Lordship. To some, this idea of Christ being our Lord is offensive. But we would do well to remind ourselves of the sobering message of Philippians 2:5-11 (LSB):

> Have this way of thinking in yourselves which was also in Christ Jesus, who, although existing in the form of God, did not regard equality with God a thing to be grasped, but emptied Himself, by taking the form of a slave, by being made in the likeness of men. Being found in appearance as a man, He humbled Himself by becoming obedient to the point of death, even death on a cross. Therefore, God also highly exalted Him, and bestowed on Him the name which is above every name, so that at the name of Jesus every knee will bow, of those who are in heaven and on earth and under the earth, and that every tongue will confess that Jesus Christ is Lord, to the glory of God the Father.

One day, every knee will bow to Christ's Lordship. I would rather bow my knee to Him in this life than to wait for the life to come, because those who wait till that day will be cast into everlasting punishment in hell. Some will object to this and say, "Well, I like the idea of taking Him as Savior, but I'm not really ready to make Him the Lord of my life." Well, Jesus warns of that kind of thinking too. He says in Luke 6:46-49 (LSB):

> Now why do you call Me, "Lord, Lord," and do not do what I say? Everyone who comes to Me and hears My words and does them, I will show you whom he is like: he is like a man building a house, who dug and went deep, and laid a foundation on the rock; and when a flood occurred, the river burst against that house and could not shake it, because it had been well built. But the one who heard and did not do accordingly, is like a man who built a house on the ground without any foundation; and the river burst against it and immediately it collapsed, and the ruin of that house was great.

Do you see why Paul makes it crystal clear in his opening that Jesus Christ is Lord? If Jesus is not Lord, then why should Timothy—or anyone else—hold fast to His truth? In my opinion, this failure to acknowledge Jesus as Lord is *the* reason why we are seeing the rapid decline of holding fast to the truth among professing Christians. We have left the most important truth: that Jesus is Lord! And because we have left the truth of His Lordship, we have left the truth of His Word. But He *is* Lord and His word *is* truth, and we are commanded to hold fast to what we have been taught: to preach the Word, to study the Word, and to live the Word.

## Summary

In these first couple of verses in Paul's final letter to Timothy, we have seen the persons Paul mentioned: Paul, Jesus, God, and Timothy. Two are finite beings; two are infinite beings. We have seen the promise Paul mentioned: that of life eternal—and I trust that if you do not have the assurance of life eternal, you will soon bow your knee and call upon the name of the Lord. (You can refer to the gospel presentation at the back of this book.) Lastly, we have seen the peace Paul mentioned. Peace is the result of having received the grace and mercy shown to us from God our Father through our Lord Jesus Christ. Does the peace of God rule in your heart? If today you are facing sorrow over the prospect of losing someone you love, like Timothy was, or any other difficulty, as a daughter of the King, you can bank on the person of Christ, the promise of eternal life, and the peace of God.

There is a song I've grown to love, entitled "He Will Hold Me Fast," which reminds me of the unshakable truths we've been considering. This beautiful song was first written in 1906. Additional lyrics and a more modern tune have been added in recent years, I encourage you to look up the modern rendition by Matthew Merker. Here are the original stanzas:

> When I fear my faith will fail, Christ will hold me fast;
> When the tempter would prevail, He can hold me fast.
>
> *Refrain*
> He will hold me fast, He will hold me fast;
> For my Savior loves me so, He will hold me fast.
>
> I could never keep my hold, He will hold me fast;
> For my love is often cold, He must hold me fast.
>
> I am precious in His sight, He will hold me fast;
> Those He saves are His delight. He will hold me fast.
>
> He'll not let my soul be lost, Christ will hold me fast;
> Bought by Him at such a cost, He will hold me fast.[3]

He is, indeed, holding fast those who are His. But, my friend, are you holding fast to the truth? We are living in an age where there is an ever-growing departure from the truth, and you and I must reclaim that truth! Paul's second letter to Timothy is a much-needed source of truth for our age. Will you join me, with our Master, as we together determine to hold fast to the truth?

---

3 Ada Ruth Habershon. "He Will Hold Me Fast." Public Domain, 1906.

# QUESTIONS TO CONSIDER

1. (a) Read 2 Timothy 1:1-2 and note any words that are repeated. (b) Why do you think Paul writes about forth Jesus in these two verses?

2. Memorize 2 Timothy 1:1 (I would encourage you to memorize the entire epistle of 2 Timothy. It is short, and it will bless you immensely!)

3. (a) Read all of 2 Timothy. What theme would you assign to this short epistle? (b) If the "time for *your* departure" was at hand, what words would you want to pass on to others?

4. (a) What facts do you learn about Timothy from the following verses? Acts 16:1-5; 17:14-15; 19:22; 20:4; Romans 16:21; 1 Corinthians 4:17; Philippians 2:19-23; 1 Thessalonians 3:1-2; 1 Timothy 1:2; 5:23; 6:20; Hebrews 13:23. (b) How would you summarize Timothy's character?

5. (a) What does the promise of eternal life mean to you? (b) What would it mean to you if you were facing death?

6. (a) In what ways do you see Christendom departing from the truth? (b) In what ways do you personally hold fast to the truth?

7. What do you hope to gain from this study? Please write your thoughts in the form of a prayer request.

# The Qualities of Those Who Marked Timothy's Life

*2 Timothy 1:3-5*

THE week I was studying for this chapter happened to be right before Mother's Day. In fact, just before I sat down to begin this chapter, which was on a Thursday, my son, who lives in another state, called me. Since Mother's Day was coming up in just three days, I jokingly said, "Is this my pre-Mother's Day call?" He said, "Kind of." He then invited me to meet him halfway for an early Mother's Day lunch (he lives three hours away). I accepted, we chatted a moment, and then I began my studies for this chapter.

Mother's Day is a Hallmark card opportunity in the secular world we live in, but in the spiritual world, Mother's Day should be a wholehearted opportunity for Christian mothers to soberly evaluate their high calling before God. I hope Mother's Day has not become a time for you and I to be indulgent but to be diligent in pondering our God-given role. Many Christian women in our day have vacated their responsibilities as a parent and are leaving a grim legacy for their children. It is the wise mother who will consider her biblical role as a mother and endeavor to fulfill that role with godly fear. In this chapter, we will look not only at a godly mother but also a godly grandmother and a godly spiritual father who influenced young Timothy. Let's consider the text together, verses 3-5 of chapter one.

> I thank God, whom I serve with a pure conscience, as my forefathers did, as without ceasing I remember you in my prayers night and day, greatly desiring to see you, being mindful of your tears, that I may be filled with joy, when I call to remembrance the genuine faith that is in you, which dwelt first in your grandmother Lois and your mother Eunice, and I am persuaded is in you also.

Our outline for this chapter will have us taking a look at *Timothy's*

*Spiritual Father* (vv 3-4) and *Timothy's Physical Mother and Grandmother* (v 5). We began our study of 2 Timothy in our last chapter, and we learned that the persons mentioned in those opening verses were Paul, Timothy, Jesus, and God. We also learned of the promise mentioned, that of eternal life. And, lastly, we learned that peace was mentioned. Peace is the result of the grace and mercy shown to us by God our Father.

After his initial greetings in verses 1-2, Paul begins the body of his letter. As he does, we are struck by the first quality of this man who sits in a Roman prison chained to two soldiers, with little water or food, the sickening stench from nearby toilets, male and female prisoners incarcerated together, not to mention the sexual immorality that frequently went on in such arrangements. With what words does Paul begin his letter to Timothy? "I'm miserable here and I want out of this place"? No! Look at what he writes:

## Timothy's Spiritual Father *2 Timothy 1:3-4*

> I thank God, whom I serve with a pure conscience, as my forefathers did, as without ceasing I remember you in my prayers night and day, (2 Timothy 1:3)

There are at least *six* qualities that describe Paul. *The first quality of this godly apostle, who poured his life into Timothy, is thankfulness.* What an example for you and me to follow! Paul himself wrote, in 1 Thessalonians 5:18, that we are to be thankful in all things because this is God's will for our lives. This is not only an example for us to follow, but a great way to begin a letter or a greeting to someone. Paul chooses to be thankful in the midst of difficult circumstances and in the face of death. He chooses to dwell on things that are lovely and good and pure and not on things that are unlovely and awful and evil.

To whom does Paul give this thanks? He says *I thank God*, and this is important because even when we are thankful for another person, we can always thank God for making that person and gifting him or her for His glory. Everything you and I have, every spiritual gift we possess, is because of God and God alone. My friend, we must never forget that, lest our hearts be lifted up in pride and we become obsessed with ourselves, like the culture we live in! In his letter to the church at Rome, Paul writes something similar, "First, I thank my God through Jesus Christ for you all, because your faith is being proclaimed throughout the whole world." (Romans 1:8, LSB). He recognizes the faith of the church at Rome, but it's not them he thanks—it's God.

Not only is Paul thankful, but *the second quality of this man is that he is a servant.* He says this God—I give thanks to Him. He is the One *I serve.* He's saying that he is God's servant. The word *serve* means to minister. We can read through the Pauline epistles, and it goes without saying that what we find there is a man who is a slave of the Lord. Paul served in the worst of circumstances and sometimes with the worst of people. He traveled in dangerous areas, just to get the gospel to those who needed it. He risked his life for others and for the God he served. Paul's life was one of a living sacrifice for the God who had saved him.

Note also how Paul serves God: *with a pure conscience.* This means that Paul's conscience was clean; it was morally pure. *This is the third quality of Paul: he had a pure conscience.* In Acts 24:16 (LSB), Paul says, "In view of this, I also do my best to maintain always a conscience without fault both before God and before men." The conscience is that internal part of us that gives us a moral sense of right and wrong. Ladies, your conscience is a part of you that you want to keep clean. You don't want to defile your conscience; you don't want to go against your conscience, lest you end up with what Paul describes as a seared conscience. He mentions this in his first letter to Timothy in 1 Timothy 4:1-2 (LSB): "But the Spirit explicitly says that in later times some will fall away from the faith, paying attention to deceitful spirits and doctrines of demons, by the hypocrisy of liars, who have been seared in their own conscience." Keep your conscience clean; keep short accounts with God and man.

Paul then writes of the fact that his *forefathers* also served God with a pure conscience. In Acts 24:10-14 (LSB) we read,

> And when the governor had nodded for him to speak, Paul answered:
> "Knowing that for many years you have been a judge to this

> nation, I cheerfully make my defense, since you are able to ascertain the fact that no more than twelve days ago I went up to Jerusalem to worship. And neither in the temple, nor in the synagogues, nor across the city did they find me carrying on a discussion with anyone or causing a riot. Nor are they able to prove to you of what they are now accusing me. But this I confess to you, that according to the Way, which they call a sect, I do serve the God of our fathers, believing everything that is in accordance with the Law and that is written in the Prophets."

Paul's fathers, or forefathers, would have been Abraham, Isaac and Jacob. Paul was a Jew and would have been well-versed in the Law, the first five books of Moses. Paul was brought up at the feet of Gamaliel, as he mentions in Acts 22:3, a renowned teacher, highly esteemed among his peers. Rabbis would teach their students by memorization and by questions and answers. Most of their students would have the first five books of Moses memorized (see Psalm 1). I am certain that Paul learned much about the integrity and holiness of his forefathers through his memorization of the Law.

Before we go on, I'd like to highlight the reality that Paul was himself discipled and he actively discipled Timothy and a number of other men. This is imperative for all of us—for every believer. We all should be discipled by others, and we all should be discipling others. This is a biblical principle that is taught often in the Word of God. In fact, Paul will write of this very pattern and responsibility in 2 Timothy 2:1-2: "You therefore, my son, be strong in the grace that is in Christ Jesus. And the things that you have heard from me among many witnesses, commit these to faithful men who will be able to teach others also."

Paul is not only a thankful man; he is not only a servant; he is not only a man who possesses a clean conscience; but he is also a man of prayer, as evidenced by what he writes next. Paul says *without ceasing I remember you in my prayers night and day. This is the fourth quality of the man who poured his life into Timothy: he was a praying man.* Paul tells Timothy that he *remembers* to pray for him, which means he has a recollection recital. This is something he does over and over again, and he does it *without ceasing*, which means that his praying for Timothy is continual and uninterrupted. This is one of the commands Paul writes of in 1 Thessalonians 5:17; he says there that we are to pray without ceasing. Now, obviously this doesn't mean that this is a non-stop activity, 24 hours a day, but that it is a reoccurring event in the life of Paul. It means that his mind and heart go to God in prayer throughout the day and the night. Paul's thoughts are heavenward, and he offers up *prayers* for Timothy, which means Paul makes requests for Timothy. Timothy was on Paul's mind, and whenever Timothy came to Paul's mind, Paul prayed. Those into whom we pour our lives are often on our minds and in need of our prayers. I am sure that the nights were often long for Paul there in prison, but again, instead of dwelling on his awful situation, he chose to dwell on his awesome Savior and to petition Him on behalf of his son in the faith. Certainly, there would have been countless petitions for Timothy regarding his timidity, his fears, his need to hold fast to the truth. Again, Paul sets an example for you and me not to be anxious about anything or anyone but to pray instead. Paul tells us in Philippians that when we do that, the peace of God guards our hearts and our minds in Christ Jesus (Philippians 4:6-7). But, when we choose to worry instead of praying, we become like the world: without peace. We must petition the throne of grace to find mercy in our time of need (Hebrews 4:16). In verse 4, there are two more qualities mentioned regarding the apostle Paul.

> greatly desiring to see you, being mindful of your tears, that I may be filled with joy, (2 Timothy 1:4)

Paul writes to Timothy that he is *greatly desiring to see* him. To greatly desire is to have a great yearning. The reason for Paul's great desire to see Timothy is that Paul is *mindful* of Timothy's sadness, Timothy's *tears* over losing his mentor. Ladies, we cannot help but see that *the fifth quality of this man, Paul, is that he was a man of loving compassion.* His heart was tender and warm, not calloused and cold. He hurt with the hurts of others. Again, Paul writes in Romans 12:15 that we are to rejoice with those who rejoice and weep with those who weep. We are to consider others as more important than ourselves, as he writes in Philippians 2:3.

Now, did Paul actually see Timothy cry at some point? What exactly is Paul referring to in this verse? It could be that Paul is remembering the following account in Acts 20:17-38 (LSB). (Timothy would have been present with Paul at this time, as evidenced by the beginning of the chapter).

> Now from Miletus he sent to Ephesus and called to him the elders of the church. And when they had come to him, he said to them,
>
> "You yourselves know, from the first day that I set foot in Asia, how I was with you the whole time, serving the Lord with all humility and with tears and with trials which came upon me through the plots of the Jews; how I did not shrink from declaring to you anything that was profitable, and teaching you publicly and from house to house, solemnly testifying to both Jews and Greeks about repentance toward God and faith in our Lord Jesus Christ. And now, behold, bound by the Spirit, I am on my way to Jerusalem, not knowing what will happen to me there, except that the Holy Spirit solemnly testifies to me in every city, saying that chains and afflictions await me. But I do not make my life of any account nor dear to myself, so that I may finish my course and the ministry which I received from the Lord Jesus, to testify solemnly of the gospel of the grace of God.
>
> "And now, behold, I know that all of you, among whom I went about preaching the kingdom, will no longer see my face. Therefore, I testify to you this day that I am innocent of the blood of all. For I did not shrink from declaring to you the whole purpose of God. Be on guard for yourselves and for all the flock, among which the Holy Spirit has made you overseers, to shepherd the church of God which He purchased with His own blood. I know that after my departure savage wolves will come in among you, not sparing the flock; and from among your own selves men will arise, speaking perverse things, to draw away the disciples after them. Therefore be watchful, remembering that night and day for a period of three years I did not cease to admonish each one with tears. And now I commend you to God and to the word of His grace, which is able to build *you* up and to give you the inheritance among all those who have been sanctified. I have coveted no one's silver or gold or clothes. You yourselves know that these hands ministered to my own needs and to those who were

> with me. In everything I showed you that by laboring in this manner you must help the weak and remember the words of the Lord Jesus, that He Himself said, 'It is more blessed to give than to receive.'"
>
> And when he had said these things, he knelt down and prayed with them all. And they began to weep aloud and falling on Paul's neck, they were kissing him, being in agony especially over the word which he had spoken, that they would not see his face again. And they were accompanying him to the ship.

It could be that Paul is referring to this event or to one that we have no record of; perhaps, he is referring to the moment when Timothy and Paul had to say goodbye to one another just before Paul's final arrest. Whatever the circumstance, Timothy likely knew that it would probably be the last time he would see his mentor alive. We must not think ill of Timothy and his tears. The Bible speaks often of tears, and even Jesus wept at the death of his friend Lazarus (John 11:35). I think we often expect people to be robotic in the grief process and would do well to consider that even in the Old Testament we see people mourning for 30 days and even 70 days (Numbers 20:29 and Genesis 50:3). In 2 Kings, we have the account of two other men, Elisha and Elijah, who were also in a mentoring relationship. Elijah was Elisha's spiritual father and, as we know, Elijah was taken up in a whirlwind to Heaven and Elisha saw Elijah no more, and the Word says that Elisha rent his clothes in two—a clear sign of mourning (2 Kings 2:11-12). His mentor was gone. He wept bitterly. We also read of David and Jonathan, whose souls were knit together in deep friendship; when Jonathan died, David wrote a lament in 2 Samuel 1 and wept for his friend.

*We come next to the sixth and final quality of the man who poured his life into Timothy: that Paul was a man of joy.* It was so that he might *be filled with joy* that Paul wanted to see Timothy again. I am certain that this was not a selfish joy that Paul writes of. Rather, it was the kind of joy one has when they see the joy of another—in this case, the joy Paul would have experienced at seeing Timothy's joy. Paul was facing his death, and nothing would bring him more joy than to see Timothy one last time, and to see Timothy's joy in that moment. To be *filled with joy* means that Paul would be filled all the way up with gladness and calm delight. Paul's joy would not come as a result of some monetary gift or release from prison, but it would come when he saw the joy of others. In this, we see Paul rejoice with those who rejoice (Romans 12:15)!

But Paul's joy was prompted not only at the thought of Timothy being joyful. It was also prompted at the thought of Timothy's rich spiritual heritage, one which originated with his mother and grandmother. This was doubling Paul's joy! Notice what he writes in verse 5, and with this we turn from the qualities of Timothy's spiritual father to the qualities of his mother and grandmother.

## Timothy's Physical Mother and Grandmother *2 Timothy 1:5*

> when I call to remembrance the genuine faith that is in you, which dwelt first in your grandmother Lois and your mother Eunice, and I am persuaded is in you also. (2 Timothy 1:5)

Paul's joy not only was because of the hope of seeing Timothy and contributing to Timothy's joy but also because of Timothy's faith. Paul puts it like this: *when I call to remembrance the genuine faith that is in you.* In other words: "When I remember your faith, which is genuine or sincere, it brings me joy." It is worth noting that Paul also writes of this genuine faith in 1 Timothy 1:5: "Now the purpose of the commandment is love from a pure heart, from a good conscience, and from sincere faith." He also writes of it again in 1 Timothy 4:6: "If you instruct the brethren in these things, you will be a good minister of Jesus Christ, nourished in the words of faith and of the good doctrine which you have carefully followed." Paul was not in doubt of the man that Timothy was. In fact, in Paul's letter to the Philippians, he highlights several qualities of Timothy's that are worth noting. Philippians 2:19-24 (LSB):

> But I hope in the Lord Jesus to send Timothy to you shortly, so that I also may be in good spirits when I learn of your circumstances. For I have no one else of kindred spirit who will genuinely be concerned about your circumstances. For they all seek after their own interests,

> not those of Christ Jesus. But you know of his proven worth, that he served with me in the furtherance of the gospel like a child serving his father. Therefore I hope to send him immediately, as soon as I evaluate my own circumstances, and I am confident in the Lord that I myself also will be coming shortly.

Timothy was a servant; he was a kindred spirit of Paul's; he was selfless; he was sincere; he consistently served with Paul as a son would with his father; and he was serving together with Paul in the gospel. And to think, this is just one portion of Scripture regarding this young man, Timothy. Paul had traveled with Timothy and observed his life. Paul knew Timothy to be a man of sincere faith; he knew Timothy by his fruits. Oh, that God would give us more Timothys for our day!

Now, where did Timothy first learn about Christianity? This faith, Paul says, *dwelt first* in Timothy's *grandmother* and *mother. Lois* is a name which means Christian woman, and *Eunice* means victorious. The word *dwelt* is in the past tense, rather than the present tense, which tells us that Timothy's mother and grandmother were no longer living. But, evidently, Paul seemed to have known both of these women. In Acts 16:1 (LSB), we read, "Now Paul also arrived at Derbe and at Lystra. And behold, a disciple was there, named Timothy, the son of a Jewish woman who was a believer, but his father was a Greek." As to how these two women came to faith, we are uncertain because the Scriptures do not tell us, but we do know they greatly influenced Timothy. In the biblical world, families often lived together or in a common area, so Timothy's grandmother would have been very involved in his life and may have even lived in the same home with him. We know that Timothy's father was a Greek and it appears that he was an unbeliever, but both Timothy's mother and grandmother evidently taught him the Word of God. Paul writes of this in 2 Timothy 3:15, when he says, "from childhood you have known the Holy Scriptures, which are able to make you wise for salvation through faith which is in Christ Jesus." One man helps us here:

> Even though fathers were responsible for their sons' education, Judaism and Greco-Roman aristocrats wanted mothers to be knowl-

> edgeable so they could impart knowledge to their young children. (This is true even though Judaism did not provide women advanced education in the law, and even though Greco-Roman society generally reserved rhetorical and philosophical training for men.) Until the age of seven a Roman boy's mother was his main formative influence; many thought that children should not be taught reading until age seven, but others wished to begin it much earlier, even at the age of three. Jewish Scripture education began by the age of five or six, although this education always emphasized memorization and recitation more than reading skills.
>
> The "faith" of Timothy's mother and grandmother was Jewish (Jewish Christian by the time Paul met them—Acts 16:1). Jewish fathers were primarily responsible for their son's instruction in the law, but Timothy's father was a Gentile (Acts 16:1, 3). Those without a living religious father also learned from grandmothers if they were still living (cf. Tobit 1:8).
>
> Most education included corporal discipline, but some ancient education experts stressed instead encouraging the child, making him or her feel successful, provoking competition and making learning enjoyable (Quintilian). Ancient writers differed on whether public instructors or home schooling was better, provided the former held classes small enough to permit private instruction.[4]

When we consider the character qualities of Timothy's mother and grandmother, it is clear that they were God-fearing women who possessed genuine faith and were passionate about passing it on to their offspring. Paul is clear that not only did this faith dwell in Timothy's mother and grandmother, but it also dwelt in Timothy as well. Paul says: *and I am persuaded* [it] *is in you also.* There was no doubt about it; genuine faith dwelt in Timothy. The word *dwelt* means to inhabit. We know that the dear Holy Spirit dwells in us and that genuine faith produces fruits, or evidences, that one is truly of God. Paul was convinced that Timothy was the real deal, not like Demas, who forsook Paul, having loved the present world. Demas denied the faith; Timothy was in the faith.

---

4 Craig S. Keener, *IVP Bible Background Commentary: New Testament* (Downers Grove: InterVarsity Press, 1993), 617, Biblesoft.

## Summary

As we consider those who marked Timothy's life, we think of Paul first, Timothy's spiritual father. What qualities did Paul possess? He was a thankful man; a servant; a man with a clear conscience; a man of prayer; a man of loving compassion; and a man of joy. Wouldn't it be wonderful to have someone like that pouring their life into you? And wouldn't it be wonderful if you and I possessed these qualities so that others could follow our example?

Next, we have the qualities of Timothy's mother and grandmother. They were God-fearing women who not only possessed genuine faith but were passionate about passing it on to their offspring. Ladies, we must emulate these godly women and endeavor to pass on the truth to the next generation—especially when we consider that 70% of all parents are in the workforce today. We need women who are committed, yes, to their children, but more than that, women who are committed to the Word of God. Susanna Wesley was one of those mothers.

> Susanna Wesley delivered 19 children. ... Early in her life, she vowed that she would never spend more time in leisure entertainment than she did in prayer and Bible study. Even amid the most complex and busy years of her life as a mother, she still scheduled two hours each day for fellowship with God and time in His Word, and she adhered to that schedule faithfully. The challenge was finding a place of privacy in a house filled to overflowing with children.
>
> Mother Wesley's solution to this was to bring her Bible to her favorite chair and throw her long apron up over her head, forming a sort of tent. This became something akin to the "tent of meeting," the tabernacle in the days of Moses in the Old Testament. Every person in the household, from the smallest toddler to the oldest domestic helpers, knew well to respect this signal. When Susanna was under the apron, she was with God and was not to be disturbed except in the case of the direst emergency. There in the privacy of her little tent, she interceded for her husband and children and plumbed the deep mysteries of God in the Scriptures. This holy

> discipline equipped her with a thorough and profound knowledge of the Bible.[5]

From this devoted mother and godly woman came Samuel, John, and Charles Wesley, who have left tremendous legacies for the Christian world. Oh, my friend, we need women who are committed to hours each day in the Scriptures and with the Savior—and not to social media. May our desire be as that of one woman, who penned these words in her hymn "O Give Us Homes."

> O give us homes built firm upon the Savior
> Where Christ is Head and Counselor and Guide
> Where ev'ry child is taught His love and favor
> And gives his heart to Christ the Crucified
> How sweet to know that though his footsteps waver
> His faithful Lord is walking by his side
>
> O give us homes with godly fathers, mothers
> Who always place their hope and trust in Him
> Whose tender patience turmoil never bothers
> Whose calm and courage trouble cannot dim
> A home where each finds joy in serving others
> And love still shines tho' days be dark and grim
>
> O give us homes where Christ is Lord and Master
> The Bible read, the precious hymns still sung
> Where pray'r comes first in peace or in disaster
> And praise is natural speech to ev'ry tongue
> Where mountains move before a faith that's vaster
> And Christ sufficient is for old and young
>
> O Lord, our God, our homes are Thine forever
> We trust to Thee their problems, toil, and care
> Their bonds of love no enemy can sever

5 Taken from *Only One Life* by Jackie Green, Lauren Green, and Bill High. Copyright © 2018 by Jackie Green, Lauren Green and Bill High. 207-208. Used by permission of HarperCollins Christian Publishing. www.harpercollinschristian.com.

If Thou art always Lord and Master there
Be Thou the center of our least endeavor
Be Thou our guest, our hearts and homes to share[6]

# QUESTIONS TO CONSIDER

1. Read 2 Timothy 1:3-5. (a) What people are mentioned in these verses and what do you learn about them? (b) How do you think Timothy would have received these words from Paul?

2. Memorize 2 Timothy 1:5.

3. (a) Paul writes to Timothy in 2 Timothy 1:3 regarding the fact that he prays night and day for him. What would be some of the prayer requests that Paul might have prayed for his son in the faith? (You might need to do some further study about Timothy from the Word of God to get your answers.) (b) Why do you think it is necessary to pray for those we mentor? (This could be another woman, a child, or a grandchild.)

4. (a) Paul also mentions in 2 Timothy 1:5 that Timothy's faith was genuine. In what ways did Timothy's life demonstrate genuine faith? (Again, you will need to do some further study from the Word of God to discover this answer.) (b) What are the marks of genuine faith? Demonstrate your answer from the Scriptures.

5. (a) Timothy's mother and grandmother had great influence on his Christian faith, according to 2 Timothy 1:5 and 2 Timothy 3:15. What other mothers or grandmothers mentioned in the Bible had a godly impact on their children or grandchildren? (b) What mothers or grandmothers in the Bible influenced their children or grandchildren for evil? (c) What lessons, either good or bad, do you learn for your own life by these examples?

6. (a) Who are the people who have had or are having an influence on you in your spiritual walk? (b) What qualities of Christ in them have impacted you? (c) What are some ways we as women can influence the younger generation (our children, grandchildren, or others) for the gospel?

7. Either write a prayer of thanks to God for those who have influenced your life or write a prayer of petition regarding those whom God has placed in your life who you are influencing.

# Five Truths Which Must Be Remembered When Using Our Spiritual Gifts

*2 Timothy 1:6-7*

THROUGHOUT my years of ministry to women, I have been blessed to have many of them come alongside and work together with me in service to the Lord. It has been a joy that has regularly encouraged my heart. However, there have also been those within the body who possess many talents and spiritual gifts but have remained "pew-sitters" year after year, rarely using what God has gifted them with for His glory and for the benefit of others. A number of common excuses are offered for this failure to serve the Lord and His people: "I don't have time"; "I am not as gifted as so and so"; "I am afraid of messing up"; "my past sins render me useless"; "there's no place for me to serve here"; among others. But, as we come to the third chapter in our study of Paul's second letter to Timothy, we encounter a passage that should offer encouragement to all those "excuse-makers." The reason I say this is that young Timothy evidently had some personal fears in regard to exercising his gifts. In the verses we'll study in this chapter, Paul gives to Timothy, and to you and me, some encouragement to stop making excuses and start exercising our gifts. Paul does this by way of reminding Timothy of five truths pertaining to the use of one's spiritual gifts. Let's listen in as Paul writes to Timothy in 2 Timothy 1:6-7:

> Therefore I remind you to stir up the gift of God which is in you through the laying on of my hands. For God has not given us a spirit of fear, but of power and of love and of a sound mind.

In our previous chapter, we considered the qualities of the people who had marked Timothy's life spiritually. One of those individuals was the apostle Paul, who was Timothy's spiritual father—a thankful man; a servant; a man with a clear conscience; a man of prayer; a man of loving compassion; and a man of joy. The other two individuals who marked Timothy's life spiritually were his grandmother Lois and his mother Eunice; we learned that these were God-fearing women who not only possessed genuine faith but were passionate about passing it on to their children. Those of us who pour our lives into others, whether children or other women, naturally want those we have invested in to pass on to others the things we have taught them. We want our spiritual children to make a difference in the world we live in, especially as it relates to the gifts and talents God has given them. Paul desired this very thing for his disciple, Timothy. But, evidently, Timothy needed some encouragement to use his gifts, just as you and I do at times.

In this chapter, we will discover five truths that must be remembered when using our spiritual gifts. I have put these five truths in the form of an acrostic, **GIFTS** (they will not be presented in this order), so that you will hopefully remember them the next time you are hesitant or fearful to use your spiritual gifts. Let's consider the first truth, in verse 6, which must be remembered as it pertains to our spiritual gifts.

> Therefore I remind you to stir up the gift of God which is in you through the laying on of my hands. (2 Timothy 1:6)

Paul begins this portion of his letter with the word *therefore*, which causes us to consider what he has said just before this word. Paul is saying, "Therefore, because not only I, but your mother and grandmother also, have instructed you in the things of God, then do not become useless, Timothy, but rather, become useful in your service to God." So, Paul reminds Timothy *to stir up the gift of God which is in* him. Paul is saying that it is his aim to *remind* Timothy, which means Paul is calling Timothy to remember this important truth. Timothy is no different from you and I, in the sense that we, too, need to be reminded of spiritual truths. How often we forget the things that we have learned! And Paul was not the only writer in Scripture who wrote of this need to be reminded; Peter mentions in 2 Peter 3:1-2 (LSB),

> This is now, beloved, the second letter I am writing to you in which I am stirring up your sincere mind by way of reminder, that you should remember the words spoken beforehand by the holy prophets and the commandment of the Lord and Savior spoken by your apostles.

In fact, there are numerous examples in the Word of God which pertain to our need to be reminded of spiritual truths.

What is Paul reminding Timothy of? *The first thing Paul reminds Timothy of is the **S** on your acrostic:* Paul reminds Timothy to ***Stir** up the gift of God which is in him.* The words *stir up* mean to rekindle, and the metaphor used here is that of a fire. When we build a fire for warmth or enjoyment, we have to stir it up and add more fuel to it or it will go out. So it is with our spiritual gifts. We can't just sit around and do nothing. We must rekindle the flame by adding fuel so that we might excel in the use of our gifts. Many believers become lazy and selfish with their time and energy and are content with just getting by. We must never be content with the status quo, but we are to stir up the gift of God which is in us. The Christian life is one of progress and growth; it is one of pressing on; it is one of producing much fruit for God and His Kingdom. Paul writes to Timothy in 1 Timothy 4:14 (LSB), "Do not neglect the gift within you, which was given to you through prophetic utterance with the laying on of hands by the council of elders." Peter writes in 1 Peter 4:10-11 (LSB), "As each one has received a gift, employ it in serving one another as good stewards of the manifold grace of God—whoever speaks, as one speaking the oracles of God; whoever serves, as one serving by the strength which God supplies; so that in all things God may be glorified through Jesus Christ, to whom belongs the glory and might forever and ever. Amen." We are to use the gifts God has given us and never let the passion and drive with which we use them go out.

Before we go on to the next truth, I'd like to point out an interesting contrast: fire is used to rekindle this flame, so to speak, in the use of our gifts, and fire will be used to test how we used those gifts—whether we worked in our own strength or according to the grace of God. Paul says in 1 Corinthians 3:9-15 (LSB),

> For we are God's fellow workers; you are God's field, God's building. According to the grace of God which was given to me, like a wise master builder I laid a foundation, and another is building on it. But each man must be careful how he builds on it. For no one can lay a

> foundation other than the one which is laid, which is Jesus Christ. Now if anyone builds on the foundation with gold, silver, precious stones, wood, hay, straw, each man's work will become evident, for the day will indicate it because it is revealed with fire, and the fire itself will test the quality of each man's work. If any man's work which he has built on it remains, he will receive a reward. If any man's work is burned up, he will suffer loss, but he himself will be saved, yet so as through fire.

A word to those who are aging: Don't let your flame go out, but rekindle it. You are at the peak of your life in ministering to others with wisdom and experience. We need the older men and women to keep serving God to the end. Jay Adams says in his book, *Wrinkled But Not Ruined*, "The most dangerous tendency of all relating to the matter of retirement is the tendency to retire from Christianity! It is a sad thing to meet those who have been active and useful in the past but who are now hardly even attending church, even though they are able to. They have stopped thinking, stopped serving, stopped growing."[7]

Now, note that this gift is from *God.* A spiritual gift is a special endowment given by God to those who belong to Him. This is done by the Spirit of God, as Paul mentions in 1 Corinthians 12, which is an important portion of Scripture dealing with our spiritual gifts. In 1 Corinthians 12:11 (LSB) Paul writes, "But one and the same Spirit works all these things, distributing to each one individually just as He wills." The gift or gifts you and I possess are from God the Holy Spirit and they have been given to us for His glory. Jesus says, in John 15:8 (LSB), "My Father is glorified by this, that you bear much fruit, and so prove to be My disciples." And then again, in John 15:16 (LSB), "You did not choose Me but I chose you, and appointed you that you would go and bear fruit, and that your fruit would abide, so that whatever you ask of the Father in My name He may give to you." I want to emphasize that this gifting is from God, because there is present within the church in our day, a mentality that aims at becoming a so-called "celebrity Christian," whatever that is.

7 Jay Adams, *Wrinkled But Not Ruined* (Woodruff: Institute for Nouthetic Studies, 2023), 33-34.

Ladies, there are no celebrities in God's Kingdom; we celebrate Him alone. We are servants, and whatever we have it is only because He gave it to us. Paul warns us in 1 Corinthians 4:6-7 (LSB):

> Now these things, brothers, I have applied to myself and Apollos for your sakes, so that in us you may learn not to go beyond what is written, so that no one of you will become puffed up on behalf of one against the other. For who regards you as superior? What do you have that you did not receive? And if you did receive it, why do you boast as if you had not received it?

The sobering account of Herod, in Acts 12, also serves as a warning for us in this regard. Herod allowed the crowds to call him a god and did not correct their error, but rather took the glory for himself and, as punishment for his idolatry, he was eaten by worms and died!

Another thing worthy of noting about this gift of which Paul is speaking is that it is *in* Timothy, and, by extension, that means that the gifts God has given to us are also *in* us. This means it is in a fixed position and it is in a place of rest. This is an exciting truth because it reminds us that the Holy Spirit is in us, the very Holy Spirit who also never leaves us, and, according to 1 Corinthians 12:11, it is He who gives to every man individually as He wills.

Now, what does it mean when Paul says that this gift was given to Timothy *through the laying on of my hands*? Does this mean that Paul had some power to bestow spiritual gifts to Timothy? No, because only the Spirit of God has that. Rather, it is a reference to Timothy's ordination service where Paul laid his hands on Timothy; as Paul did that, Timothy would have been made aware of or reminded of the seriousness of his calling and the responsibility to use his gifts. Paul refers to this laying on of hands in his first letter to Timothy, where he writes in 1 Timothy 4:14 (LSB), "Do not neglect the gift within you, which was given to you through prophetic utterance with the laying on of hands by the council of elders." I can recall many an ordination service like this, and I have often been moved as I have watched the church leadership lay their hands on a chosen elder or deacon. I have thought to myself how that elder or deacon is entering into a very high calling from God, one which lays tremendous responsibility upon them, and I imagine that the one who is being ordained also gives sober thought—or, at least, should—to using their gifts for the glory of God.

Timothy, perhaps, is like some of us who are fearful when it comes to using our gifts. I mean, what if I mess up? What if people hate me because of my boldness for Christ? Well, Paul encourages Timothy that this fear he has is not from God. Instead, God has given Timothy something a tad different from fear. Let's consider verse 7 and the other four truths that need to be remembered about the use of our gifts.

> For God has not given us a spirit of fear, but of power and of love and of a sound mind. (2 Timothy 1:7)

One of the things I am often asked about when I travel to speak is if I get fearful when in front of the audiences. My usual answer is something along the lines of, "Rarely, but at times I do, when I know that the message is hard or that the audience is unlikely to receive it." Someone once told me years ago, when I got nervous singing before others, that my focus was on myself and not on God or on the people to whom I am ministering. That has stuck in my mind throughout these years, and it has been a good reminder that my fear is self-focused. (By the way, before we unpack this verse, I would like to say that this verse is often used out of context. I have heard it used in regard to a myriad of things, but it's important to keep in mind that the context of it is the use of one's spiritual gifts. We are not to be fearful of using them and there are reasons for that, which Paul details for us in the surrounding verses.)

Paul begins this verse with the word *for*, which is a great word in light of verse 6. Timothy is to stir up the gift in himself, to not be timid or stagnant about it. Why? Paul says *for*, or because, God has not given Timothy *a spirit of fear. This is the second truth to be remembered and the **F** on your acrostic: **F**ear regarding the usage of our gifts is not from God.* The word *not* here is an absolute negative. No matter what we might think or even what we may be taught, an ungodly fear is not from God. The words *spirit of fear* mean a spirit of timidity or a spirit of bondage. *Fear* produces bondage when we serve; love produces freedom when we serve. Romans 8:15 reminds us, "For you did not receive the spirit of bondage again to fear, but you received the Spirit of adoption by whom we cry out, 'Abba, Father.'" Paul mentions Timothy's fear in 1 Corinthians 16:10-11 (LSB), "Now if Timothy comes, take care that he is with you without fear, for he is doing the Lord's work, as I also am. So let no one despise him. But send him on his way in peace, so that he may come to me, for I expect him with the brothers." So, this fear of Timothy's wasn't a one-time occurrence but an ongoing issue that needed to be addressed. (The apostle John speaks of this principle in 1 John when referring to the Day of Judgment. He writes, in 1 John 4:17-19 (LSB):

> By this, love has been perfected with us, so that we may have confidence in the day of judgment, because as He is, so also are we in this world. There is no fear in love; but perfect love casts out fear, because fear involves punishment, and the one who fears is not perfected in love. We love, because He first loved us.

The context here is not spiritual gifts but the day in which we stand before God. For those of us who know God, our love has been perfected and we will have no fear on that day. Those who do not know God, however, will fear, and they should, because all of us will stand before Him. But John makes it clear that perfect love casts out fear. When we love God and others as we should, there should not only be no fear of judgment but also no fear in serving, either.) In fact, did you know that fear is not from God?

I remember, years ago, one of my mentors gave me an assignment to do: a word study on fear. I looked up every verse in the Bible that dealt with fear (and there are a lot!), and I learned a sobering truth: that the only thing we are to fear is God (and there is one mention of fearing our parents)—and that's it. I was pricked in my heart when I realized that fear was a sin that had hindered my devotion to my Lord.

My other mentor, decades ago, called me one morning and said she wanted to come over. I thought it was odd but told her to come on over. She came in, walked right through the house, sat down at my kitchen table, and said to me in her strong southern accent, "Susan ... this fear of flying you have is a *sin*!" But her words did not stop there; she went on to say, "And, by Tuesday, I want you to give me 10 reasons why it is safer to fly than to drive." And with that, she stood up, got her purse, and left. I remember thinking at that moment, "Boy, I sure don't like *her* very much!" But God used that rebuke and that assignment to show me, once again, how awful my sin of fear was in His sight, and how gracious it was of my Lord to use someone who loved me enough to confront me. He knew that years from then I would be traveling and speaking, nationally and internationally, and would have to fly numerous times a year.

Paul was a gracious mentor (just like mine were), and he did not want Timothy to be fearful. Fear is crippling to ministers of Christ. We don't know why Timothy was timid, but I can imagine that, as Paul's spiritual son, Timothy might have found it intimidating to follow such a remarkable man. Timothy may not have thought he could measure up to Paul the apostle. But Paul tells us in 2 Corinthians 10:12 (LSB), "For we do not dare to classify or compare ourselves with some of those who commend themselves, but when they measure themselves by themselves and compare themselves with themselves, they are without understanding." Also, Timothy may have been fearful of the persecution he would incur as he served the Lord. No doubt he had witnessed many of Paul's persecutions and knew that a zealous pursuit and use of his gifts would likely bring suffering for Christ.

So, God has not given us a spirit of fear; this is the negative. But now Paul ends with the positive, with three more truths for us to remember. He begins with the word *but*, which is a word of strong contrast. There are two Greek words that are translated as *but*, and this is the stronger of the two. Paul is emphasizing that fear is not what has been given to us by God; instead, God has given us something else. The first thing He has given us is power. *This is the third truth to remember and the* ***G*** *on your acrostic.* ***G****od gives us His power as we use our gifts.* What is *power*, and what does it have to do with using our gifts? The word power refers to a miraculous power, a dynamite power, that only comes from God—a power that is given to us to do above and beyond what we think is possible. We should often remind ourselves of the words of Jesus in John 15:5 (LSB), "I am the vine, you are the branches; he who abides in Me and I in him, he bears much fruit, for apart from Me you can do nothing." Earlier this year, this truth hit home to me when I was teaching in another state. I had had only one hour of sleep, traveled most of the day to get where I was going, and when it was time for me to teach I had been up for almost 20 hours. I remember praying while the women were singing, "Lord, help me. I am so tired. I do not know how I can physically do this." Do you know what happened? I did teach and with unction and power from God. In fact, when I finished speaking, I went to the back of the room and the lady who travels with me gave a thumbs up! (She never does that!) Only the power of God can enable us to use our gifts like that! We must never endeavor to use our spiritual gifts in our own power—we will most certainly fail when we do. But when we serve in His power, He is able to do, for His glory, above all we can ask or think.

Secondly, instead of fear, God has given us love. *This is the fourth truth to be remembered and the **I** on your acrostic: It is **I**mperative that we love others and God when using our gifts.* The word for *love* in this verse is *agape. Agape* love is a love that gives rather than gets. This would be a love for God and a love for others. One man says,

> If we have love for lost souls and for the people of God, we will be able to endure suffering and accomplish the work of God. Selfishness leads to fear because, if we are selfish, we are interested only in what we will get out of serving God, and we will be afraid of losing prestige, power, or money. True Christian love, energized by the Spirit (Rom 5:5), enables us to sacrifice for others and not be afraid. The Spirit gives love (Gal 5:22).[8]

Peter speaks of this in 1 Peter—and note that Peter's words are in the context of using one's spiritual gifts. 1 Peter 4:8-11 (LSB) states,

> Above all, keep fervent in your love for one another, because love covers a multitude of sins. Be hospitable to one another without

8 Excerpted from *The Bible Exposition Commentary on the New Testament* © 1989 Warren W. Wiersbe. Used by permission of David C Cook. May not be further reproduced. All rights reserved. 241.

> grumbling. As each one has received a gift, employ it in serving one another as good stewards of the manifold grace of God—whoever speaks, as one speaking the oracles of God; whoever serves, as one serving by the strength which God supplies; so that in all things God may be glorified through Jesus Christ, to whom belongs the glory and might forever and ever. Amen.

Paul tells us in 1 Corinthians 13:13 (LSB), "But now abide faith, hope, love—these three; but the greatest of these is love." My friend, if we do not have love for God and others when we're using our gifts, we are nothing. When Paul writes of the fruit of the Spirit in Galatians 5:22-23, it is love that is the heading and from love flow all the other fruit. When we are filled with God's Spirit, we love others. As Jesus said in John 13:35, love will be the mark by which others know we belong to God. Others will know if we love them or not. And, of course, God knows whether we love Him and others!

Thirdly, instead of fear, God has given us a sound mind. *This is the fifth and final truth and the* ***T*** *on your acrostic:* ***T****hinking as Christ (being sober-minded) is imperative when using our gifts.* The words *sound mind* mean to be disciplined in our minds, to be sober-minded. This is a qualification for all elders and deacons; they cannot minister to the flock if they are not serious and sensible in their shepherding of the flock. But it is also a qualification for all of God's children, as Titus 2:1-5 makes clear. When we are thinking as Christ thinks, with sound minds, it helps us to speak the words of God and not false, off-the-wall ideas that we think we have cleverly devised. I've heard some bizarre things from some so-called Bible teachers in our day. And, at times, I have wondered if some of them are on drugs because their teachings are so odd. They are far from being of sound mind!

This *being of sound mind* applies to the use of other gifts besides speaking gifts. For example, when you are using your gift of hospitality, you need a sound mind, and you need to be sensible. You don't need to lavish a ridiculous amount of food and gifts on your guests, but you don't want to leave them hungry at mealtimes or make them feel unwelcome, either. You must be sensible. Or, for example, when you are using your gift of mercy, you must possess a sound mind. As you exercise mercy, you must be careful not to enable people but must meet the needs they genuinely have. Let's take another gift, the gift of exhortation. You and I need to remember that we are to exhort others in a spirit of meekness, as Paul says in Galatians 6:1-2 (KJV). We must not exhibit an attitude of superiority or pride. Christ never exhorted others in such a manner. One more example would be the gift of administration. When using that gift, you must be careful to not micromanage people or to act like a bull in a china closet. Instead, using the gift of administration with a sound mind means you must do so with meekness, and meekness is strength under control. You can see how being of sound mind, or being sober-minded, when using our gifts is essential. When we use our gifts, we must do so under the power and influence of the Holy Spirit and not outside of His control.

## Summary

As we close, let's revisit the five truths that Timothy needed to remember, because they are the same truths you and I must remember as well regarding our own spiritual gifts. First, **G**od gives us His power as we use our gifts. Do you draw upon the dynamite power of God when you use your gifts for His service and glory? Or, are you drawing upon your own strength when you serve? Do you pray before and while you use your spiritual gifts? Do you thank God after some act of service for His enabling you to use your gift for His glory? These things will serve to remind us that it is His power we must use when we are exercising our spiritual gifts.

Second, it is **I**mperative that we love others and we love God when we are using our gifts. What are your motives when you use your gifts? Have you stopped long enough to evaluate whether you are using your gifts out of love for others and for God or out of love for yourself? Is it your desire that God be recognized in what you do? Do you love others enough to sacrificially give of yourself to them? That sacrificial giving might come in the form of an act of mercy, hospitality, speaking the truth in love, teaching, or an admonition, etc.

Third, we need to remind ourselves that **F**ear of using our gifts is not from God. Do you become anxious or fearful when you are using your gifts? If so, have you ever asked yourself why that is? Remember, fear is produced by wrong-thinking about ourselves, about God, and about others. Love, however, is a product of right-thinking about ourselves, about God, and about others.

Fourth, when using our gifts, we must **T**hink as Christ thinks; we must be of sound mind. Are you using self-control when you use your gifts? Do you stop long enough to ask God to help you do and speak as He would? To do that, it is necessary that we have a steady diet of the Word of God so that we know how Jesus would act and what He would say.

Lastly, we must remember to **S**tir up the gifts that are in us. Have you let the flame go out in your service to God? Are you more zealous for Him this year than you were last year? Are you serving Him more fervently than you have previously? What are you doing to stir up the gift that is in you?

Frances Havergal was one of the most dedicated Christian women of the 19th century. Though she was ill most of her life, she was active in service to the Lord. She began memorizing the Bible at the age of four, and she memorized the New Testament, the Psalms, Isaiah, and the Minor Prophets before her death at the age of 43. She also wrote numerous hymns, poems, and gospel tracts. Ms. Havergal did not allow the flame to go out—but she certainly went out in a blaze of glory! She stirred up the gift that was in her; she did not have a spirit of fear, but one of love, of power, and of a sound mind. In fact, she is the writer of my favorite hymn, "Take my Life and Let it Be," which is written about the use of one's spiritual gifts. As we close, let's use her words as a prayer to the Lord as we think about using our gifts for Him.

> Take my life and let it be consecrated, Lord, to thee.
> Take my moments and my days; let them flow in endless praise,
> Let them flow in endless praise.

Take my hands and let them move at the impulse of thy love.
Take my feet and let them be swift and beautiful for thee,
Swift and beautiful for thee.

Take my voice and let me sing always, only, for my King.
Take my lips and let them be filled with messages from thee,
Filled with messages from thee.

Take my silver and my gold; not a mite would I withhold.
Take my intellect and use every power as thou shalt choose,
Every power as thou shalt choose.

Take my will and make it thine; it shall be no longer mine.
Take my heart it is thine own; it shall be thy royal throne,
It shall be thy royal throne.

Take my love; my Lord, I pour at thy feet its treasure store.
Take myself, and I will be ever, only, all for thee,
Ever, only, all for thee.[9]

9 Francis Havergal, "Take My Life and Let It Be", Public Domain, 1874.

# QUESTIONS TO CONSIDER

1. (a) Read 2 Timothy 1:6-7. Why would Paul need to remind Timothy to stir up the gifts that were given to him by God? (b) What are some of the other reminders Paul passes on to Timothy? (c) If you could pass on five truths to those you disciple, what would they be, and why?

2. Memorize 2 Timothy 1:6-7.

3. Paul mentions to Timothy, in 2 Timothy 1:7, that God has not given us a spirit of fear but has given us power, love, and a sound mind. With that in mind, read Exodus 3-4 and answer the following questions. (a) Who was fearful to obey what God asked of him? (b) What were the excuses he gave? (c) What counsel did God give him? (d) What principles do you glean from this story, especially regarding fear in serving the Lord?

4. Instead of fear, God gives us power, love, and a sound mind as we use our gifts. (a) Read 1 Corinthians 13 and write down what happens when we don't use our gifts in love. (b) Why is it important that our spiritual gifts be exercised with the power of God, according to 1 Corinthians 2:1-5? (c) Why is it necessary that we be of sound mind (or sober-minded), according to 1 Peter 4:7-11? (By the way, this passage is dealing with the use of our spiritual gifts.)

5. (a) Do you know what your spiritual gifts are? If so, are you excelling and growing in using them, or are you becoming stagnant in your service to God? (If you do not know what your gifts are, I would encourage you to find out what they are and begin serving in your church. God created you for good works for His glory!) (b) How can one overcome any fear they might have when using their gifts?

6. (a) Do you think it is sinful to not use your spiritual gifts? Use Scripture to prove your answer. (b) How can we encourage believers who are not using their gifts to begin using them?

7. How can you improve your service to God and to others? In what ways should you be excelling in the spiritual gifts you possess? Please put your needs in the form of a prayer request.

# The Mighty Power of God!

*2 Timothy 1:8-11*

IN the early 1700s, Isaac Watts wrote a hymn entitled “I Sing the Mighty Power of God.” In around 1015 B.C., King David wrote Psalm 145, in which he joyfully sings of making known the power of God. We sing about the power of God, we might talk about the power of God, but what is the power of God and what does it have to do with 2 Timothy, with Paul, with Timothy, with the church at Ephesus, and with you and me? This chapter should prove to be a great encouragement to each of us as we meditate on what God’s power can do. If we truly ponder these five truths pertaining to the power of God, it should minimize our discouragement and maximize our courage as we face the daily challenges of life as children of God. Let’s read the text we’re going to study together:

> Therefore do not be ashamed of the testimony of our Lord, nor of me His prisoner, but share with me in the sufferings for the gospel according to the power of God, who has saved us and called us with a holy calling, not according to our works, but according to His own purpose and grace which was given to us in Christ Jesus before time began, but has now been revealed by the appearing of our Savior Jesus Christ, who has abolished death and brought life and immortality to light through the gospel, to which I was appointed a preacher, an apostle, and a teacher of the Gentiles. (2 Timothy 1:8-11)

In our last chapter, we considered five truths that must be remembered as we consider using our spiritual gifts: God gives us His power as we use our gifts; it is essential that we love others and love God when we’re using our gifts; fear of using our gifts is not from God; in using our gifts, we must think as Christ, that is, we must be of sound mind; and, lastly, we are to stir up the gifts that are in us. In this chapter, we will consider five aspects of the power of God: *God’s Power in Suffering* (v 8); *God’s Power to Save Us* (v 9); *God’s Power to Slay Death* (v 10a);

*God's Power to Shine Light on the Gospel* (v 10b); and *God's Power to Give Spiritual Gifts* (v 11). The verses we'll cover in this chapter convey only a smidge of what the Bible has to say about the power of God. The *Questions to Consider* at the end of this chapter point you to consider other Scriptures that deal with God's power. But even those Scriptures barely plumb the depths of what God's Word says about God's power! It would be a fabulous word study to consider all that the Bible has to say about the power of God—and I would encourage you to do just that.

As we begin considering verses 8-11 of 2 Timothy 1, it's important for us to keep in mind that Paul has just written to Timothy of the need for him to stir up the gift within him, and that Paul has encouraged Timothy with the reality that God will grant to Timothy the power he will need while he is ministering. In these verses, Paul is continuing to write about the power of God, and here Paul focuses on the effects of that power. Let's consider the first effect of the mighty power of God, from verse 8.

## God's Power in Suffering *2 Timothy 1:8*

> Therefore do not be ashamed of the testimony of our Lord, nor of me His prisoner, but share with me in the sufferings for the gospel according to the power of God, (2 Timothy 1:8)

Here, Paul is saying to Timothy: "*Therefore*—because God has granted us gifts and the ability and power to use them—then you need not be ashamed to testify of Him. God's power will sustain you, Timothy, even if while using your gifts you incur suffering." And, believe me, the apostle Paul knew well of suffering for the sake of the gospel; almost every time he used his spiritual gifts, he ended up in prison! When Paul says *do not be ashamed*, it is as though Paul is saying, "God forbid that we should ever be ashamed!" The aorist tense of the Greek here indicates that Timothy is not guilty of this yet, but Paul must have had concerns that it could be possible, and so he warns Timothy. Perhaps, looming in Paul's mind is the shame that drove Peter or Judas. Matthew's Gospel records the account of Peter's denial of Christ in Matthew 26:69-75 (LSB).

> Now Peter was sitting outside in the courtyard, and a servant-girl came to him and said, "You too were with Jesus the Galilean." But he denied it before them all, saying, "I do not know what you are talking about." And when he had gone out to the gateway, another servant-girl saw him and said to those who were there, "This man was with Jesus of Nazareth." And again he denied it with an oath, "I do not know the man." A little later the bystanders came up and said to Peter, "Surely you too are one of them; for even the way you talk gives you away." Then he began to curse and swear, "I do not know the man!" And immediately a rooster crowed. And Peter remembered the word which Jesus had said, "Before a rooster crows, you will deny Me three times." And he went out and cried bitterly.

Judas was far more brazen than Peter in his denial of the Lord; Judas betrayed Jesus for just 30 pieces of silver, and we know that after that betrayal he hung himself. Being ashamed is a dangerous place to be for a Christian. It can begin when we are lethargic in serving the Lord, which is perhaps why Paul tells Timothy to stir up the gift within him. Don't become spiritually lazy, my friends! It is the beginning of what could be a spiritual downfall. Being isolated from other believers can lead to spiritual poverty, which then results in being ashamed of your faith. Consider Proverbs 18:1 (LSB), "He who separates himself seeks his own desire, he breaks out in dispute against all sound wisdom." In 2 Timothy 4:12, Paul will explain that he is not ashamed because he knows the One in whom he believes.

When Paul speaks here in verse 8 about *the testimony of our Lord*, the word for *testimony* refers to given evidence, that is, evidence that Jesus is *Lord*. Paul knew that Jesus was Lord—there was no doubt in his mind—and that firm belief gave him boldness, not shame. In Romans 1:16 (LSB), Paul says, "For I am not ashamed of the gospel, for it is the power of God for salvation to everyone who believes, to the Jew first and also to the Greek." There are many ways that we can exhibit being ashamed of being a Christian. We might remain silent when we should be speaking up for what is right; we might look like the world; we might be embarrassed to mention the Lord's name publicly or to pray in public; we might accept the world's ideas as our own. It's sad to think that we would be ashamed of the One who has given us life and saved us from sin and death. Rather than being filled with pride, which causes us to then be ashamed of Christ, we should be thankful and humbled that we are called by His name.

Paul writes that Timothy is not to be ashamed of the Lord, but he also is not to be ashamed of Paul, as evidenced by the words *nor of me His prisoner.* At the time Paul was writing to Timothy, Paul was in prison for the gospel. In fact, Paul spent 25% of his life in prison. We must remember that at this time it was costly to be a Christian; many were imprisoned for their faith and many died for their faith. Timothy may have been ashamed or fearful to identify with Paul. Like Paul, Timothy probably understood that he too would also end up in prison because of his association with Christ. But, instead of being ashamed, Timothy is to share in Paul's sufferings. To *share with me in the sufferings* means that Paul is asking Timothy to suffer hardship along with him. When you think about it, those who are not willing to suffer for Christ's sake are also those who are ashamed to be associated with Him. The ones who are bold and unashamed are the ones who are also willing to suffer. Peter says in 1 Peter 4:16, "Yet if anyone suffers as a Christian, let him not be ashamed, but let him glorify God in this matter."

Notice that the suffering Paul speaks of here is because of *the gospel.* Timothy needed to be reminded of what Paul wrote to the church at Philippi, in Philippians 1:29 (LSB), "For to you it has been granted for Christ's sake, not only to believe in Him, but also to suffer for His sake." Jesus tells us in Luke 14:25-33 that we must each consider the cost of being a disciple. In Acts 14:22 (LSB), we read of Paul and Barnabas' ministry, in which they were "strengthening the souls of the disciples, encouraging them to continue in the faith, and saying, 'Through many afflictions we must enter the kingdom of God.'" And Paul will make it clear later in this epistle, in 2 Timothy 2:12-13, that "if we suffer, we shall also reign with him: if we deny him, he also will deny us: If we believe not, yet he abideth faithful: he cannot deny himself" (KJV). My friend, we can also take encouragement, just as Timothy could, that we are not alone in our sufferings. You and I have brothers and sisters all over the world who are suffering physically for the sake of the gospel. Peter speaks to this very reality when he addresses the persecuted Christians of his day, in 1 Peter 5:9b (LSB), by saying, "that the same experiences of suffering are being accomplished among your brethren who are in the world." We not only share salvation with all of our brothers and sisters in Christ, but we also share suffering.

Paul says that this suffering for the gospel is *according to the power of God*. What does he mean here? He's just written of the power we have when we use our gifts, and it is that same power that helps us in our sufferings. *The first thing we see in these verses about the mighty power of God is that it helps us in our sufferings.* What did Paul say in 2 Corinthians 12:7-10 (LSB) about the power of God during his sufferings?

> Because of the surpassing greatness of the revelations, for this reason, to keep me from exalting myself, there was given me a thorn in the flesh, a messenger of Satan to torment me—to keep me from exalting myself! Concerning this I pleaded with the Lord three times that it might leave me. And He has said to me, "My grace is sufficient for you, for power is perfected in weakness." Most gladly, therefore, I will rather boast in my weaknesses, so that the power of Christ may dwell in me. Therefore I am well content with weaknesses, with insults, with distresses, with persecutions and hardships, for the sake of Christ, for when I am weak, then I am strong.

When we go through suffering, Christ's power rests upon us. In our weakness, we are made strong. In 2 Timothy 4:16-18, just a few chapters from this point in Paul's letter, he will write again of this power during suffering:

> At my first defense no one stood with me, but all forsook me. May it not be charged against them. But the Lord stood with me and strengthened me, so that the message might be preached fully through me, and that all the Gentiles might hear. Also I was delivered out of the mouth of the lion. And the Lord will deliver me from every evil work and preserve me for His heavenly kingdom. To Him be glory forever and ever. Amen!

Paul's words are an excellent reminder for us that no suffering is wasted. Suffering is for us precious time to draw near to the Lord! Oh, that we had the mindset of Paul as he writes to the church at Philippi: "that I may know Him and the power of His resurrection and the fellowship of His sufferings, being conformed to His death, in order that I may attain to the resurrection from the dead" (Philippians 3:10-11, LSB). Paul wanted to suffer so that He might know Christ more. He even speaks in Colossians of pursuing a path of suffering so that he can fill up that which is lacking in Christ's sufferings (Colossians 1:24). We sure have veered far from the doctrine of suffering in our day of easy-believism, easy-road Christianity, which wants a sugar-coated Bible! Paul continues in verse 9 with another aspect of the power of God.

## God's Power to Save Us *2 Timothy 1:9*

> who has saved us and called us with a holy calling, not according to our works, but according to His own purpose and grace which was given to us in Christ Jesus before time began, (2 Timothy 1:9)

The *who* in *who has saved us* refers back to the last word of verse 8—God! God *has saved us*! Listen to what Paul writes in 1 Corinthians 1:18 (LSB): "For the word of the cross is foolishness to those who are perishing, but to us who are being saved, it is the power of God." My friend, we have no power to save ourselves; our works are as filthy menstrual rags (Isaiah 64:6), but our God has power to save us with His precious blood. *This is the second aspect of God's mighty power: it saves us!* But He doesn't only save us; He also has *called us with a holy calling*. You might wonder what this means. Our brother Peter sheds light on this as he writes in 1 Peter 1:15-16, "but as He who called you is holy, you also be holy in all your conduct, because it is written, 'Be holy, for I am holy.'" The One who has called us to salvation, that is, God, is *holy*. Therefore, He expects those whom He has *called* to live in holiness of life.

Now, Paul makes it clear that it is not by our works that we are saved. He writes in Ephesians 2:8-9 (LSB). "For by grace you have been saved through faith, and this not of yourselves, it is the gift of God; not of works, so that no one may boast." And, again, in Titus 3:5 (LSB), "He saved us, not by works which we did in righteousness, but according to His mercy, through the washing of regeneration and renewing by the Holy Spirit." Anyone who believes or teaches that salvation is by works is cursed, according to Galatians 1:8-9. Instead of our works, salvation is *according to His own purpose and grace. His own purpose* means what He intends to happen, and *His grace* is the gift of salvation given to us. And note that this was *given to us in Christ Jesus before time began.* Paul tells the church at Ephesus in Ephesians 1:4 (LSB), "just as He chose us in Him before the foundation of the world, that we would be holy and blameless before Him in love." We were chosen before the foundation of the world, before time began. Paul moves on to yet two more aspects of the power of God in verse 10.

## God's Power to Slay Death *2 Timothy 1:10*

> but has now been revealed by the appearing of our Savior Jesus Christ, who has abolished death (2 Timothy 1:10a)

We might read this and ask, "What is it that has been revealed?" The idea here is that our salvation was planned before time *but has now been revealed,* or made manifest, *by the appearing of our Savior Jesus Christ.* Remember when the angel spoke to Joseph and told him not to be afraid of taking Mary as his wife? The angel was explaining to Joseph what would transpire, and in Matthew 1:21 (LSB), the angel says, "And she will bear a Son; and you shall call His name Jesus, for He will save His people from their sins." That once-hidden mystery, the gospel, is now revealed by God sending His Son in the flesh to save us from our sins.

So, what happened when Jesus came to save us from our sins? Well, numerous things transpired, but here in this text Paul says that, first of all, Christ abolished death. This means He rendered it useless. Those who know Christ will no longer be subject to eternal death; death has no sting for them. My friend, this is amazing power from God, is it not? *Only God's mighty power can slay death—this is the third aspect of His power.* There is no other religion that promises this; only the true God can destroy death!

## God's Power to Shine Light on the Gospel *2 Timothy 1:10*

> and brought life and immortality to light through the gospel, (2 Timothy 1:10b)

Another thing that happened when Jesus came was that He *brought life and immortality to light through the gospel.* This means His coming has shined light on the gospel. Paul knew of this amazing power because he experienced on the Damascus road both literal light and spiritual light shining on him. In fact, when Jesus called Paul, Jesus made clear to Paul that he would be a spokesman to share this good news. In Acts 26:17-18, Paul relates how the Lord said to him on that Damascus road,

> I will deliver you from the Jewish people, as well as from the Gentiles, to whom I now send you, to open their eyes, in order to turn them from darkness to light, and from the power of Satan to God, that they may receive forgiveness of sins and an inheritance among those who are sanctified by faith in Me.

Jesus was saying to Paul that those who repented under Paul's ministry would have their eyes opened and the light of their understanding turned on, so that they would no longer be under the power of Satan but of God. Who can shine light on the gospel? Only God. And only His mighty power can take people who are dead in their trespasses and sins and shine the light of life on them. *This is the fourth aspect of God's power: He shines light on the gospel.* There is one more aspect of God's power mentioned in verse 11 and with this we close.

## God's Power to Give Spiritual Gifts *2 Timothy 1:11*

> to which I was appointed a preacher, an apostle, and a teacher of the Gentiles. (2 Timothy 1:11)

Here, Paul says *to which I was appointed*, that is, chosen. And to whom was he appointed to make these things known? *To the Gentiles.* In Acts 9:15-16, the Lord instructed a disciple named Ananias to minister to Paul immediately following his conversion, relieving Ananias' fears of

Paul and explaining this specific calling the Lord had placed upon Paul: "But the Lord said to him, 'Go, for he is a chosen vessel of Mine to bear My name before Gentiles, kings, and the children of Israel. For I will show him how many things he must suffer for My name's sake.'" And what did God appoint Paul to be? *A preacher, an apostle, and a teacher.* Did you know that only God has the ability to give us such spiritual gifts? No one on earth can grant you the power of a spiritual gift. Consider Ephesians 4:8-13:

> Therefore He says: "When He ascended on high, He led captivity captive, And gave gifts to men." (Now this, "He ascended"—what does it mean but that He also first descended into the lower parts of the earth? He who descended is also the One who ascended far above all the heavens, that He might fill all things.) And He Himself gave some to be apostles, some prophets, some evangelists, and some pastors and teachers, for the equipping of the saints for the work of ministry, for the edifying of the body of Christ, till we all come to the unity of the faith and of the knowledge of the Son of God, to a perfect man, to the measure of the stature of the fullness of Christ.

*God has power to give spiritual gifts. This is the fifth aspect of His mighty power.*

Now, what are these gifts? The first one mentioned is *preacher*, which is simply one who heralds the gospel. In Ephesians 3:8, Paul writes, "To me, who am less than the least of all the saints, this grace was given, that I should preach among the Gentiles the unsearchable riches of Christ." The second one mentioned is *apostle*, which means one sent by God. Paul begins most of his epistles by saying, "Paul, an apostle of Christ Jesus." Paul knew he had been sent by God with a message. He was God's ambassador. The third gift Paul mentions is *teacher.* A teacher is one who instructs others by explaining truth in a methodical manner to his or her audience. In the New Testament, we have numerous accounts of Paul teaching others, and he must have loved doing so. In fact, we have one account, in Acts 20, of Paul preaching for so long that at midnight a young man named Eutychus fell asleep and fell out of the third-story window in which he had been sitting. Paul checked on the young man, because they all thought he was dead, then fell on him, embraced him, and raised him up. But not even that could stop Paul from teaching—he continued on till daybreak!

Consider again that Paul's calling was *to the Gentiles.* This would be amazing, in and of itself, because Paul was a Jew. One man says of this,

> As a herald Paul must announce and loudly proclaim that gospel. As an apostle he must say and do nothing except that which he has been commanded to say and to do. And as a teacher he must impart carefully instruction in the things pertaining to salvation and the glory of God, and he must admonish unto faith and obedience. For this threefold gospel-task, Paul has been divinely appointed or commissioned.[10]

As one who was appointed to these three things, teacher, preacher, and apostle, Paul knew and experienced the suffering which came with the job. He knew that we must, through much tribulation, enter the Kingdom of God. Paul was not immune to suffering, and the more he used his gifts, the more suffering he incurred. In fact, he will write in the very next verse, 2 Timothy 1:12, "For this reason I also suffer these things; nevertheless I am not ashamed, for I know whom I have believed and am persuaded that He is able to keep what I have committed to Him until that Day." Paul was Timothy's mentor, and Paul wanted Timothy to remember that he needed to pass on to others those things that had been taught to him by Paul as an apostle, a preacher, and a teacher.

## Summary

God's power has countless aspects to it, and if you and I were to read from Genesis to Revelation, we could probably make note of thousands of aspects of His power. In this chapter, we have learned of five aspects of that power. The first one mentioned here is that His power enables us in our suffering. Have you ever suffered for the sake of Christ? If not, why not? Are you ashamed of being a Christian? Are you willing

10 William Hendriksen, *New Testament Commentary: Exposition of The Pastoral Epistles* (Grand Rapids: Baker Book House, 1957), 234.

to be a fool for Christ's sake? When you do suffer for His sake, do you draw upon the power God grants as you go through suffering? Jesus Himself, while He was going through the suffering of the cross that was before Him, cried out to God to help Him. In Hebrews 5:7-8 (LSB), we read this:

> He, in the days of His flesh, offered up both prayers and supplications with loud crying and tears to the One able to save Him from death, and He was heard because of His reverence. Although He was a Son, He learned obedience from the things which He suffered.

Did you notice there that Jesus learned obedience by the things He suffered? Suffering not only draws us close to Christ, but we learn through it and one of the things we learn is obedience. Perhaps a good assignment would be to read the biographies of those who have gone before us, so that we might learn of the sufferings they incurred for the gospel but also of the amazing power God granted them during their horrific sufferings. God has power to help you during your suffering—will you draw upon that power?

Secondly, God's power saves us. Have you experienced the saving power of our God? What has God's power saved you from? Is your life different today than when you were born again? How has His power given you victory over sin? Have you thanked God for His mighty power that has saved you from death, from sin, and from hell?

Thirdly, God's power slayed death; it destroyed death. This is an amazing truth—death has no sting anymore! We will be changed in a moment, in a twinkling of an eye, as Paul says in 1 Corinthians 15. And this will all be done by the power of God. Because of God's mighty power, death no longer has a hold on you and me. The grave will have no hold on us!

Fourthly, God's power shines light on the gospel! When was your gospel moment, when God, in His amazing power, shined the light of the gospel on your heart and gave you faith to believe? I pray that you and I never get over that incredible miracle! Knowing this power should give us freedom in sharing the gospel because we know that it is not up to us, but it is up to God's power to shine the light of the truth of the gospel into the hearts and minds of those with whom we share. He did it for us, and He can do it for others. We must simply be faithful vessels to go and share that gospel.

Lastly, God's power has granted us spiritual gifts. What are your spiritual gifts, and are you using them? Have you stopped to think that it was God's power that granted you those gifts? It takes power to use a weak vessel made of dust for His glory. He takes weak men and women and makes them strong with His power for His glory. God's mighty power granted you the gifts that are within you. He made Paul a preacher, an apostle, and a teacher. What has He made you, and how are you serving Him?

As you go through this week, you might talk about the power of God, you might even sing about the power of God, but will you experience the power of God? Martin Luther once said, "But the power of God cannot be so determined and measured, for it is uncircumscribed and immeasurable, beyond and above all that is or may be. On the other hand, it must be essentially present at all places, even in the tiniest tree leaf."

## QUESTIONS TO CONSIDER

1. Read 2 Timothy 1:8-11. (a) What are the commandments in this passage? (b) What are the warnings in this passage? (c) What are the promises in this passage?

2. Memorize 2 Timothy 1:8.

3. (a) What is God's power able to do, according to 2 Timothy 1:8-11? (b) What other things do you learn about the power of God from Deuteronomy 9:29; Psalm 78:26; Jeremiah 10:12; Luke 4:36; 5:24; 12:5; 21:27; John 10:18; 1 Peter 1:5; and Revelation 19:1? (c) When you think about the power of God helping you in your suffering, how do the truths in these verses encourage you? (d) Can you recall a time when God's power aided you during a time of suffering? How did His power aid you in that difficulty? (e) How would you describe God's power?

4. (a) According to the following verses, what happens when we partake in and endure the sufferings of our Lord? Philippians 3:10; Colossians 1:24; 2 Timothy 2:11-12; and 1 Peter 4:12-16? (b) Why do some people have difficulty with being willing to suffer for the Lord?

5. Cite an example in Scripture where God's power was manifested on an individual or a situation. How does that example encourage you in your daily walk?

6. (a) What could have been some of the reasons that Timothy was ashamed? (b) What is the danger of being ashamed of the Lord, according to Matthew 26:69-75 and Mark 8:38? (c) What are some ways we exhibit being ashamed of our Lord?

7. What has God's power done in your life? Write a praise to the Lord for His mighty power to share with your group.

# Holding Fast to the Truth

*2 Timothy 1:12-14*

THROUGHOUT the last few decades of my life, as I've read or reviewed my memorization of 2 Timothy, whenever I come to chapter one, verse 12, I find myself wanting to sing a hymn that I have known since childhood. Originally published in 1883, "I Know Whom I Have Believed" is a beautiful hymn written by Major Daniel Webster Whittle.

> Whittle was named after American politician (and dictionary compiler) Daniel Webster. Whittle reached the rank of major in the American Civil War, and for the rest of his life was known as "Major" Whittle. During the war, Whittle lost his right arm, and ended up in a prisoner of war camp. Recovering from his wounds in the hospital, he looked for something to read, and found a New Testament. Though its words resonated with him, he was still not ready to accept Christ. Shortly after, a hospital orderly woke him and said a dying prisoner wanted someone to pray with him. Whittle demurred, but the orderly said, "But I thought you were a Christian; I have seen you reading your Bible." Whittle then agreed to go. He recorded what took place at the dying youth's bed side:
>
> I dropped on my knees and held the boy's hand in mine. In a few broken words I confessed my sins and asked Christ to forgive me. I believed right there that He did forgive me. I then prayed earnestly for the boy. He became quiet and pressed my hand as I prayed and pleaded God's promises. When I arose from my knees, he was dead. A look of peace had come over his troubled face, and I cannot but believe that God who used him to bring me to the Savior, used me to lead him to trust Christ's precious blood and find pardon. I hope to meet him in heaven.[11]

After the war, Whittle became an evangelist and wrote many hymns, but "I Know Whom I Have Believed" speaks most clearly about the truth revealed to him that day.

---

11 "Hymns & Music :: Biography for Daniel Webster Whittle." *Blue Letter Bible*. https://www.blueletterbible.org/hymns/bios/bio_w_h_whittle_dw.cfm. Accessed March 11, 2024.

The chorus of Whittle's hymn is based on the text of 2 Timothy 1:12 (KJV): "for I know whom I have believed, and am persuaded that he is able to keep that which I have committed unto him against that day." Having written more than 200 hymns over the course of his life, Whittle went home to be with his Lord on March 4, 1901.

*I know whom I have believed.* What a profound confession by the apostle Paul! Is this a statement you can echo with Paul in full confidence? How could Paul himself be certain of this Christian confession? Well, let's consider some answers to that last question as we look at 2 Timothy 1:12-14.

> For this reason I also suffer these things; nevertheless I am not ashamed, for I know whom I have believed and am persuaded that He is able to keep what I have committed to Him until that Day. Hold fast the pattern of sound words which you have heard from me, in faith and love which are in Christ Jesus. That good thing which was committed to you, keep by the Holy Spirit who dwells in us.

As we study these verses together, our outline will include: *Paul's Confession Before Timothy* (v 12), in which we will observe a fivefold confession; and *Paul's Charge to Timothy* (vv 13-14), in which we will observe a twofold charge. In our last chapter, we considered the mighty power of God and saw five aspects of His power: His power to aid in suffering; His power to save us; His power to slay death; His power to shine light on the gospel; and His power to give spiritual gifts. Paul has just highlighted, in verse 11, a few of the spiritual gifts that were given to him by God to use for His service. In verse 12, Paul now speaks to Timothy of the suffering for God that comes along with that service to God. Let's consider Paul's fivefold confession before Timothy, in verse 12.

## Paul's Confession Before Timothy *2 Timothy 1:12*

> For this reason I also suffer these things; nevertheless I am not ashamed, for I know whom I have believed and am persuaded that He is able to keep what I have committed to Him until that Day. (2 Timothy 1:12)

Paul begins with the words *for this reason*, which require us to look back at what he has just written in verse 11. The *reason* Paul says *I also suffer these things* is that God appointed Paul to be a preacher, an apostle, and a teacher. Paul is saying that his appointment by God comes with suffering. When Jesus was talking to Ananias about Paul, Jesus said, in Acts 9:15-16 (LSB), "Go, for he is a chosen instrument of Mine, to bear My name before the Gentiles and kings and the sons of Israel; for I will show him how much he must suffer for My name." Paul was appointed to suffer, and, my friend, you and I are not exempt from suffering either. In 2 Timothy 3:12, Paul writes, "Yes, and all who desire to live godly in Christ Jesus will suffer persecution." One man wisely wrote regarding Paul's suffering,

> Though Paul has been subject to ignominy, he has not disgraced himself. Along with others, such as Joseph, Jeremiah, Daniel, John the Baptist, and Peter, he has joined the ranks of prisoners for the best cause. After all, the place of dishonor may be the place of highest honor. Was not Jesus crucified between two malefactors?[12]

Paul suffered many things for the sake of the gospel. He did not consider it drudgery to suffer for the Lord, the One who had saved him. It was Paul's joy to go through suffering for the Lord. *This is the first statement of Paul's fivefold confession: I suffer.* And, my friend, Paul's statement of suffering was not for self-pity, but for his Savior.

*Paul goes on to mention his second confession: I am not ashamed.* He has already admonished Timothy in verse 8 not to be ashamed of the testimony of Christ. Paul wants Timothy to follow his example, and so he makes it clear: *nevertheless*, even though it is true that I suffer, *I am not ashamed*. One man says of this, "Confidence as to the future drives away shame."[13]

Paul goes on to set forth why he is not ashamed and mentions his third

---

12 William Hendriksen, *Pastoral Epistles*, 254.

13 Andrew Robert Fausset, Robert Jamieson, David Brown, et al., "Jamieson, Fausset, and Brown Commentary on the Whole Bible" *CCEL*, https://ccel.org/ccel/jamieson/jfb/jfb.xi.xvi.ii.html, accessed 2/23/24.

confession. He says *I know whom I have believed. This is Paul's third confession before Timothy.* Paul is not in doubt about his salvation; he *knows*, he is absolutely persuaded about the Christ in whom he believes. The word *believe* means to commit and put trust in, and it is in the perfect tense, which indicates that this was a past action with present, ongoing results. Our salvation occurred sometime in the past, but its effects are ongoing.

Before we go on to Paul's fourth confession, if you find that you are in doubt regarding your own commitment to the Lord, I would highly encourage you to carefully read over 1 John, James, and the Sermon on the Mount (Matthew 5-7). These three portions of Scripture are replete with self-examination passages that will aid you in truthfully examining yourself. When Paul wrote to the church at Corinth, in 2 Corinthians 13:5-6 (LSB), he encouraged this very kind of self-examination: "Test yourselves to see if you are in the faith; examine yourselves! Or do you not recognize about yourselves that Jesus Christ is in you—unless indeed you fail the test? But I hope that you will realize that we ourselves do not fail the test."

*Paul goes on to mention a fourth confession to Timothy: I am persuaded that He is able to keep what I've committed to Him.* Paul is absolutely convinced that his salvation is secure with God. Paul has no doubts about what God can do. *He is able* means that God is strong; He can do it. It's the same idea Paul writes about in Philippians 4:11-13 when he writes about learning to be content and declares that he can do all things through Christ who strengthens him. In other words, Paul can be content because of the strong power of God. It's not Paul's power; it's God's power. That same idea is here in 2 Timothy 1:12. Peter also writes, in 1 Peter 1:5, that we "are kept by the power of God through faith for salvation ready to be revealed in the last time." It is not Paul who *keeps* what has been committed to God, but it is God who does it.

In the next phrase, however, Paul says God is able to keep *what I have committed to Him*. You might be thinking, "Well, now I am really confused. God is able to keep us, but we make a commitment to Him, right?" Man is responsible; God is responsible. We are in a covenant relationship with Him: we with Him, and He with us. *Here we have Paul's fifth confession before Timothy: I have committed myself to His Lordship.* The commitment Paul made was to the gospel, the saving grace bestowed upon him. Didn't he just say, "I know whom I have believed"? He's declaring, "I am committed!" In fact, to believe is to make a commitment to someone, in this case, to the Lord. The word *committed* means to put a deposit into something for safekeeping. Paul knows that the commitment he has made is kept by God, who is able to keep our souls safe. It is God who guards us or preserves us. The word *keep* is a military term which refers to a soldier keeping guard over something. If a soldier is not attentive during his watch, he could lose his life. Our God is far more attentive than any human soldier; He is never inattentive in His watch over us and guarding of our souls. Listen to Psalm 121 (LSB) and be encouraged:

> I will lift up my eyes to the mountains; from where shall my help come? My help comes from Yahweh, who made heaven and earth. He will not allow your foot to stumble; He who keeps you will not slumber. Behold, He who keeps Israel will not slumber and will not sleep.
>
> Yahweh is your keeper; Yahweh is your shade on your right hand. The sun will not strike you by day, nor the moon by night. Yahweh will keep you from all evil; He will keep your soul. Yahweh will keep your going out and your coming in from now until forever.

Did you notice what the Psalmist said? The Lord, Yahweh, shall keep your soul! Our brother Peter writes of this very thing, in 1 Peter 1:3-5 (LSB), when he says,

> Blessed be the God and Father of our Lord Jesus Christ, who according to His great mercy has caused us to be born again to a living hope through the resurrection of Jesus Christ from the dead, to obtain an inheritance incorruptible and undefiled and unfading, having been kept in heaven for you, who are protected by the power of God through faith for a salvation ready to be revealed in the last time.

We are kept by the power of God!

Paul ends his fivefold confession before Timothy by saying that the keeping and guarding of the commitment he has made to God is *until that Day.* The *Day* that Paul is referring to is The Day of Judgment. Paul will speak of this later on in this letter, in 2 Timothy 4:6-8, where he writes, “For I am already being poured out as a drink offering, and the time of my departure is at hand. I have fought the good fight, I have finished the race, I have kept the faith. Finally, there is laid up for me the crown of righteousness, which the Lord, the righteous Judge, will give to me on that Day, and not to me only but also to all who have loved His appearing.” This keeping of Paul’s soul will be not only until the day he stands before God but throughout all eternity.

Paul’s persuasion regarding his commitment to Christ had results: he was unashamed of Christ, he was willing to suffer for Christ, and he was committed to Christ. And because Paul wanted these same results for his spiritual son Timothy, Paul had in mind some charges for Timothy that would aid in his steadfast commitment to the Lord. So, we turn from Paul’s confession before Timothy, in verse 12, to Paul’s charge to Timothy, in verses 13 and 14.

## Paul’s Charge to Timothy *2 Timothy 1:13-14*

> Hold fast the pattern of sound words which you have heard from me, in faith and love which are in Christ Jesus. (2 Timothy 1:13)

*The first charge Paul gives to Timothy is to hold fast the pattern of sound words.* What does it mean to *hold fast*? The idea is that of continuing to adhere to something, to remain tightly secured. Paul charges Timothy to hold fast to *the pattern of sound words.* The term *pattern* here has to do with a plan or an outline of a building. If you hire an architect to design a building, you are trusting that architect to create precise plans. If those plans are not precise, the building will be faulty and may even crumble. So it is with doctrine. We must follow a precise diet set forth in Scripture. If we do not, we will be faulty in our faith—at best—and our end may result in crumbling. If our foundation is not set solely upon Christ and His Word, the results will be a great fall, as Jesus mentions at the end of His Sermon on the Mount (Matthew 7:24-29). *Sound words* are those which are uncorrupted or pure. We might even say they refer to healthy doctrine. A passage often taken out of context, which deals with this same topic, is 1 Thessalonians 5:20-22 (LSB): "Do not despise prophecies, but examine all things; hold fast to that which is good; abstain from every form of evil." The idea in these verses is that we are not to despise the preaching of the Word; but, rather, as we hear the Word of God taught, we are to test it. We are to test teachers, as well, as John says in 1 John 4, where he tells us not to believe everything we hear but to test it. We are to be like the Berean believers in Acts 17:10-11 who not only listened to the Word being taught but also searched the Scriptures to make sure the things they were hearing were accurate. Having tested what we are hearing, we are to then *hold fast to what is good* in what we've heard taught. We are to hold fast to the sound teaching, but we are also to abstain from that which is evil. In other words, anything other than sound doctrine is evil and we are to get away from it.

Also, it is required of an elder that he hold fast to sound teaching. Consider how Titus 1:9 (LSB) describes elders as those who are "holding fast the faithful word which is in accordance with the teaching, so that he will be able both to exhort in sound doctrine and to reprove those who contradict." Ladies, I want to encourage you to guard what you hear. If the teaching you are receiving is not from the Word of God, then it is not healthy. While I was studying for this very chapter, I received a heartbreaking email from a woman I have never met. I won't go into the details but suffice it to say that she was more concerned about someone's feelings being hurt than with the truth of Scripture. I responded to her by reminding her that we must hold fast to truth even if it costs us something.

In the next phrase, Paul clarifies that this pattern of sound words to which Timothy was to hold fast had come from Paul himself; he says *which you have heard from me*. When I pour my life into another person, which is what we call discipleship, I am to teach that person sound things. In fact, in Titus 2:3-5, where it states that older women are to teach younger women, one of the requirements of the older woman is that she is to be a teacher of good things. When we instruct those younger than us, we are to teach them sound doctrine. Paul will write in just a few short verses, in 2 Timothy 2:1-2, "You therefore, my son, be strong in the grace that is in Christ Jesus. And the things that you have heard from me among many witnesses, commit these to faithful men who will be able to teach others also." He not only wants Timothy to hold fast to what has been taught from his lips, but he wants him to pass those things on to faithful men. Again, this is what we call discipleship. I would strongly encourage you that if you are not a part of that process, either discipling someone or being discipled, you should start. I have the joy of having two women who pour into my life, and I have the joy of pouring myself into many women through discipleship. It is joy unspeakable! (For the most part!)

Paul then adds the words *in faith and love which are in Christ Jesus.* The idea here is that we hold fast to these sound words in faith and love. Here, *faith* refers to our faith in our Lord, and *love* refers to our love for Him and others. Holding fast to the truth requires both faith and love. I was just talking with someone recently who was sharing the heartbreaking news with me that their daughter doesn't think she believes anymore. She made a verbal commitment to Christ at one time but no longer has faith. Lenski wisely says, "True love will never offer anything unhealthy. Can it be love when it does?"[14]

Ladies, this should cause us to pause to consider the multitude of false teachers we have today. They are not motivated by love but by greed; they desire to make merchandise of those who give them an ear (2 Peter 1:3, KJV). Peter mentions these things in 2 Peter 2:1-3 (LSB) when writing about false teachers. He says,

> But false prophets also arose among the people, just as there will also be false teachers among you, who will secretly introduce destructive heresies, even denying the Master who bought them, bringing swift destruction upon themselves. And many will follow their sensuality, and because of them the way of the truth will be maligned. And in their greed they will exploit you with false words, their judgment from long ago is not idle, and their destruction is not asleep.

They deny the Lord; they don't believe in Him. They don't love others, but,

14 R. C. H. Lenski, *Commentary on the New Testament: Timothy*, 771.

rather, exploit them with deceit. It is interesting to note that in his first letter to Timothy, Paul writes, "And the grace of our Lord was exceedingly abundant, with faith and love which are in Christ Jesus" (1 Timothy 1:14). Faith and love come from God, and we are to exhibit both of these qualities. Not only does Paul instruct Timothy in these verses to hold fast to sound teaching, but he now adds a second charge to him in verse 14.

> That good thing which was committed to you, keep by the Holy Spirit who dwells in us. (2 Timothy 1:14)

*The second charge to Timothy is to keep the good things which were committed to him.* Paul mentioned something similar in verse 12, when he wrote, "for I know whom I have believed and am persuaded that He is able to keep what I have committed to Him until that Day." Now what is this *good thing* Paul is referring to? He is referring to the sound doctrine he mentioned in verse 13. Paul is saying this good thing, this sound doctrine, was *committed* or deposited *to you.*

> The "entrusted deposit" (1:12, 14) was originally a monetary image, although other writers had also applied it to teaching; one was responsible to safeguard or multiply any money given one for safekeeping. Jewish teachers felt that they were passing on a sacred deposit to their disciples, who were expected to pass it on to others in turn (cf. 2:2).[15]

This is the desire of all who pass on good things to those they teach. It was Paul's desire for Timothy and he writes of it in 1 Timothy 6:20-21 (LSB): "O Timothy, guard what has been entrusted to you, turning aside from godless and empty chatter and the opposing arguments of what is falsely called knowledge—which some, while professing, have gone astray from the faith."

Note that even though Paul says it is Timothy's responsibility to *keep* what has been committed to him, it is by the enabling of the *Holy Spirit* that Timothy is able to do this; it is, ultimately, the Holy Spirit who does this work in Timothy. It is the same idea we saw in verse 12.

---

15 Craig S. Keener, *Bible Background Commentary*, Biblesoft.

Man has responsibility to do his part, and God does His part. Paul is not in doubt about Timothy's commitment. Rather, Paul is careful to say of the Holy Spirit that He *dwells in us*; this precious part of the Godhead dwells within Paul and Timothy; He inhabits them both. And, my friend, if you belong to the Lord, He inhabits you also! What a profound and sobering thought!

## Summary

Paul's fivefold confession to Timothy is this: I suffer; I am not ashamed; I know whom I have believed; I am persuaded that He is able to keep my salvation secure; and I am committed to His Lordship. If you were to write a fivefold confession, what would it say? I suffer for the sake of Christ, or I shrink at the thought of suffering for Him? I am not ashamed, or I am ashamed? I know whom I have believed, or I am in doubt about my belief? I am persuaded He is able to keep what I have committed to Him, or I am in doubt about God's ability to keep me? I am committed, or I am half-way committed or not committed at all? Paul's confession before Timothy is a far cry from much of what we see among professing Christians today.

Paul's twofold charge to Timothy is this: he is to hold fast to sound doctrine, and he is to keep the good things that have been committed to him. Are you holding securely to the truth? In what ways are you feeding yourself spiritually? How much sound doctrine do you digest each day? Who are the teachers you are listening to? When you hear something that doesn't measure up to Scripture, do you dismiss it? Are you caught up in the novel religious ideas of our day? How are you keeping those things that have been committed to you, and who are you passing them on to? Do you hear a sermon and quickly forget what you heard, or do you ponder it deeply? Do you pass truth on to others?

My dear sister, we need Pauls and Timothys in our day. We need men and women who will forsake all for the gospel, who will lose their lives to save them. We need young people who will listen to the wisdom of godly older men and women as they instruct them in the truths of Christ. Are you willing to lose your life for the gospel? Will you pass on sound doctrine to the next generation?

As we close this chapter, let's consider the words to the song I mentioned in the opening, and, as we do, let's make that confession that Paul made before Timothy.

I know not why God's wondrous grace
To me He hath made known,
Nor why, unworthy, Christ in love
Redeemed me for His own.

*Refrain:*
But I know Whom I have believed,
And am persuaded that He is able
To keep that which I've committed
Unto Him against that day.

I know not how this saving faith
To me He did impart,
Nor how believing in His Word
Wrought peace within my heart.

I know not how the Spirit moves,
Convincing men of sin,
Revealing Jesus through the Word,
Creating faith in Him.

I know not what of good or ill
May be reserved for me,
Of weary ways or golden days,
Before His face I see.

I know not when my Lord may come,
At night or noonday fair,
Nor if I walk the vale with Him,
Or meet Him in the air.[16]

---

16 Daniel W. Whittle, "I Know Whom I Have Believed", Public Domain, 1883.

# QUESTIONS TO CONSIDER

1. (a) What are the doctrinal truths that Paul is convinced of, according to 2 Timothy 1:12-14? (b) What are Paul's desires for his spiritual son, Timothy?

2. Memorize 2 Timothy 1:13.

3. Read 2 Corinthians 6:1-10; 11:16-33; 12:7-10, then answer the following questions. (a) What are some of the sufferings that the apostle Paul endured? (b) What attitudes do you detect in Paul's descriptions of his sufferings? (c) What are some sufferings you see fellow believers going through? (d) What attitudes have you observed in others in their sufferings that have encouraged you in your own sufferings?

4. (a) Paul says in 2 Timothy 1:12 that he is persuaded that God is able to keep that which he has committed unto Him. What else is Paul persuaded of, according to Romans 8:38-39 and 2 Timothy 1:5? (b) What things are you convinced of regarding your Christian faith?

5. (a) According to Psalm 19:7-11 and 1 Peter 2:2, why is it essential to hold fast to sound doctrine? (b) What happens if we receive false teaching, according to Jeremiah 23:16; Matthew 24:11; Titus 1:10-11; 2 Peter 2:1-3; 3:17-18? (c) Are you listening to doctrine that is true or false? How do you know? (d) In what ways do you hold fast to sound teaching?

6. (a) What doctrinal truths are you convinced of? (You might want to write a confession of your faith in a sentence or two!) (b) How do you plan to hold fast to the truth you have been taught?

7. After studying this chapter, what has the Lord challenged or convicted you of? Please write a prayer request to share with your group.

# What Will You Be Remembered For: A Disciple or a Defector?

*2 Timothy 1:15–18*

THE night before I sat down to write this chapter, my husband and I received a phone call informing us that his sister had passed away. It was a sobering reminder for us of the reality that we all are going to die. Times like that move me to reflect on my own life, the brevity of it, and to make it count for eternity. One of the questions I immediately asked my husband after we learned of his sister's death was, "Do you think your sister was a Christian?" He said that he doubted it. Her life reflected what Jesus said in the parable of the soils in Mark 4:3-9 (LSB):

> "Listen to this! Behold, the sower went out to sow; and it happened that as he was sowing, some seed fell beside the road, and the birds came and ate it up. And other seed fell on the rocky ground where it did not have much soil; and immediately it sprang up because it had no depth of soil. And after the sun rose, it was scorched; and because it had no root, it withered away. And other seed fell among the thorns, and the thorns came up and choked it, and it yielded no crop. And other seeds fell into the good soil, and as they grew up and increased, they were yielding a crop and produced thirty, sixty, and a hundredfold."
>
> And He was saying, "He who has ears to hear, let him hear."

A few verses later, in Mark 4:13-20 (LSB), Jesus explained this parable to His disciples:

> And He said to them, "Do you not understand this parable? How will you understand all the parables? The sower sows the word. And these are the ones who are beside the road where the word is sown: when they hear, immediately Satan comes and takes away the word which has been sown in them. And in a similar way, these are the ones

> being sown on the rocky places: those who, when hearing the word, immediately receive it with joy; and they have no root in themselves, but are only temporary; then, when affliction or persecution arises because of the word, immediately they fall away. And others are those being sown among the thorns; these are the ones who have heard the word, but the worries of the world, and the deceitfulness of riches, and the desires for anything else enter in and choke the word, and it becomes unfruitful. And those are the ones which were sown on the good soil: they who hear the word and accept it and are bearing fruit, thirty, sixty, and a hundredfold."

Many are like my husband's sister. They hear the Word of God, they endure for a little while, but then the cares of life, the deceitfulness of riches, persecutions, and other distractions come, and they defect. They are spurious believers. The gospel never penetrated their hearts to bring forth fruit.

Death should cause us as believers to reflect on many things. How am I living my life? What changes do I need to make in order that my life will count for eternity? Another question we might reflect on, especially as we attend a memorial service is, "What will *I* be remembered for?" Unfortunately, in the case of my husband's sister, she was a defector—one who earlier in her life professed to have faith in Christ but did not bear fruit. What will *you* be remembered for? As we come to the end of chapter one of Paul's second letter to Timothy, we will find a vivid contrast between those who were defectors from the faith and one who was a disciple of the faith. Let's read the text together.

> This you know, that all those in Asia have turned away from me, among whom are Phygellus and Hermogenes. The Lord grant mercy to the household of Onesiphorus, for he often refreshed me, and was not ashamed of my chain; but when he arrived in Rome, he sought me out very zealously and found me. The Lord grant to him that he may find mercy from the Lord in that Day—and you know very well how many ways he ministered to me at Ephesus. (2 Timothy 1:15-18)

Our outline for this chapter will include *The Characteristic of a Defector* (v 15) and *The Characteristics of a Disciple* (vv 16-18). In our last chapter, we considered Paul's fivefold confession to Timothy: I suffer, I am not ashamed, I know whom I have believed, I am persuaded that He is able to keep that I have committed to Him; and I am committed to His Lordship. Next, we considered Paul's twofold charge to Timothy: to hold fast to sound doctrine, and to keep the good things that have been committed to him. It's interesting that Paul's final words in the previous verse, verse 14, were about the Holy Spirit who dwells in believers. The reason I mention that is because now Paul mentions two men—not himself and Timothy, who were genuine disciples of the Lord indwelt by His Spirit, but two other men in whom the Holy Spirit did not dwell, who were defectors from the faith.

## The Characteristic of a Defector *2 Timothy 1:15*

> This you know, that all those in Asia have turned away from me, among whom are Phygellus and Hermogenes. (2 Timothy 1:15)

Paul reminds Timothy of something he already knows: *that all those in Asia turned away from* Paul. Paul uses the word *all* in a general sense, not a literal sense. He is not saying that every single human being in Asia turned away from him, but that all those associated with him in his ministry, who were from Asia, had turned away from him. There are numerous examples of this kind of literary use of the term *all* in Scripture. Consider Paul's use of it in 1 Corinthians 9:22b (LSB), where he writes, "I have become all things to all men, so that I may by all means save some." We know that Paul doesn't mean this literally but is using the term *all* in a general sense; otherwise, we might say that Paul had compromised his convictions to win some. Consider also 1 Corinthians 13:7 (LSB), where Paul writes that love "bears all things, believes all things, hopes all things, endures all things." Again, we could interpret this to mean ridiculous ideas like the thought that Paul is encouraging us to love to the extent of allowing for the ongoing sinfulness of others. Yet another example is found in Ephesians 6:21, where Paul writes, "But that you also may know my affairs and how I am doing, Tychicus, a beloved brother and faithful minister in the Lord, will make *all* things known to you." Tychicus did not make known to the Ephesians every single thing that could possibly be known; otherwise we could say that Tychicus made known to them what makes the world round or the sky blue. Paul is saying here in 2 Timothy 2:15 that Timothy knew of what took place in Asia, how Paul was forsaken by all his ministry associates from Asia, and Paul now singles out two of the men who turned away, *Phygellus and Hermogenes.* Interestingly, the name *Phygellus* means *fugitive*, and both of these men were known to have apostatized. The words *turned away* mean they turned back. The only mention of these two men in the New Testament is here in this verse. How sobering to think that the only reference to them is that they turned away from Paul and from the faith! Barnes says, "It is a sad thing when the ONLY record made of a man—the only evidence which we have that he ever lived at all—is that he turned away from a friend, or forsook the paths of true religion. And yet there are many men of whom the only thing to be remembered of them is that they lived to do wrong."[17] But Paul isn't the only one to have had men turn away from him and from the faith—so did our Lord. John writes about Jesus, in John 6:66 (LSB), that "As a result of this many of His disciples went away and were not walking with Him anymore."

While these two men are mentioned by name here, they were clearly not the only ones who turned away. Toward the end of this letter, in 2 Timothy 4:9-16, Paul specifically names others who had also departed from him:

> Be diligent to come to me quickly; for Demas has forsaken me, having loved this present world, and has departed for Thessalonica—Crescens for Galatia, Titus for Dalmatia. Only Luke is with me. Get Mark and bring him with you, for he is useful to me for ministry. And Tychicus I have sent to Ephesus. Bring the cloak that I left with Carpus at Troas when you come—and the books, especially the parchments.
>
> Alexander the coppersmith did me much harm. May the Lord repay him according to his works. You also must beware of him, for he has greatly resisted our words.

17 Albert Barnes, "Barnes' New Testament Notes," *CCEL*, https://ccel.org/ccel/barnes/ntnotes/ntnotes.xix.i.xv.html. Accessed February 27, 2024.

> At my first defense no one stood with me, but all forsook me. May it not be charged against them.

So, what is the characteristic of a defector? A defector turns away from the faith; they apostatize from the faith. But, thankfully, not all turned away from Paul; not all departed from the faith. There was one man who did not. His name was Onesiphorus. So, we turn from the defectors of the faith to a genuine disciple of the faith. There are five characteristics of a genuine disciple listed for us in these verses, and I have put them in the form of an acrostic: **MERCY**. A genuine disciple of the Lord will receive mercy from the Lord. Paul mentions twice in these few verses his desire that God would grant Onesiphorus mercy, so that's why I thought it an appropriate word to use for the acrostic.

## The Characteristics of a Disciple *2 Timothy 1:16-18*

> The Lord grant mercy to the household of Onesiphorus, for he often refreshed me, and was not ashamed of my chain; (2 Timothy 1:16)

Paul's desire was for the *Lord* to *grant mercy* not only to *Onesiphorus* himself but for all who were in his *household*, which would be his family. *Mercy* is divine compassion. Paul is saying, "Lord, grant divine compassion to this man and all that live with him." As we will see in the coming verses, Onesiphorus had shown Paul mercy and now Paul prays for mercy to be granted to Onesiphorus and his entire household. I was thinking, as I was studying this passage, that I could not recall ever asking God to show mercy to someone's entire family. I have asked God to show mercy to our nation, and to individuals, but not a family. Perhaps this is something we should consider praying, since we have this Pauline example.

So, who is *Onesiphorus*? His name means profit-bearer, a helper. This is the only letter in the New Testament in which he is mentioned. Near the end of this letter, in 2 Timothy 4:19, Paul mentions Onesiphorus a second time when Paul writes, "Greet Prisca and Aquila, and the household of Onesiphorus." It is possible that Onesiphorus was a deacon, but we cannot be certain of that.

Why would Paul desire that God would grant mercy to this man and to his household? Paul says it is because Onesiphorus often *refreshed me. This is the **R** on your acrostic: A genuine disciple of the Lord **R**efreshes others.* The word *refresh* means to cool again, to relieve others of their distress. We might say that this person is a breath of fresh air. In 1 Corinthians 16:17-18 (LSB), Paul mentions three men—Stephanas, Fortunatus, and Achaicus—and says of them, "they have refreshed my spirit and yours. Therefore recognize such men" (1 Corinthians 16:18). In Philemon 1:7, Paul writes to Philemon, "we have great joy and consolation in your love, because the hearts of the saints have been refreshed by you, brother." What a blessing to think of those who refreshed Paul as he worked so diligently to serve the Lord! Proverbs 11:25 reminds us, "The generous soul will be made rich, and he who waters will also be watered himself." You know, my friend, we often long for others to refresh us or to water us in the weariness of life, but who are you and I refreshing? Who are we encouraging? Remember the words of our Lord when He said that it is more blessed to give than to receive (Acts 20:35)! Onesiphorus was a refresher of souls—are you?

Not only did Onesiphorus refresh Paul, but Paul goes on to say of him that *he was not ashamed of my chain.* Onesiphorus was not ashamed of Paul's imprisonment. *This is the **C** on your acrostic: A genuine disciple is **C**ourageous.* Remember, Paul had admonished Timothy to not be ashamed of the fact that Paul was in prison, back in verse 8, and now Paul is giving Timothy an example of someone he can emulate who is not ashamed. Timothy lacked courage. I know in my own life, in those areas where I am weak, it is good for me to have the example of someone to follow. This was a difficult time for Paul in prison; many forsook him, and many forsook the faith. Paul loved Timothy dearly—they were united in spirit—and he did not want his son in the faith to defect like others had. Paul goes on to mention two more qualities of a genuine disciple in the next verse:

> but when he arrived in Rome, he sought me out very zealously and found me. (2 Timothy 1:17)

Onesiphorus evidently went to Rome where Paul was in prison, and when he arrived, he *sought* to find Paul and did so *very zealously*, Paul says. We need to understand that there would have been countless prisoners in Rome, and it is thought that Paul was not being held in a public prison, so the search would have even been greater. Onesiphorus was not going to give up trying to locate Paul. *This is the **E** on your acrostic: A genuine disciple is **E**arnest.* This guy was earnest. He was diligent. He was not going to give up on this mission to find Paul. After a few unsuccessful attempts to find Paul, I am sure that it would have been tempting to give up—but not this guy! My friend, when God calls us to do something, we should finish the task, no matter how hard it may be. So many Christians today are lazy; they fail to be zealous in their God-given calling. They fail to do everything to the glory of God. We want a comfy, cushy lifestyle on our comfy, cushy couch. Few will take the hard road of denial and discipline. Onesiphorus was one who was earnest. He was not going to give up. And what was the result? Paul said Onesiphorus *found me*! The earnest, diligent search paid off. *This is the **Y** on your acrostic: A genuine disciple **Y**ields his life.* Onesiphorus knew that his association with the apostle Paul might mean his own death. At this time, Nero was reigning and the persecution against Christians was tremendous. Paul was in prison for the gospel, and Onesiphorus' association with him could have resulted in persecution and death. What did Jesus say in John 15:13 (LSB)? "Greater love has no one than this, that one lay down his life for his friends." And in Mark 8:35-38 (LSB), Jesus soberly warns us:

> For whoever wishes to save his life will lose it, but whoever loses his life for My sake and the gospel's will save it. For what does it profit a man to gain the whole world, and forfeit his soul? For what will a man give in exchange for his soul? For whoever is ashamed of Me and My words in this adulterous and sinful generation, the Son of Man will also be ashamed of him when He comes in the glory of His Father with the holy angels.

My sister, a genuine disciple of the Lord will yield her life for others and for the gospel.

Onesiphorus is also a reminder of what Jesus warns of in Matthew 25:31-46 (LSB):

> But when the Son of Man comes in His glory, and all the angels with Him, then He will sit on His glorious throne. And all the nations will be gathered before Him; and He will separate them from one another, as the shepherd separates the sheep from the goats; and He will put the sheep on His right, and the goats on the left.
>
> Then the King will say to those on His right, "Come, you who are blessed of My Father, inherit the kingdom, which has been prepared for you from the foundation of the world. For I was hungry, and you gave Me something to eat; I was thirsty, and you gave Me something to drink; I was a stranger, and you invited Me in; naked, and you clothed Me; I was sick, and you visited Me; I was in prison, and you came to Me." Then the righteous will answer Him, saying, "Lord, when did we see You hungry, and feed You, or thirsty, and give You something to drink? And when did we see You a stranger, and invite You in, or naked, and clothe You? And when did we see You sick, or in prison, and come to You?" And the King will answer and say to them, "Truly I say to you, to the extent that you did it to one of these brothers of Mine, even the least of them, you did it to Me."
>
> Then He will also say to those on His left, "Depart from Me, accursed ones, into the eternal fire which has been prepared for the devil and his angels; for I was hungry, and you gave Me nothing to eat; I was thirsty, and you gave Me nothing to drink; I was a stranger, and you did not invite Me in; naked, and you did not clothe Me; sick, and in prison, and you did not visit Me." Then they themselves also will answer, saying, "Lord, when did we see You hungry, or thirsty, or a stranger, or naked, or sick, or in prison, and did not take care of You?" Then He will answer them, saying, "Truly I say to you, to the extent that you did not do it to one of the least of these, you did not do it to Me." And these will go away into eternal punishment, but the righteous into eternal life.

Onesiphorus demonstrated his genuine commitment to the Lord by doing exactly what Jesus described—visiting those in prison, specifically Paul. I recall a time early in my husband's ministry when a man in our church was put in prison for about 20 years. To my knowledge, my husband was the only one who visited him from our church during those years. And, later, in another church my husband pastored, we had a young man who was in prison, and to my knowledge, once again, my husband was the only one in our congregation who visited him. Barnes writes,

> What was the employment of Onesiphorus is not known. It may have been that he was a merchant, and had occasion to visit Rome on business. At all events, he was at pains to search out the apostle, and his attention was the more valuable because it cost him trouble to find him. It is not everyone, even among professors of religion, who in a great and splendid city would be at the trouble to search out a Christian brother, or even a minister, who was a prisoner, and endeavor to relieve his sorrows. This man, so kind to the great apostle, will be among those to whom the Saviour will say, at the final judgment, "I was in prison, and ye came unto me;" Matt 25:36.[18]

In James 2:13 (LSB), James has sobering words for us in this regard, "For judgment will be merciless to one who has shown no mercy. Mercy triumphs over judgment." Paul has one more thing to say about this man, Onesiphorus, and it is the final characteristic of a disciple in our acrostic. (These are certainly not the only characteristics of a disciple of Christ; they're just the ones mentioned in this text.)

> The Lord grant to him that he may find mercy from the Lord in that Day—and you know very well how many ways he ministered to me at Ephesus. (2 Timothy 1:18)

Paul is so overcome with Onesiphorus' kindness toward him that Paul asks the Lord to grant mercy to Onesiphorus once again. This is the second time Paul requests this for Onesiphorus, and this time Paul adds *in that Day*. This is a reference to the *Day* of Judgment. Paul has already made reference to that day in verse 12. Some have taken this phrase to mean that Onesiphorus is dead and that this is a proof text regarding praying for the dead. But we have no evidence in this text to

---

18 Albert Barnes, "Barnes' Notes," *CCEL*, https://ccel.org/ccel/barnes/ntnotes/ntnotes.xix.i.xvii.html. Accessed February 27, 2024.

demonstrate that Onesiphorus was dead, and we have no proof texts anywhere in the Scriptures teaching us to pray for the dead! Because Paul was in prison, he would be unable to reward or to show kindness to this dear saint, but God on that day could show mercy to the one who had shown Paul so much mercy. God would reward Onesiphorus for his kindness to Paul. The Scriptures are clear that we will be rewarded in Heaven for our works (1 Corinthians 3:12-15) and, certainly, this man will be shown mercy on that day. And, as we've already seen demonstrated in the epistle of James, those who show mercy will be shown mercy, and those who do not show mercy will not be shown mercy (James 2:13).

Paul concludes his remarks to Timothy by saying *and you know very well how many ways he ministered to me at Ephesus. This is the **M** on your acrostic: A disciple of Christ **M**inisters to others.* Onesiphorus *ministered* to Paul. This is the same word that is used elsewhere in the New Testament for deacon. It means to serve, to be a table waiter. Paul is saying, "Onesiphorus served me; he waited upon me." Paul had many needs in prison, and Onesiphorus was faithful to minister to him. Paul would have had little food or water available to him; if it was winter, he would have needed warm clothing. Onesiphorus ministered to Paul in his needs. No wonder Paul asks for God to grant him mercy on that day! Perhaps Paul had in mind something Jesus said in Mark 9:41 (LSB): "For whoever gives you a cup of water to drink in My name because you are of Christ, truly I say to you, he will not lose his reward." God doesn't forget those who serve Him and serve others. In Hebrews 6:10 (LSB), we are reminded that "For God is not unrighteous so as to forget your work and the love which you have shown toward His name, in having ministered and continuing to minister to the saints."

## Summary

Paul reminds Timothy of two things: those who defected from the faith, and one who displayed the faith. Paul leaves these vivid contrasts to Timothy as a sober reminder to fulfill his calling and to do it with all diligence. Paul does not want Timothy to be slack and lazy and ashamed of his God-given calling.

> The contrast between the faithful and the unfaithful, the strong and the weak, the trustworthy and the unreliable, is striking. The many in Asia (v. 15) portray the very things Paul had been warning Timothy against—cowardice, shame, self-indulgence, infidelity. Onesiphorus, on the other hand, demonstrated the characteristics Paul had been recommending to Timothy—courage, love, self-discipline, boldness, and faithfulness. Clearly the negative and the positive examples were designed to strengthen Timothy's resolve to be counted among those who were willing to stand shoulder to shoulder with the apostle.[19]

What about you, my friend? When you leave this life and enter the next, will you be remembered as one who defected from the faith or as one who was a genuine disciple of the faith? What are you doing now to discipline yourself unto godliness? Are you following the example of Onesiphorus? When you consider the five characteristics Paul mentions of Onesiphorus, would you say those characteristics describe you?

Are you **M**inistering to others, especially those in need? Who have you ministered to this past week? Who have you served? This might perhaps be a family member, a neighbor, or someone in your local church. The needs are many, but oftentimes, the ministers are few.

Are you **E**arnest like Onesiphorus was, when he earnestly searched for Paul? If you are a teacher of the Word of God, are you diligent in your studies or do you study just enough to get by? If you have administrative gifts, do you use them with excellence? Are you earnest in hospitality, in serving, in giving, or in whatever calling God has placed upon your life?

Do you spend your days trying to **R**efresh others in their struggles, or do you secretly desire that others would tend to your needs? Are you actively seeking out those within your body who need help? Who have you refreshed this week?

What about **C**ourage? Are you bold in your witness for Christ? Or are

19 Excerpted from *The Bible Knowledge Commentary: New Testament* © 1983 John F. Walvoord and Roy B. Zuck. Used by permission of David C Cook. May not be further reproduced. All rights reserved.

you ashamed of those who stand for what is right, what is righteous according to God's standards? Are you trying to fit in with those who want the broad way that encompasses all religious ideas? Are you a compromiser, or are you courageous?

What about **Y**ielding your life for another? Do you die to yourself daily for the sake of others? For the Lord? Would you sacrifice your literal life for the sake of another? Would you sacrifice your life for the gospel? For your Lord?

Defectors are "me-minded"; disciples are ministry-minded. Defectors are enemies of God; disciples are earnest for God. Defectors ruffle others; disciples refresh others. Defectors are cowards; disciples are courageous. Defectors yield their lives only for themselves; disciples yield their lives for others. What will you be remembered for? A defector of the faith or a disciple of the faith?

# QUESTIONS TO CONSIDER

1. (a) Read 2 Timothy 1:15-18. What are the contrasts between the two men mentioned in verse 15 and the one man mentioned in verses 16-18? (b) Why do you think Paul wants God to have mercy on Onesiphorus on that day (see verses 16-18)?

2. Memorize 2 Timothy 1:16.

3. Paul mentions in 2 Timothy 1:16 that Onesiphorus often refreshed him, meaning that Onesiphorus ministered to Paul during his sufferings. (a) Read the following passages and answer these questions: Who is being refreshed? Who is doing the refreshing? What are the circumstances? Exodus 17:8-16; 1 Samuel 25:4-35; 1 Kings 19:1-8; Jeremiah 38:1-13; Matthew 4:1-11; 27:27-32. (b) What are some principles you can glean from these verses for your own life?

4. (a) Who else in Scripture defected from the faith and what do you learn from their example? Endeavor to list at least two examples. (b) What are the best ways to make sure we are making our calling and election sure, according to 2 Peter 1:3-11?

5. In 2 Timothy 1:18, Paul mentions to Timothy that Onesiphorus ministered to him at Ephesus. (a) Read Acts 19:23-41 and note what you find in those verses that might indicate the circumstances surrounding this ministry. (b) In what practical ways might Onesiphorus have ministered to Paul at this time?

6. (a) Share about a time in your life when someone refreshed you while you were going through a trial or difficulty. (b) Whom do you encourage in the ministry, and how do you refresh them? (c) In what ways have others refreshed you, and how has it been an encouragement to you? Make it your goal each day to be an encouragement to at least one person (Be an Onesiphorus!).

7. After meditating on the truths in this chapter, how do you think you can be a better encouragement to others? Write your thoughts in the form of a prayer request. (And remember to be a doer of the Word and not just a hearer of it!)

# The High Call to Disciple

*2 Timothy 2:1-2*

THE verses we will be considering in this chapter have special meaning for me for several reasons. One reason is that discipling women has been one of the greatest joys of my life. To be able to pour my life into another individual and to watch them grow and then go on to disciple others has been a rich blessing for me. A second reason these verses have special meaning for me is that I saw them lived out in my husband's life. Many years ago, on one of my husband's milestone birthdays—his 50th, I believe—I gifted him with a framed collection of photos of his mentor and himself. The photo of my husband's mentor was positioned at the top and my husband's photo was positioned at the bottom, and between those two photos were the particular verses we'll be considering in this chapter. That frame still hangs in my home as a reminder of the one who poured his life into my husband and of my husband's faithfulness to disciple others. What verses are these? Let's read them together.

> You therefore, my son, be strong in the grace that is in Christ Jesus. And the things that you have heard from me among many witnesses, commit these to faithful men who will be able to teach others also. (2 Timothy 2:1-2)

Our outline for these verses will include *The Character of Those Who Disciple* (v 1); *The Curriculum We Use to Disciple* (v 2a); and *The Character of Those Who Are Discipled* (v 2b). We considered, in our previous chapter, two men who defected from the faith, Phygellus and Hermogenes. In contrast to these two unfaithful men, was Onesiphorus, a genuine disciple of the faith. Onesiphorus manifested the genuineness of discipleship by ministering to others, earnestly sacrificing for others, refreshing others, being courageous, and yielding his life. This man would be a wonderful example for Timothy to emulate. As we move on to the verses we'll cover in this chapter, Paul reminds Timothy of the high call of discipleship by first highlighting the character of those who disciple others. Let's look at this verse together.

## The Character of Those Who Disciple *2 Timothy 2:1*

> You therefore, my son, be strong in the grace that is in Christ Jesus. (2 Timothy 2:1)

*You therefore*, because of the bad example of the two men who turned away along with so many in Asia and because of the good example of faithful Onesiphorus, you, Timothy, *my son*, are to *be strong*. You are to be strong in the faith. You are to resist the temptation to turn from the truth. What does it mean to *be strong*? It means to empower or to enable (in a good way!).

> The verb be strong is an imperative, making it a command. Yet it is a command tempered by Paul's deep love for Timothy, his son. There was tenderness in Paul's heart because there is tenderness in God's heart. Even the Lord's strongest commands are given in love. He admonishes His children firmly but lovingly, and that is the way Paul admonished his spiritual son Timothy. Because Timothy had "sincere faith" and was nourished in that faith by his godly mother and grandmother (1:5), because he was specially gifted by God and ordained by the laying on of Paul's' hands (v.6) and the hands of the Ephesians' elders (1 Tim. 4:14), and because of the abundant resources mentioned in the remainder of chapter 1, Timothy had no reason for not being strong. Paul was saying to Timothy, "My son, the Lord's work in Ephesus depends on you, it's divinely appointed and divinely endowed minister." The effectiveness of his ministry depended not simply in his having that call and those resources but in his faithfully using them in God's power and to God's glory.[20]

This strength is an ongoing power because it comes from Christ. His power is unlimited. Psalm 147:5 (LSB) reminds us, "Great is our Lord and abundant in power; His discernment is infinite." My friend, you and I can only be strong in the grace that *is in Christ Jesus*. Without

---

20 John MacArthur, *The MacArthur New Testament Commentary: 2 Timothy* (Chicago: Moody Press, 1995), 37-38.

Him, we can do nothing. It is interesting that the first mention of discipleship in the New Testament is in Matthew 28:19-20 (LSB). Jesus says, "Go therefore and make disciples of all the nations, baptizing them in the name of the Father and the Son and the Holy Spirit, teaching them to keep all that I commanded you; and behold, I am with you always, even to the end of the age." When Jesus says, "I am with you always," it is a promise for Him to be with us in the discipleship process. God is the One who gives us the strength we need, even as we disciple others. The Lord told Joshua the same things when he stepped into his role as successor to Moses, in Joshua 1:6-7 (LSB),

> Be strong and courageous, for you shall cause this people to inherit the land which I swore to their fathers to give them. Only be strong and very courageous to be careful to do according to all the law which Moses My servant commanded you; do not turn aside from it to the right or to the left, so that you may be prosperous wherever you go.

Just as Moses passed the baton to Joshua, so Paul is now passing the baton to Timothy.

Paul says be strong *in the grace* that is in Christ Jesus. *Grace* is divine influence upon the heart. As Christ told Paul in 2 Corinthians 12:9b (LSB), "My grace is sufficient for you, for power is perfected in weakness." Paul now tells Timothy the same thing. God's grace is perfect in your weakness, Timothy. In all the fears you might have as you minister to others, draw upon the grace of God. It is enough for you, Timothy. *So, what is the character of those who disciple? They must be strong in the grace that is in Christ Jesus.* I am certain these words from Paul must have encouraged Timothy to continue on after Paul's death. But, Timothy might have been wondering, "What do I teach to others?" Paul anticipates this question and goes on to talk about the curriculum Timothy is to use in discipleship, in verse 2.

## The Curriculum We Use to Disciple *2 Timothy 2:2*

> And the things that you have heard from me among many witnesses, commit these to faithful men (2 Timothy 2:2a)

*And the things that you have heard from me*—Paul made mention of this back in 2 Timothy 1:13, when he wrote, "Hold fast the pattern of sound words which you have heard from me, in faith and love which are in Christ Jesus." And Paul will write again of this in 2 Timothy 3:14, when he says, "But you must continue in the things which you have learned and been assured of, knowing from whom you have learned them." What are *the things* that Timothy had heard from Paul? He mentions some of them in 2 Timothy 3:10-11: "But you have carefully followed my doctrine, manner of life, purpose, faith, longsuffering, love, perseverance, persecutions, afflictions, which happened to me at Antioch, at Iconium, at Lystra—what persecutions I endured." Not only did Timothy hear Paul's teachings, but there were other witnesses as well. *The curriculum we use in discipleship is biblical truth.*

What is Timothy to do with what Paul has taught him? Paul says *commit these* things *to faithful men.* The word *commit* means to deposit as a trust for protection. When we deposit something, we don't bury it. When we deposit something in a bank, it's for the purpose of investing, of multiplying what we have deposited, right? So it is with truth. We don't take in spiritual truth and bury it; instead, we invest it in others so that they too can pass it on to others. We multiply! (Paul has already mentioned this word commit in 1:12 and 14.)

## The Character of Those Who Are Discipled *2 Timothy 2:2*

> commit these to faithful men who will be able to teach others also.
> (2 Timothy 2:2b)

Note what kind of men Timothy is to make this deposit in—*faithful men. This is the character of those we disciple.* These should be genuine believers who are faithful to what they believe in and who are also trustworthy. This is the opposite of Phygellus and Hermogenes, who defected from the faith. I have discipled many women who are not faithful and it is difficult, and, in my humble opinion, it is an unprofitable use of precious time that the Lord has given to all of us. I have also found that those relationships usually don't last long.

What a joy to think that Paul deposited biblical truth into Timothy, and Timothy gets the privilege of doing the same with other faithful men—and the joy is that those men will then go on to teach others also. While Paul urges Timothy to do this, evidently Timothy had already demonstrated faithfulness in doing so. Consider Paul's commendation of Timothy in 1 Corinthians 4:17 (LSB): "For this reason I have sent to you Timothy, who is my beloved and faithful child in the Lord, and who will remind you of my ways which are in Christ, just as I teach everywhere in every church." Who knows how many millions of God's children have been discipled throughout the ages, beginning with the apostle Paul!

We too have been entrusted with precious, rich truths from God's Word, and our responsibility is not to keep them to ourselves but to take what we have learned and pass it down to others. What truths are you passing down to others? Are you passing down sound doctrine? I fear for this generation, as it seems many have traded theology for technology. I fear for them that their faith will fail in the day of adversity because their time was spent in trivial games and the trite pursuits of social media.

I want to take the rest of this chapter to consider another passage which is key to disciple-making, especially for us as women. Paul mentions this concept of discipleship to another spiritual son, Titus, in Titus 2:1-5, and I would like to use the same outline we just used in thinking through this text: *The Character of Those Who Disciple* (Titus 2:3); *The Character of Those Who Are Discipled* (Titus 2:4a); and *The Curriculum We Use to Disciple* (Titus 2:4b-5).

> But as for you, speak the things which are proper for sound doctrine: that the older men be sober, reverent, temperate, sound in faith, in love, in patience; the older women likewise, that they be reverent in behavior, not slanderers, not given to much wine, teachers of good things—that they admonish the young women to love their husbands, to love their children, to be discreet, chaste, homemakers, good, obedient to their own husbands, that the word of God may not be blasphemed. (Titus 2:1-5)

Let's first consider the character of those who should be discipling others.

## The Character of Those Who Disciple *Titus 2:3*

> the older women likewise, that they be reverent in behavior, not slanderers, not given to much wine, teachers of good things — (Titus 2:3)

Before we look specifically at the character of those who are to be discipling others, notice that Paul gives this as a command and not an option. The pattern set forth here is that older men are to teach younger men, and older women are to teach younger women. The word *admonish* in verse 4 means to school or train. Paul is saying in verse 3 that *older women* are to school or train younger women. Now, we must ask the question, "What does *older* mean?" In its most basic sense, it means older in age. We all are older than someone, right? We can all be teaching someone younger than us. Unfortunately, we live in an age where we put the older women on shelves, thinking they have nothing to offer the younger women. But with age comes experience, wisdom, and the secrets of godly living. Older women can save the younger women a lot of grief and heartache. But to say that this woman is *older* could also mean that this woman is older in the Lord. In other words, this older woman has more spiritual maturity than the woman she disciples. The younger woman's main role should be discipling her children and pouring her life into them. But this does not exclude her from fulfilling the Great Commission to go and make disciples. It is good for younger women to invest their lives in young people other than their own children. I am very grateful for the men and the women who invested in my children when they were teenagers and were still living at home. It was a huge blessing because many times they were able to impact my children in ways that their father and I could not.

Notice that Paul lists four elements that he assumes will be characteristic of these older women who are involved in teaching or discipling younger women. First, he says they must be *reverent in* their *behavior.* In the Greek, this means behavior that is becoming as a priest. She must be a holy woman or a priestess, we might say. She must have a godly, separated life.

Second, this older woman must *not* be a *slanderer.* This means that she should not be involved in gossip or slander. John Calvin once said, "Talkativeness is a disease of women, and it gets worse with age." Unfortunately, his words are too often true.

Third, this older woman who is discipling a younger woman must *not* be *enslaved to much wine.* You might be thinking, "Say, what?!" We need to remember that Paul wrote this book to Titus, who was ministering on the isle of Crete. Paul and Timothy had previously been ministering on the isle of Crete together, and for reasons unknown to us the apostle Paul left young Titus to minister there. The isle of Crete was not a wonderful place to minister; it was a place full of wickedness. We would not call it the "Bible Belt," that is for sure. "Sinner's Square" might be a better name for it. In fact, consider what Paul writes about Crete in Titus 1:12-13: "One of them, a prophet of their own, said, 'Cretans are always liars, evil beasts, lazy gluttons.' This testimony is true. Therefore rebuke them sharply, that they may be sound in the faith." Drunkenness was a problem on the isle of Crete, so Paul tells Titus that these older women should not be *enslaved to much wine* (Titus 2:3, LSB). I would draw a principle from Paul's words here: Any woman who is enslaved to any sin that she is not actively trying to fight would be wise not to engage in training younger women. In discipleship, we become like the one we're learning from, for good or for bad. It is not uncommon for the younger woman to eventually mimic the sin patterns she observes in the older woman who is discipling her. Sinful habits that an older woman practices will be mimicked by the person she is discipling.

Fourth, Paul says this older woman is to be a *teacher of good things.* We should expect older women to teach younger women good things, and we certainly would not want her to be teaching bad things. *So, what is the character of those who disciple? We would say they are older women who are godly or reverent in behavior, not enslaved to wine (or any other sin), not involved in slander, and who teach good things.* In verses 4 and 5, Paul gives us a list of what those good things are. Before we look at those good things, though, let's consider the character of the women who are to be discipled.

## The Character of Those Who Are Discipled *Titus 2:4*

> that they admonish the young women (Titus 2:4a)

What is the character of the women we disciple? Here, Paul tells Titus specifically in verse 4 that older women are to *admonish the young women*. This could be someone who is younger in age than you, or it could just be someone who is younger in the Lord. Many women whom I have discipled are older than me in physical age, but younger in spiritual age. I have also discipled young women who seemed to have the maturity to be discipling me. Often, discipleship is a mutual learning process, and Proverbs 27:17 captures that idea when it tells us that "iron sharpens iron." I would also add that what Paul told Timothy back in 2 Timothy 2:2 applies in this scenario as well—that this woman must be faithful. *When we consider the 2 Timothy and Titus passages together, we would describe the character of those we disciple as faithful women who possess genuine saving faith.*

## The Curriculum We Use to Disciple *Titus 2:4-5*

> that they admonish the young women to love their husbands, to love their children, [5]to be discreet, chaste, homemakers, good, obedient to their own husbands, that the word of God may not be blasphemed. (Titus 2:4-5)

Next, let's consider the curriculum we use in discipleship, the list of good things Paul says the older women are to teach to the younger women. Often, people will ask me about the discipling ministry at our church, and one of the questions I can usually count on them asking is "What curriculum do you use?" The exciting thing is that the curriculum is right here in Titus 2. There are some materials that I have found to be helpful, but there is some very dangerous stuff out there too. Please be careful as you choose material to aid you in the discipling process. You want to make sure the outside books you use are biblical and doctrinally sound. Paul will identify seven things for older women to teach younger women.

The *first* thing in Paul's curriculum of things that an older woman is to teach to a younger woman is something that shows up in the KJV and the LSB, but not in the NKJV or other translations: to be *sober* or sober-minded. In the KJV, the first phrase of verse 4 is translated as "that they teach the young women to be *sober*," and in the LSB, that same phrase is translated as "so that they may instruct the young women in *sensibility*" (emphases mine). The Greek root word for sober or sensible is *sophron,* and it means to be of sound mind, self-controlled, and to limit one's freedoms. A sober woman is a woman who exercises self-control, with proper restraints on all her passions and desires. Someone has said that it means to bring her to her senses, to wise her up to her wifely duties. Younger women need to be taught to be serious, to be sensible, and to use good judgment. They need to learn how to keep their passions under control! I remember, when I was a young woman, that I needed help in getting my emotions under control. There were times my poor husband couldn't even look at me a certain way without tears flowing. I also remember getting angry at him for the most ridiculous things. One particular incident occurred soon after we were married: He told me he did not like the tacos I had fixed for dinner—and I didn't speak to him for three days! I certainly was not behaving as a woman with her emotions under control. I needed my passions to be brought under control by the help of an older woman who would invest her life in me and help me in putting off my sinful attitudes.

This self-control would not only include a woman's emotions but also her physical passions, including her sexual appetite and physical appetite. Her speech may need to be brought under control. This is one area in which nearly all women need help. We need to train young women to speak words that are edifying, words that are lovely, words that are true, and words that are of a good report. Teaching self-control would also include teaching a woman to control the financial aspect of her life. Some young women will not control their compulsive spending habits and they need to bring that area of their life under control. A woman who is sober-minded, if she is out shopping, will not purchase items she knows she cannot afford. She will live within the means that God has provided. I am convinced that many women are working today simply because they refuse to live within the means of their husband's salary.

A woman who is sober will also get her thought-life under control. She will not let her mind go out of control with unrealistic or hysterical thoughts. I remember, as a young wife and mother, that there were times my husband or my children were late getting home and, in my mind, I had them in a traffic accident and dead. I would let my mind go out of control with ridiculous thoughts to the point of having their funerals planned. All those "what ifs" are useless thinking and reveal a mind that is out of control. We need to train young women to replace useless thoughts with God-honoring thoughts. Instead of thinking, "My husband is late; he must be dead or in a traffic accident," we can think, "My husband is late; yes, that is true. He could be in a traffic jam, or he might have stopped at the store to buy me some flowers. Or, even if he is dead or in a horrible traffic accident, God will give me the grace to deal with it." We need to train women to renew their minds and thoughts with the Word of God. They should memorize His truths and meditate on them day and night. (One of the many reasons I am a big advocate of Scripture memorization is because I have seen dramatic changes in the way women think who have taken the challenge to memorize the Word and allow it to renew their thinking.)[21] Many times, a husband may not be able to reach a resisting wife, but a godly older woman is often able to come alongside her and help her restrain these out of control passions.

The *second* thing we are to pass on to the women we disciple is teaching them how to *love their husbands.* Now to understand this point, we must understand the times in which Paul's epistle to Titus was written. In biblical times, marriages were arranged and so a young bride would be forced to live with and love a man who was likely a total stranger. She would need an older woman who had already been through this and could help her learn how to love her husband. But, ladies, even in a culture where we marry for "love," we must admit that loving one's husband can be a challenge at times. The Greek root word for *love* here is *philos*. It conveys the idea of cherishing the object and showing tender affection characterized by constancy. We need to come alongside young women and teach them how to love their husbands in this way and

21 See: Susan J. Heck, *A Call to Scripture Memory* (Irvine, Three Sixteen Publishing), 316Publishing.com.

to teach them that this is a privilege, not a burden. We must disciple them in how to show love to their husbands physically, emotionally, and spiritually. We need to teach young women the importance of taking time to listen to their husbands, even when the subject matter isn't particularly interesting to the wife. We need to train wives to warmly greet their husbands at the end of the day, even when the wife has had a lousy day. And, along with that, we teach them not to greet their husbands at the door with a list of all the things that went wrong during the day before he even has a chance to say hello! As wives, our primary focus ought to be on what our husbands do, not on what they don't do. A wife should be grateful that she even has a husband.

The *third* quality that should be passed down to young women is the need to *love their children*. Now, again, think biblically with me. These women would have had arranged marriages, and in many cases, they would have been married to men they were not too fond of, and then along would come children from that union, and it may have been difficult, under those circumstances, to love those children. A young woman in such a situation would need to learn how to love her children. But nothing is new under the sun, right? Today, loving one's children can sometimes be equally as hard. Let's face it: sometimes, our children are not so lovely. Sometimes, we moms have a hard time not favoring one child over another. Sometimes, a child with a difficult disability or one who is rebellious is hard to love. And yet the command is to love our children. Again, the root word for *love* here is *philos*, which is the same kind of love that we are to show to our husbands. Loving our children with a *philos* love is shown by cherishing our children and being affectionate toward them in a consistent manner.

What are some of the best ways to show love to our children and to teach young women to love their children? In Ephesians 6:4, Paul gives us two of the best ways to show love to our children. He says, "And you, fathers, do not provoke your children to wrath, but bring them up in the training and admonition of the Lord." The KJV translates "training and admonition" as "nurture and admonition" and the LSB translates it as "discipline and instruction." What does this entail exactly? To *nurture* is to discipline or to train, and *admonition* involves words of instruction or encouragement. Let's consider this idea of nurturing or discipline first. A parent's discipline of their children is evidence of that parent's love for their child. This is one of the areas that grieves me as I disciple women. I often see mothers refusing to do what God says regarding disciplining their children. What hardships they bring on themselves! Parenting is not unnecessarily difficult, if you will do it God's way. Proverbs 22:15 says, "Foolishness is bound up in the heart of a child; the rod of correction will drive it far from him." Proverbs 23:13-14 says, "Do not withhold correction from a child, for if you beat him with a rod, he will not die. You shall beat him with a rod, and deliver his soul from hell." Let me tell you, ladies, I had a father who believed in discipline, and I am not dead! Proverbs 29:15 tells us, "The rod and rebuke give wisdom, but a child left to himself brings shame to his mother." I don't know about you but that's the way I feel when I see a child out of control at the grocery store, the mall, or any other public place. It's not the poor child that we must blame, but it is the parents. If parents don't discipline their children, then you have to ask, "Do they really love them?" Proverbs 13:24 (LSB) is very clear, "He who holds back his rod hates his son, but he who loves him disciplines him diligently." In Hebrews 12:6, we have an interesting verse which tells us that our Heavenly Father disciplines those who are His because He loves them: "For whom the Lord loves He chastens, and scourges every son whom He receives." The writer goes on in verse 8 to say, "But if you are without chastening, of which all have become partakers, then you are illegitimate and not sons." Ladies, the Lord loves us enough to discipline us, and if we are not being disciplined by Him, then it proves that we are not His children. If you are discipling a young woman, and she does not discipline her children, then it is in serious question whether she loves her children or not.

The second way in which we love our children that Paul mentions in Ephesians 6:4 is that of *admonition*. This means by words of instruction or encouragement. The most encouraging and instructing words that mothers can give to their children are the words of God. We should instruct and encourage our children in spiritual things, teaching them biblical principles. We should do that when we stand and when we sit and when we are lying down—everywhere and in every circumstance—as

Deuteronomy 6:7 states. We need to be there to listen to their problems and to answer their questions. We should pray with them and for them. We must show them affection and tell them we love them. These are all ways we can show love and encouragement to our children. We must not tear them down by yelling at them and calling them unkind names. There are enough children in this world who are unloved, and we need to instruct young women to be different from the world—to love their children.

Next, we read in our text that a young woman is to be taught is *to be discreet*, in verse 5. The Greek term for *discreet* here is actually the same term used back in verse 4 and translated there as sober or sensible or sensibility. In fact, in the LSB, this term in this verse is translated as sensible, just as it was back in verse 4. The concepts are the same: young women are to be taught that they need to be sensible and how they are to do that. I'm not sure why the translators of the NKJV and other translations chose to leave out the term sober or sensible in verse 4, but perhaps it is because the idea is repeated here in verse 5. I won't go into the details of what this term means here since we already dealt with it at length when we looked at verse 4.

The *fourth* area of instruction in our discipling curriculum is to teach young women to be *chaste*, as seen in verse 5. This means to be pure in their hearts and in their lives. It also includes being free from defilement. The isle of Crete, as I mentioned earlier, was especially known for ungodliness, and so the older women needed to come alongside the younger women and teach them how to be pure. And, oh, how needed this is in our day as well! The world around us is filled with immorality, unholiness, and impurity. It is essential that we teach the younger women among us how to avoid impure things, to walk within their houses with perfect hearts, and to set no wicked things before their eyes, as the Psalmist says in Psalm 101. In 1 Thessalonians 4:7, Paul says that "God did not call us to uncleanness, but in holiness." Countless young women are addicted to pornography, which they find readily available on the internet, and the results of it are disastrous. It's been said that the average woman watches 21 hours of television per week; and that's not including social media or streaming platforms. It saddens me to say it, but it's true: Many of us know what's on television for the week or trending on social media, but we don't know where the simplest things are in the Bible.

Young women also need instruction in how to be pure in their speech, their time, their thought lives, and even in choosing the right friends. Paul says in 1 Corinthians 15:33, "Do not be deceived: 'Evil company corrupts good habits.'" I have seen women spiral downward in their walk with God just because they have chosen the wrong friends to spend the bulk of their time with.

The *fifth* thing on our curriculum is to teach young women to be *homemakers*. The word here for homemakers comes from two Greek words, which mean housekeeper or keeper at home. This is a woman who looks after the domestic concerns of the house, as well as her duties to the family. She is the woman mentioned in Proverb 31:27 (LSB), where it says of her: "She watches over the ways of her household, and does not eat the bread of idleness." Ladies, our first duty should be to our home and to the people who live in it. To be able to rear children to the glory of God and to invest in eternal matters instead of things that are going to burn up someday is a godly goal for women. Teaching a younger woman how to be a keeper of her home might include teaching her how to clean house, how to organize things, how to cook, how to plan a menu, how to grocery shop, and how to be hospitable. Some young moms were never taught these things by their own mothers; they don't have a clue how to prepare healthy meals, how to provide a peaceful and happy home environment, or how to manage their time. All of these things would fall under the category of teaching women to be keepers at home.

The *sixth* quality that we must pass down to younger women as we disciple them is goodness. Paul says we are to teach them to be *good*. This word means to be benevolent, profitable, or useful, and the good is for the benefit of others. Again, this reminds me of the woman mentioned in Proverbs 31, where it says in verse 20 (LSB) that "She extends her hand to the poor, and she stretches out her hands to the needy." We need to teach young women to see the needs in their immediate families, their church families, and in their neighborhoods. And then we need to teach them how to extend their hands to be beneficial to others. We need to teach them how to sacrifice their time and energy and maybe even their resources to benefit someone else. We need to teach young women to live for others and show them practical ways to do that. We have become a very selfish, isolated society and we need to teach young women to look out for the interests and needs of others.

The *seventh* and last area in our curriculum is number seven on Paul's list of things that we should be teaching young women to do. Notice what Paul says: *obedient to their own husbands*. The LSB and NASB translate this as "be subject to their own husbands," while the ESV translates it as "submissive to their own husbands," and the terms subject and submissive capture the idea in this term well. In our culture, which has become increasingly focused on self and one's rights, we have to fight hard against the attitude that declares, "No one is going to tell me what to do!" The Greek word for *obedient* or submissive means to place in an orderly fashion under, much like military personnel are placed in order by rank. With this in mind, we might liken the husband to a five-star general and the wife to a four-star general, or the husband to the president and the wife to the vice president. This same term is also used in Ephesians 5:22-23, where Paul says, "Wives, submit to your own husbands, as to the Lord. For the husband is head of the wife, as also Christ is head of the church; and He is the Savior of the body." Paul explains to us the reason it is so important that we teach women to submit to their husbands: the husband-wife relationship is intended to represent Christ and His church. The husband is the head of the wife, just as Christ is the head of the church. In Colossians 3:18, Paul also says, "Wives, submit to your own husbands, as is fitting in the Lord." And, in 1 Peter 3:1, Peter tells wives that they must be subject even to their unsaved husbands: "Wives, likewise, be submissive to your own husbands, that even if some do not obey the word, they, without a word, may be won by the conduct of their wives." Now, ladies, this does not mean that a woman is a doormat, or that she can never express an opinion or an idea. The reason submission can be difficult is because of the curse that we inherited from our Mother Eve. When Adam and Eve sinned, they each got cursed for their disobedience. The woman received two curses. In Genesis 3:16 (LSB), we read, “To the woman He said, ‘I will greatly multiply your pain and conception, in pain you will bear children; your desire will be for your husband, and he will rule over you.’” God told Eve her desire would be to rule over Adam, but instead he would rule over her!

A woman needs help in learning how to let her husband lead their family—and how to do that graciously, not giving him the silent treatment for days when she disagrees with him. Women need instruction in how to make gracious appeals when they disagree with their husbands. I have seen women make important decisions without consulting their husbands and some have gone so far as to purposely defy their husbands’ wishes. This is an awful indictment on the role of the wife, and it brings shame to the name of Christ!

Now, I do want to say that there is an exception to the command that wives submit to their husbands, and that exception would be if a woman’s husband asked her to do anything that is a direct violation of the Word of God. This, and only this, is where she would have to graciously decline her husband’s wishes and choose to obey God over her husband, a principle clearly set forth in Acts 5. There, Peter and the other apostles were forbidden to share the gospel, which is directly from God, and they responded with: “We must obey God rather than men” (Acts 5:29, LSB). Consider this example: If a woman’s husband asked her to look at pornography with him, she would have to decline, as she would have biblical precedent for that; Ephesians 5:3 (LSB) is very clear on this: “But sexual immorality or any impurity or greed must not even be named among you, as is proper among saints.” But young women sometimes need help in discerning what is a sin issue and what is a preference issue, and this is why it is wise for them to have older women in their lives to help them discern these things.

*So, what is the curriculum we use in discipleship? We teach the younger women to be sober-minded, to love their husbands, to love their children, to be chaste, to be keepers at home, to be good, and to be submissive to their own husbands.* Now, this obviously does not mean that these are the only things we disciple in. We also mentor younger women in the whole of Scripture, as Jesus said in Matthew 28:19-20. This means that we who are older women should know what God says and be able to instruct a younger woman in the things of the Lord. This may seem like an impossible task, but, with the help of our Lord, it really is not![22] We women often pass down recipes, clothes, furniture, and heirlooms, all of which are perishing. Why not pass down something that is not perishing, like sound doctrine? Warren Wiersbe once said, "The task of the local church is not to preserve the truth, as in a museum; but to live it and to teach it to the generations to come."[23] Will you, by God's grace and power, pass the baton of truth down to the next generation?

---

22 For a more thorough understanding on this topic, see: Susan J. Heck, *A Call to Discipleship* (Irvine, Three Sixteen Publishing), 316Publishing.com.

23 Excerpted from Wiersbe's Expository Outlines on the New Testament © 1992 Warren W. Wiersbe. Used by permission of David C Cook. May not be further reproduced. All rights reserved. 645.

# QUESTIONS TO CONSIDER

1. (a) What does Paul call Timothy in 2 Timothy 2:1? (b) What other things does Paul say about Timothy in Philippians 2:19-24; 1 Timothy 1:2; 1:18; and 2 Timothy 1:2?

2. Memorize 2 Timothy 2:2.

3. (a) What do Matthew 28:18-20 and Titus 2:1-5 say about discipling others? (b) How would you define discipleship?

4. (a) Paul mentions that Timothy is to pass on to other men the things he has taught him. Skim Acts 16-20 and note the truths Timothy heard from Paul's teaching that needed to be passed down to others. (b) What truths do you think are essential to pass down to the next generation? (c) What valuable truths have been passed on to you by others?

5. (a) According to 2 Timothy 2:2, what is to be the character of those whom Timothy should disciple? (b) Why is faithfulness an important character quality for God's children, according to Psalm 31:23; Luke 16:10-12; 1 Timothy 1:12; Revelation 2:10; 17:14? (b) Why do you think faithfulness is essential when discipling others?

6. (a) Are you currently being discipled or discipling another person? (By the way, this does not have to be a formal discipleship; it might even be a child or grandchild.) (b) What value have you seen in mentoring another person or being mentored by someone? (For those who are not involved I would highly encourage you to prayerfully consider doing so!)

7. Life is brief, and we must make moments with others count for eternity. Who can you pour your life into? Who can pour their life into you? Come with a prayer request that reflects your desires in this area of discipleship.

# Have *You* Counted the Cost of Following Christ?

*2 Timothy 2:3-7*

RECENTLY, I was speaking at a conference where there were numerous churches represented. I rarely speak before an audience where I fail to give the gospel in some form or another, and, knowing this would be a mixed audience with many different denominations present, I took quite a bit of time in sharing the gospel in its fullness. One of the ladies from the conference spoke to me the next day, saying that her whole table was stirred and convicted because they had never heard the gospel presented like that before. She went on to say that they had never heard they needed to submit to Jesus as Lord of their lives. She said they had talked about the message all the way home and decided they might not be saved. We chatted a bit, and I could tell she was deeply troubled. I knew I might not have any other time to speak to her and so I graciously told her they needed to repent and believe the gospel and be saved.

It's sad to say, but this is not uncommon in our day. Pastors are failing to give their sheep not only sound doctrine but the gospel and all its implications. Have *you* considered the gospel in all its fullness and the implications of Christ's Lordship? My friend, have you truly considered the cost of being a Christ-follower? Paul has something to say to Timothy about this very thing, and we will see it in this chapter as we continue our study of 2 Timothy. Let's read what Paul has to say.

> You therefore must endure hardship as a good soldier of Jesus Christ. No one engaged in warfare entangles himself with the affairs of this life, that he may please him who enlisted him as a soldier. And also if anyone competes in athletics, he is not crowned unless he competes according to the rules. The hardworking farmer must be first to partake of the crops. Consider what I say, and may the Lord give you understanding in all things. (2 Timothy 2:3-7)

Our outline, as we consider these verses, will include: *The Suffering Soldier* (vv 3-4); *The Submissive Athlete* (v 5); *The Sweating Farmer* (v 6); and *The Strong Admonition* (v 7). In our last chapter, we considered the high call of discipleship. We considered two passages: one in 2 Timothy 2 and one in Titus 2. From the passage in 2 Timothy, we learned that the character of those who disciple is that they must be strong in the Lord. The character of those into whom we pour our lives is that they must be faithful, genuine believers. And the curriculum we use is sound biblical truth. As we looked at the Titus passage, we learned those who disciple are older women who are godly, not given to wine, not slanderers, and teachers of good things. The ones into whom they pour their lives are young women who are faithful. And the curriculum we use: we teach them to be sober-minded, to love their husbands and children, to be discreet, chaste, keepers at home, good, and obedient to their own husbands.

Now, as we turn to 2 Timothy 2:3-7, Paul continues to admonish Timothy (and us) regarding what it takes to be a follower of Christ. These words of Paul follow the call for Timothy to disciple. If we are going to disciple someone else, we must have lives worth emulating. Timothy needed to count the cost of being a disciple, and, my dear sister, you and I must too. I fear that many well-meaning Christians are sitting in our pews today with no clue as to what genuine Christianity looks like; they simply have not stopped long enough to count the cost of being a disciple of Christ. Let's consider what Paul has to say regarding that cost. He begins by likening that cost to the suffering of a soldier, in verses 3 and 4.

## The Suffering Soldier *2 Timothy 2:3-4*

> You therefore must endure hardship as a good soldier of Jesus Christ. (2 Timothy 2:3)

Paul begins this section by saying *you therefore*, you Timothy, *endure hardship. Therefore* points back to what Paul has said in the previous verses. Those who pass on sound doctrine must be strong in Christ Jesus. This is not for the weak. Christianity is not for the faint-hearted. It not only takes the strength of the Lord to disciple others, but it also takes God's strength to be a suffering soldier, a submissive athlete, and a sweating farmer. Christianity is not peaches and cream. There is enough of that in many of our so-called churches, but that does not represent real Christianity.

So, Paul is saying, "Timothy, you must endure hardship." Paul has already told Timothy that he needed to share in his sufferings, in suffering for the gospel, back in 2 Timothy 1:8. Evidently, hardship was a challenge for young Timothy, just as it is for many a Christian. Suffering for Christ is not easy, but, my friend, that is the calling of a good soldier. We must remain steadfast in the hardships of life. We have the strength of our Lord to help us, and, if we would allow it, it's a precious time of drawing near to our Savior and partaking of His sufferings. No suffering is ever wasted in the Lord!

Paul uses the analogy of *a good soldier*, which means a virtuous warrior. You may be wondering why Paul would use the analogy of a good soldier. Well, we must remember that Paul was in prison chained to a Roman soldier, so he would have witnessed, to some extent, the kinds of hardships soldiers would undergo. Soldiers often go without food and sleep; they don't see their families while they are away from home; they endure the physical hardships of exercise and daily training routines; they're exposed to the elements of the earth—cold, heat, storms, snow; they daily must put on armor and take it off again; they must keep their weapons sharpened and ready for battle. Being a soldier is not for the fainthearted. Enlisting involves the realization that you might lose your life. Enlisting in Christianity involves the realization, my friend, that we not only die daily to ourselves, but we might also lose our physical lives as well. If you want to save your life, you will lose it, Jesus said, in Matthew 10:39. In Philippians 2:25 (LSB), Paul gives us an example of one who was a good soldier. He says, "But I regarded it necessary to send to you Epaphroditus, my brother and fellow worker and fellow soldier, who is also your messenger and minister to my need." If you recall, Epaphroditus almost lost his life traveling more than 800 miles from Philippi to Rome to bring a monetary gift to Paul. A soldier is willing to risk his life for the sake of others. In Philemon 1:2, Paul also mentions another man with this same willingness: "to the beloved

Apphia, Archippus our fellow soldier, and to the church in your house." Evidently, Archippus exemplified the life of a good Christian soldier. Paul continues to write about the life of a good soldier in verse 4. He says,

> No one engaged in warfare entangles himself with the affairs of this life, that he may please him who enlisted him as a soldier. (2 Timothy 2:4)

*No one*, not one single person, who is a soldier *entangles himself with the affairs of this life*. The Greek rendering here means not even one. I realize that well-meaning believers will tell you otherwise—but, my friend, well-meaning believers are not the standard for our faith. Our God is the standard, and He says not one of us can claim salvation and simultaneously be intentionally entangling ourselves in this life. Soldiers must engage in warfare, which means they are involved in military campaigns. Fighting a war is serious business. In order to do that, a soldier cannot be *entangled*, which means to be entwined in the affairs of this life. *The affairs of this life* would include the transactions of this life, all secular pursuits. Roman soldiers were not permitted to get married or to have a trade while serving as a soldier. A couple of Old Testament passages to consider, in relationship to this idea, are: Deuteronomy 20:5-7 (LSB),

> The officers also shall speak to the people, saying, "Who is the man that has built a new house and has not dedicated it? Let him go and return to his house, lest he die in the battle and another man dedicate it. Who is the man that has planted a vineyard and has not begun to use its fruit? Let him go and return to his house, lest he die in the battle and another man begin to use its fruit. And who is the man that is engaged to a woman and has not married her? Let him go and return to his house, lest he die in the battle and another man marry her."

Consider also Deuteronomy 24:5 (LSB): "When a man takes a new wife, he shall not go out with the army nor be charged with any duty; he shall be free at home one year and shall give gladness to his wife whom he has taken." Soldiers must serve without distraction, or they will not be effective. Now, Paul is not saying that a good soldier of Jesus Christ cannot have an occupation, because Paul himself was a tent-maker. We also know that the Word clearly states that if we are unwilling to work, then we shouldn't eat (2 Thessalonians 3:10). Paul is saying, however, that we should not be entangled, or all wrapped up in and consumed with, the affairs of this life. In Colossians 3:2, Paul says that we are to set our minds on things above and not on things of this earth. James calls those who love the world adulterers and adulteresses—enemies of God (James 4:4). John says that if we love the world then the love of the Father is not in us (1 John 2:15-17). If we want to be good soldiers, we must serve the Lord without distraction, or we will not be effective. Too many well-meaning Christians today are involved in all kinds of outside pursuits and it is sucking their devotional and spiritual life dry. I heard about one well-known minister who once said regarding certain frivolities of this life: "Others may; *I* may not." He also said he had little need in his life to be entertained. This man has done amazing things for the Kingdom of God. He has served as a good soldier, not allowing the world to distract him. Jesus Himself said, in the Sermon on the Mount, that you cannot serve two masters; you will hate the one and love the other (Matthew 6:24). As much as we think we can love God and love the world at the same time, we cannot. If you are enlisted in the army, you serve the army. If you are enlisted in the Kingdom of God, you serve King Jesus. He has enlisted us in His army.

Perhaps reading this is difficult for you. My dear sister, consider what Paul says next: *that he may please him who enlisted him as a soldier*. We do this so that we can *please* the One who has enlisted us as a soldier. Do you stop long enough to think deeply about the reality that God chose you before the foundation of the world and that it is He who has enlisted you? Why would we not desire to please the One who has chosen us to be in His army? Why would we be entangled in this life, which is fleeting and perishing? When we think of it, it doesn't make rational sense. The soldier in the army is working for the one who has enlisted him. That is his employment! He can't be distracted with other things; he has a job to do to fight for his country and to win the battle. You and I also cannot be distracted; we too have a war to fight, a spiritual one, one in which we endeavor to win the battle and to please the One who has chosen us.

*The first example Paul gives when we consider the cost of being a disciple of Jesus is of the suffering soldier. The suffering soldier endures hardship, doesn't entangle himself with the affairs of this life, and is eager to please the one who has enlisted him.* Paul moves from the illustration of the suffering soldier to that of the submissive athlete.

## The Submissive Athlete *2 Timothy 2:5*

> And also if anyone competes in athletics, he is not crowned unless he competes according to the rules. (2 Timothy 2:5)

Paul gives another analogy and this time it is the submissive athlete. Paul says of the submissive athlete that *he competes according to the rules.* If he doesn't submit to the rules, he is disqualified. Competing in the Olympic Games was, and still is, an endeavor requiring rigorous training. An athlete must be meticulous in his exercise regimen, his diet, and his training for his specific athletic event. In our day, most athletes who compete in the Olympics train 4-8 years before even making an Olympic team. And, after making a team, they must train around 32 hours each week. There is no way an Olympian will be crowned the winner if he doesn't both involve himself in rigorous practice and abide by the rules. And there are many rules and codes of conduct. In fact, I have heard of many athletes who have been disqualified due to their use of performance-enhancing drugs or other kinds of improper conduct. No athlete will be *crowned* if he doesn't compete by these rules. And it is the same in the spiritual realm. Paul writes about this in 1 Corinthians 9:24-27:

> Do you not know that those who run in a race all run, but one receives the prize? Run in such a way that you may obtain it. And everyone who competes for the prize is temperate in all things. Now they do it to obtain a perishable crown, but we for an imperishable crown. Therefore I run thus: not with uncertainty. Thus I fight: not as one who beats the air. But I discipline my body and bring it into subjection, lest, when I have preached to others, I myself should become disqualified.

We cannot run the Christian race by our own rules; we must run it by the rules set forth for us in God's Word. It is interesting that Paul mentions here in 1 Corinthians "an imperishable crown" that we are endeavoring to obtain, and in 2 Timothy he mentions the crown for which the athlete competes. The Olympian's crown is perishable; it will burn up. The Christian's crown, however, is imperishable, it is undefiled, and it is reserved in Heaven for us! 1 Peter 1:3-5 (LSB) reminds us of this:

> Blessed be the God and Father of our Lord Jesus Christ, who according to His great mercy has caused us to be born again to a living hope through the resurrection of Jesus Christ from the dead, to obtain an inheritance incorruptible and undefiled and unfading, having been kept in heaven for you, who are protected by the power of God through faith for a salvation ready to be revealed in the last time.

Hebrews 12:1-2 (LSB) also reminds us of how we ought to run this race:

> Therefore, since we have so great a cloud of witnesses surrounding us, laying aside every weight and the sin which so easily entangles us, let us run with endurance the race that is set before us, fixing our eyes on Jesus, the author and perfecter of faith, who for the joy set before Him endured the cross, despising the shame, and has sat down at the right hand of the throne of God.

We are running a race, and we must run without those sins which weigh us down.

Now, my friend, I want to be frank with you. Consider what Paul is saying. Many today are telling us that we can run the race by our own rules; in fact, some are endeavoring to change the rules of Christianity by doing away with the Law, while others have brought into the church the doctrines of demons, mysticism, and legalism. But the rules never change. God doesn't change His requirements to suit our vain pursuits. He does not adjust to us. Paul is an example for us to follow as one who has run the race well and is assured of a crown. Listen to what he says in 2 Timothy 4:7-8, "I have fought the good fight, I have finished the race, I have kept the faith. Finally, there is laid up for me the crown of righteousness, which the Lord, the righteous Judge, will give to me on that Day, and not to me only but also to all who have loved His appearing."

*What is the cost of being a disciple of Christ? In this second illustration, we see that the submissive athlete must compete by the rules.* We've seen the example of the suffering soldier and the submissive athlete; now, Paul shows us the example of the hardworking, sweating farmer, in verse 6.

## The Sweating Farmer *2 Timothy 2:6*

> The hardworking farmer must be first to partake of the crops. (2 Timothy 2:6)

Paul draws our attention to the hard work of a farmer. If you recall, from the earliest pages of Genesis, the very first farmer in history was Adam. When Adam chose to sin with his wife, they both received curses, as did Satan. In Genesis 3:17-19 (LSB), God tells Adam what will happen to him because of his sin:

> Cursed is the ground because of you; in pain you will eat of it all the days of your life. Both thorns and thistles it shall grow for you; and you will eat the plants of the field; by the sweat of your face you will eat bread, till you return to the ground, because from it you were taken; for you are dust, and to dust you shall return.

This was not going to be an easy life for Adam; the work would be so intense that it would produce sweat. This is not the life of sitting at a computer in an air-conditioned office. Paul says the farmer is *hardworking*. This means his work is laborious; it is fatiguing. If you know anything about farming, then you know it is hard work. Most farmers put in 12-13 hours of work in a day. It's exhausting! They get up before dawn, and they go to bed late. There are rigorous chores, all related to the taking care of crops or cattle or property. And farmers don't get the weekend off because animals don't fast from Friday night till Monday morning.

What does it mean that this hardworking farmer *must be first to partake of the crops*? The farmer works hard, he labors, sweating, so that he can receive the reward, the *first*-fruits *of the crops*. Crops don't grow by osmosis. It is the farmer's labor that produces the reward of being able to enjoy the profits, whether that be in actually eating of his own crops or in receiving the monies that come from the sale of those crops. And so it is with us in the spiritual sense. We work hard for the Kingdom. This concept of laboring comes up often in Paul's letters, and it means working to the point of exhaustion (for some examples, see Philippians 1:22; 2:16; Colossians 1:29; 1 Thessalonians 2:9; 1 Timothy 4:10). In fact, in 1 Corinthians 15:58 (LSB), Paul tells the church at Corinth, "Therefore, my beloved brothers, be steadfast, immovable, always abounding in the work of the Lord, knowing that your labor is not in vain in the Lord." Our labor is not in vain. In Hebrews 6:10-12 (LSB), we read,

> For God is not unrighteous so as to forget your work and the love which you have shown toward His name, in having ministered and continuing to minister to the saints. And we desire that each one of you show the same diligence so as to realize the full assurance of hope until the end, so that you may not become dull, but imitators of those who through faith and patience inherit the promises.

Our labor produces something: it produces fruit for God's Kingdom. And, along with what rewards the Lord deems best for us in this life, we also have the reward of Heaven. Consider Paul's words in 1 Corinthians 3:5-15 (LSB):

> What then is Apollos? And what is Paul? Servants through whom you believed, even as the Lord gave to each one. I planted, Apollos watered, but God was causing the growth. So then neither the one who plants nor the one who waters is anything, but God who causes the growth. Now he who plants and he who waters are one, but each will receive his own reward according to his own labor. For we are God's fellow workers; you are God's field, God's building.
>
> According to the grace of God which was given to me, like a wise master builder I laid a foundation, and another is building on it. But each man must be careful how he builds on it. For no one can lay a foundation other than the one which is laid, which is Jesus Christ. Now if anyone builds on the foundation with gold, silver, precious

> stones, wood, hay, straw, each man's work will become evident, for the day will indicate it because it is revealed with fire, and the fire itself will test the quality of each man's work. If any man's work which he has built on it remains, he will receive a reward. If any man's work is burned up, he will suffer loss, but he himself will be saved, yet so as through fire.

The third example Paul has given us regarding the cost of being a disciple of Jesus is the sweating farmer. The sweating farmer works hard for others but also so that he can be the first to partake of his labors.

All three of these illustrations Paul uses—the soldier, the athlete, and the farmer—show that being a disciple of Jesus Christ is hard labor that pays off. But they think nothing of the time they put into fighting a war, running a race, or planting a crop. All of their efforts will yield something: for the soldier, it is a victory; for the athlete, it is the crown; for the farmer, it is the crop. And so it is with the Christian: our labors will one day be rewarded with a victorious, fruitful crown. We should think nothing of our labor for the Kingdom. In verse 7, Paul moves from these three analogies, the suffering soldier, the submissive athlete, and the sweating farmer, to a strong admonition for us.

## The Strong Admonition *2 Timothy 2:7*

> Consider what I say, and may the Lord give you understanding in all things. (2 Timothy 2:7)

*Consider* what I am saying, Timothy. Exercise your mind and think about what I am saying. Comprehend what I am saying and allow that comprehension to lead to action. Do not be merely a hearer of what I say but a doer. You and I should not be mere readers of the Word; we should be doers of it. Oh, that we would stop and ponder the words of God. We need to stop and think about the things Paul is saying to Timothy and to us: Consider that soldier, consider that athlete, and consider that farmer! And, as you do, *may the Lord give you understanding in all things*. What does that mean? May the Lord give you a mental putting-together of what I am saying. And when He does give you that mental putting-together regarding these concepts, may you then do something about it. Wisdom involves action. We must be doers of what we hear. James says that if we don't do something about what we've heard from the Word, then we have deceived ourselves into thinking that all we need to do is hear and we have deceived ourselves into thinking that we are genuine believers, when, in fact, we are not (James 1:22-25). Both Paul and Timothy would have been familiar with Psalm 1, which puts forth the godly man who meditates day and night on the Word of God—and when he does, he is like a tree that brings forth fruit and prospers in whatever he does. *So, what is the strong admonition in these verses? It is, as Paul says, to consider what I say!*

## Summary

What about you? Are you a good soldier willing to suffer hardship and be disentangled from the affairs of this life? If not, why not? Are you striving to please the One who has enlisted you in His army? Isaac Watts once wrote:

> Am I a soldier of the cross,
> A follow'r of the Lamb?
> And shall I fear to own His cause,
> Or blush to speak His name?
> Must I be carried to the skies
> On flow'ry beds of ease,
> While others fought to win the prize,
> And sailed through bloody seas?
> Are there no foes for me to face?
> Must I not stem the flood?
> Is this vile world a friend to grace,
> To help me on to God?
> Sure I must fight if I would reign;
> Increase my courage, Lord;
> I'll bear the toil, endure the pain,
> Supported by Thy Word.[24]

24 Isaac Watts, "Am I a Soldier of the Cross?" Public Domain 1721.

What about being a submissive athlete? Are you running the Christian life by your own rules? Do you know the Word so well that you know what the rules are? Have you allowed well-meaning Christian friends to influence you by their rules which are not backed up by Scripture? Are you submitting to the Lord in everything you do?

Would you describe yourself as a hard-working farmer? Do you labor to the point of exhaustion for God and others? Are you willing to sacrifice your time, energy, and money to serve the Lord and others? Jesus said something very sad in Luke 10:2 (LSB), "And He was saying to them, 'The harvest is plentiful, but the laborers are few; therefore pray earnestly to the Lord of the harvest to send out laborers into His harvest.'" There is much work for our Lord which needs to be done. Will you labor for that which is eternal?

Lastly, regarding Paul's strong admonition: Will you consider what he says? Will you think about these analogies after this chapter? Or will you move on from this chapter without pausing long enough to consider its implications?

As I was researching these three analogies, I was struck with the realization that being a soldier, an athlete, and a farmer in our day is much less like it was in Paul's day, or even in the years since Paul's time. Technology and modern conveniences have made the lives of some soldiers much more like the lives of civilians; athletes in our day often use performance-enhancing drugs to make themselves stronger or faster and allow them to avoid much of the hard work necessary to achieve their goals; and the lives of today's farmers are now often run more by modern technology, with significantly less hard, physical labor necessary to obtain a fruitful crop. I say that I was struck by this contrast because the resemblance of these modern soldiers, athletes, and farmers to modern Christianity is striking. Christians today have veered away from the hard work of following Christ. It seems we want the easy road, the easy life. We have lost the vision of working hard for the Kingdom of God. The 21st century Christian world has, in many respects, changed from the New Testament Christian world. But our God does not change. May I lovingly remind you to consider what Paul is saying, to ponder it? Let us get back to biblical Christianity. Let us not be among those to whom the Lord will say, "Depart from Me, I never knew you."

# QUESTIONS TO CONSIDER

1. (a) What are the three analogies that Paul compares the Christian life to in 2 Timothy 2:3-7? (b) Read 1 Corinthians 9 and note the three analogies Paul uses there. (c) Why do you think Paul uses these analogies in these passages?

2. Memorize 2 Timothy 2:3-4.

3. (a) According to Hebrews 6:15; 10:32-36; James 1:12; 5:11, what happens to those who endure hardships? (b) How does this encourage you in the difficulties of life, especially those which pertain to your sufferings for Christ?

4. (a) Paul compares the Christian life to that of a soldier. What are the weapons we use, according to 2 Corinthians 10:3-5; Ephesians 6:11-18; 1 Timothy 1:18-19? (b) What are some practical ways in which we can do spiritual battle?

5. (a) Paul tells Timothy to consider what he (Paul) says in 2 Timothy 2:7. Why is it essential that we meditate on the words of God, and not simply read them, according to Joshua 1:8; Psalms 1:1-6; 19:6-13; 119:11-16, 97-104; and 2 Timothy 2:7? (b) What benefits have you found in your life from meditating on Scripture (including memorizing it, which is an aspect of meditation)?

6. (a) Have you counted the cost of being a disciple of Jesus? (b) In Luke 14:26-33, what does Jesus say about considering this cost? (c) When you consider Jesus' words in Luke 14:26-33 and the apostle Paul's words in 2 Timothy 2:3-7, would you say their descriptions of being a follower of Christ match the "Christianity" of our day? (d) Why or why not? (e) Do their words reflect what is true of your own life? (f) Why or why not?

7. When you consider the three analogies Paul uses for the Christian life, which one stands out as the one most in need of improvement or correction in your life? Come with a prayer request in this regard, so that others may pray for you.

# Three Things to Remember When Afflicted

*2 Timothy 2:8-10*

MOST believers in our day have heard of and even read some of the works of Charles Spurgeon. He has indeed left a legacy for many to follow. But rarely do we hear or speak of his wife Susannah. One woman writes,

> In addition to supporting Charles in his seasons of depression and illness, Susannah suffered from severe medical issues herself and spent much of her adulthood as an invalid. She often experienced such intense seasons of pain that she could barely move. The details of her illness are still coming to light, but we know that her condition became severe enough to require surgery. One of the leading surgeons in Scotland performed an operation on Susannah that didn't go to plan. The result of the botched surgery was devastating. "Suffering instead of service," she said, "became my daily portion." But Susannah believed God was using her brokenness to refine her character. Her physical agony drew her into closer proximity with a Savior who suffered for her and with her. Even in the most excruciating circumstances, Susannah demonstrated gratitude, joy, peace, and patience. She reflected, "We talked of the Lord's tender love for His stricken child. ... I remember feeling that the Lord was very near to us." Susannah's heart, rooted in thanksgiving, trusted God to accomplish his strength through her weakness. "How very good [God] is to unworthy me," she believed. In 1873, Susannah finished reading her husband's book *Lectures to My Students.* When Charles asked her how she liked it, she replied, "I wish I could place it in the hands of every minister of England." He responded, "Then why not do so? How much will you give?" This question propelled Susannah into action. She organized a charity called "The Book Fund" to provide complimentary copies of *Lectures* to poor ministers throughout England. At first, Susannah lacked the financial resources needed to make this dream a reality. But she joyfully

> bought one hundred copies herself and mailed them out to pastors in need. When she was too ill to attend the functions of the Metropolitan Tabernacle, Susannah invested her time instead in the continuation of the Book Fund. Susannah's act of scrappy, sacrificial vision launched into motion a charity that continued until her death. As letters of thanks poured into Susannah's home, word quickly spread throughout England and numerous donations were sent to sustain her project. In one year's time, Susannah distributed 3058 theological books to impoverished pastors. Nine years later, she distributed 71,000 copies.[25]

I am certain that Susannah Spurgeon could echo with the apostle Paul his words in 2 Timothy 2:9 that, even though he was in chains, the Word of God was not in chains. Even though Susannah Spurgeon was bedridden with pain, God's Word went forth through her husband's books. Susannah Spurgeon knew that the Word of God was not bound. Let's listen in as Paul writes of some amazing truths while being chained to a soldier in prison.

> Remember that Jesus Christ, of the seed of David, was raised from the dead according to my gospel, for which I suffer trouble as an evildoer, even to the point of chains; but the word of God is not chained. Therefore I endure all things for the sake of the elect, that they also may obtain the salvation which is in Christ Jesus with eternal glory. (2 Timothy 2:8-10)

In our last chapter, we considered the cost of following Christ. And, as we did, we considered the suffering soldier, the submissive athlete, the sweating farmer, and the strong admonition. We learned that Timothy must not be fearful of the cost of following the Lord—and we mustn't either. Such fearlessness may result in more affliction, as in the case of the apostle Paul, but even in that there are wonderful truths that will aid us through those dark times. In this chapter, we will learn of three things we must remember during our affliction: *Remember that God Raised Jesus from the Dead* (v 8); *Remember that God's Word Is Not*

25 Selah Ulmer. "Three Things You Didn't Know about Spurgeon's Wife." *The Spurgeon Center*, https://www.spurgeon.org/resource-library/blog-entries/3-things-you-didnt-know-about-spurgeons-wife. Accessed February 20. 2024.

*Bound* (v 9); and *Remember that God Provided Salvation through Christ Alone* (v 10). Let's consider the first thing to be remembered, in verse 8.

## Remember that God Raised Jesus from the Dead

*2 Timothy 2:8*

> Remember that Jesus Christ, of the seed of David, was raised from the dead according to my gospel, (2 Timothy 2:8)

Paul begins by writing and telling Timothy: *remember Jesus Christ.* The word *remember* means to be mindful. Paul is saying, "Timothy, when you are suffering, I want you to call to mind Jesus Christ." Often, during times of trouble, our minds run almost everywhere but to Christ. "What if my husband dies?" "What if we can't pay this month's mortgage?" "What if my loved one's cancer results in their death?" There's nothing wrong with these thoughts but many of us stop there—or, worse, we allow our thoughts to snowball into sinful worry and anxiety. We would be wise to think thoughts like this: "My husband might die, but God will help me. He has always been faithful." "It's going to be rough to pay the mortgage this month, but we will pray and trust God and take on other jobs, if need be. God will make a way." "My loved one may die from this wasting disease, but I will enjoy each day we have and draw near to Christ in this affliction. I will also do whatever I can to make sure they are ready to meet the Lord." We need to be reminded that we have a loving Lord who has also been afflicted, who has, in fact, suffered more than any of His followers. We have a High Priest who has been touched with the feelings of our infirmities and we can go to His throne of grace and find mercy in our time of need. I am certain that Paul often went to that throne of grace while he was imprisoned, and he is here reminding Timothy to do the same. Remember Jesus, my son!

You might be wondering why, right after giving Timothy the examples of the farmer, the soldier, and the athlete, Paul calls Timothy to then remember *Jesus Christ.* One man helpfully writes,

> Because the Greek verb behind "remember" is in the active voice, it carries the idea of "continue to remember" or "keep on remembering."

> The preeminence of our Lord Jesus Christ should always be in the forefront of our minds. He is the supreme and ultimate teacher of teachers. He was the greatest soldier, the greatest athlete, and the greatest farmer, as it were. He fought the greatest battle and won the greatest victory. He ran the greatest race and won the greatest prize. He sowed the perfect seed and reaped the perfect harvest.[26]

So Paul encourages Timothy to not just remember Jesus but to remember that Jesus *was raised from the dead.* Why does Paul want Timothy to remember that Jesus was raised from the dead? Paul tells us why in 1 Corinthians 15. What an encouraging portion of God's Word! My friend, without the resurrection, our faith would be in vain, and we would still be in our sins. Without the resurrection, there would be no hope for any of us. Without the resurrection, our labor for Christ would be in vain. In fact, Paul ends 1 Corinthians 15 with these words from verse 58 (LSB): "Therefore, my beloved brothers, be steadfast, immovable, always abounding in the work of the Lord, knowing that your labor is not in vain in the Lord." When we consider the awesomeness of the resurrection, we can press on through anything and labor for the Lord with steadfastness.

It's also interesting that Paul mentions that Jesus is *of the seed of David.* Jesus came from the lineage of David. When Matthew starts his Gospel, he starts with the genealogy of Jesus, and you know how it starts? Matthew 1:1 (LSB): "The book of the genealogy of Jesus Christ, the son of David, the son of Abraham." And guess how the genealogy ends, in verse 16 (LSB)? "And Jacob was the father of Joseph the husband of Mary, by whom Jesus was born, who is called Christ." This is an important fact, with tremendous implications for us: When we're going through trials, we must remember that Jesus came in the flesh. Fully human, He was tempted in all points as we were, yet without sin. We have a High Priest who has been touched with the feelings of our infirmities. This should encourage us when we are troubled. We don't have a calloused Christ; we have a sympathetic Savior we can run to and cast our cares upon. He is available to us at all times and in all places!

26 John MacArthur, *New Testament Commentary: 2 Timothy*, 56.

Another reason Paul calls Timothy to remember that Jesus was raised from the dead and was of the seed of David is because the false teachers of the day were denying that Jesus was God. These false teachers were claiming that Jesus was human but not God. Just as the truth of Jesus' humanity is important for us to remember, so too is the truth of Jesus' deity. It is important because when we're going through difficult times, we must have a correct theology of God. If, in our minds, our God is small, our problems will seem insurmountable! If, however, we see our God as big, our problems will seem small. If our foundation is not built on Christ alone and on sound doctrine, we will be led into all types of wrong thinking and we will fail in the day of adversity.

Now, why does Paul follow these reminders of Jesus' humanity and deity by saying *according to my gospel*? Obviously, we know that the gospel is the good news of Jesus Christ, but it was entrusted to Paul, and it felt to him as if it were his own. This is only the one gospel, and Paul preached it so often that it was as if this gospel were his own. This is a phrase Paul uses several other times in his writings, Romans 2:16 (LSB) being one of them: "on the day when, according to my gospel, God will judge the secrets of men through Christ Jesus." Paul is not claiming personal authorship of the gospel, nor is he claiming exclusive personal ownership of it; he is simply stating it as the gospel he proclaims.

The first thing we must remember when going through affliction is that God raised Jesus from the dead; we must remember the resurrection. When going through trials like Paul was, we must remember that our Lord also went through tremendous suffering and pain—but the story did not end there! He was resurrected from the dead—a lifeless corpse brought to life again! And, my friend, because He lives, we shall also live. This should encourage us to press on when life is troublesome. In the midst of our afflictions, our minds can become so crowded with our circumstances that we forget our blessed hope, the blessed resurrection and glory to come. My friend, whatever God has allowed in your life this day, choose to not forget the resurrection. Because He lives, you will live also. This trial you face is momentary, a hiccup; but life in glory is eternal, forever. Paul now writes of the second thing he wants Timothy to remember, in verse 9.

## Remember that God's Word Is Not Bound *2 Timothy 2:9*

> for which I suffer trouble as an evildoer, even to the point of chains; but the word of God is not chained. (2 Timothy 2:9)

The words *for which* refer back to the previous verse. In other words, because of the gospel, Paul is suffering. When Paul says *I suffer trouble*, he is referring to hardships and afflictions. Some sufferings come upon us because of our own sin; some sufferings come upon us because of the effects of living in a fallen world. But notice that Paul's sufferings were not because of either; he was suffering because he was falsely accused. He was suffering *as an evildoer*. The term *evildoer* refers to a criminal and would be used in reference to someone who had committed gross deeds. Jesus had warned Paul of this. In Acts 9:16, we read, "For I will show him how many things he must suffer for My name's sake." And in Ephesians 6:18-20 (LSB), Paul makes it clear that he was in prison because of sharing the gospel:

> praying at all times with all prayer and petition in the Spirit, and to this end, being on the alert with all perseverance and petition for all the saints, as well as on my behalf, that words may be given to me in the opening of my mouth, to make known with boldness the mystery of the gospel—for which I am an ambassador in chains—so that in proclaiming it I may speak boldly, as I ought to speak.

Paul was innocent, just like his Lord was. Jesus was sinless. And, while Paul was not sinless, he was innocent of the accusations laid against him. He wasn't complaining about what he had to endure. No, he wanted to fill up that which was lacking in his sufferings; he wanted to know personally the fellowship of his Lord's sufferings (see Philippians 3:10 and Colossians 1:24). What a testimony! Paul's suffering was *even to the point of chains*, which means to be bound or chained. One man says,

> He was virtually cut off from all outside contact and kept chained in a dungeon (2 Timothy 1:16). He was probably held underground in the Mamertine Prison, adjacent to the Roman forum, in a

> small, dark, bare stone dungeon whose only entrance was a hole in the ceiling scarcely large enough for one person to pass through. The dungeon itself is not large; about half the size of a small one-car garage. Yet it was sometimes used to hold as many as forty prisoners. The discomfort, the dark, the stench, and the misery were almost unbearable.[27]

But, even though Paul was chained, the Word of God was not! This is the second thing we are to remember in the midst of our afflictions: God's Word isn't bound! Even though Paul was chained, the gospel is never chained. The Word of God will go forth. Paul writes of this in yet another of his prison epistles, his letter to the Philippians. In Philippians 1:12-14 (LSB), he writes,

> Now I want you to know, brothers, that my circumstances have turned out for the greater progress of the gospel, so that my chains in Christ have become well known throughout the whole praetorian guard and to everyone else, and that most of the brothers, having become confident in the Lord because of my chains, have far more courage to speak the word of God without fear.

In fact, in Philippians 4:22, he writes that even some in Caesar's own household had come to faith! The Word of God is living and active and powerful—and it will never be bound!

I think not only of Susannah Spurgeon, but, even in our day, Joni Eareckson Tada, who is bound to a wheelchair, and yet God is using her to reach millions with the truth. God's Word is not bound! Or Justin Peters, who also is bound with cerebral palsy, and yet God is using him all over the United States and the world to herald the truth about false teachers. I know that probably none of you are chained in prison, and most of you are probably not bound by a physical ailment, but some of you might feel bound to the laundry, to the house, to raising children and all that goes along with that. Some of you might feel chained in a difficult marriage or bound to a difficult job. But,

---

27 Taken from *The Book on Leadership* by John MacArthur Copyright © 2004 by John MacArthur. Used by permission of HarperCollins Christian Publishing. www.harpercolllinschristian.com.

my friend, God's Word is never bound! The Word goes out still to your kids, to your difficult husband, to your co-workers. The all-sufficient, all-authoritative Word of God is never bound. It is alive! As Martin Luther well wrote,

> That word above all earthly powers,
> No thanks to them, abideth;
> The Spirit and the gifts are ours
> Through Him who with us sideth:
> Let goods and kindred go,
> This mortal life also;
> The body they may kill:
> God's truth abideth still,
> His Kingdom is forever.[28]

Now, maybe you're wondering why in the world Paul would put himself in this position? I mean, why go into the ministry if it's nothing but trouble and persecution? Why would anyone want to suffer as a Christian? Paul writes to Timothy about why he labors and suffers, in verse 10, and in so doing, also tells us the third thing we must remember during times of distress.

## Remember that God Provided Salvation Through Christ Alone *2 Timothy 2:10*

> Therefore I endure all things for the sake of the elect, that they also may obtain the salvation which is in Christ Jesus with eternal glory. (2 Timothy 2:10)

*Therefore*, because God raised Jesus from the dead, because the Word of God is never bound, then you know what? *I endure all things for the sake of the elect*, for the gospel to go forth to the elect. The word *endure* means to patiently abide. This is not a passive word but an active word. Paul did not sit around in prison worrying about his situation or that his life would, more than likely, end soon. Paul

28 Martin Luther, "A Mighty Fortress is Our God", Public Domain, 1529.

made the most of his suffering, and, my friend, so should we. Even though he was suffering for the gospel, Paul endured with patience. He did not try to run from his suffering but embraced it and learned through it. And he did this for the sake of the *elect*, that they might *obtain the salvation which is in Christ Jesus.* This is the third thing we must remember during times of troubles: that God provided salvation through Christ alone.

Paul longed for those whom God had chosen before the foundation of the world to be saved. Paul wanted his life to be a living example of the gospel. Not only did he preach it; he also lived it. In 1 Peter 3:14-17, Peter writes of this same great truth to those who are suffering for the gospel, as well. He says,

> But even if you should suffer for righteousness' sake, you are blessed. "And do not be afraid of their threats, nor be troubled." But sanctify the Lord God in your hearts, and always be ready to give a defense to everyone who asks you a reason for the hope that is in you, with meekness and fear; having a good conscience, that when they defame you as evildoers, those who revile your good conduct in Christ may be ashamed. For it is better, if it is the will of God, to suffer for doing good than for doing evil.

Peter is saying, "Do not be afraid or troubled, even though you just might lose your life because of righteousness." And notice that he uses the word evildoers just like Paul does in 2 Timothy. These Christians to whom Peter is writing were undergoing false accusations just like the apostle Paul was. But some will look on and wonder about the hope these believers profess to have, some will ask about it, and some will be saved because of it!

It's not Paul's job, or Timothy's job, or even our job, to figure out who the elect are; it is our job to patiently endure suffering so that others might benefit as they look on. Paul had compassion for people, he loved people, and so should we—and he set an example for Timothy and for us to follow. A few years ago, I received an encouraging email from someone who attends our church. I won't share all of it, but here's just a small portion of it, as it is a sweet example of what Paul is writing about:

> I wanted to take a few minutes to write to you and just let you know everything that's been going on—maybe from a different perspective, I might add. I just wanted you to know that one of the reasons why I had the strength to go through this recent trial that lasted 16 weeks is the examples that I see in you both. My first week at GCC was the first Sunday back for you, Doug [my husband], after your stroke. I watch you every week endeavor to preach the Word when you stand or not, see or not, are dizzy or not. You've just kept doing the right thing to serve the Lord, preaching the sanctifying Word of God.

Ladies, I don't share this to toot my husband's horn or to share about our afflictions, as ours are certainly no comparison to what Paul or Christ endured. I share this because we all have our own personal trials, and we must not give in to the temptation to take a break from our Christianity just because we have a difficulty or two. No, we press on, no matter what, to what God has called us to do and to be. If we believe the gospel, we must live the gospel. Others are watching, and who knows if our trust in God during trials will move some to want to know who this is who grants us solace in our troubles. They just might embrace the gospel, and if they are elect, we can be certain that at some point they will!

Paul has endured these things so that the elect also may obtain the salvation which is in Christ Jesus. The saving grace of God is through *Christ Jesus* alone. And Paul adds that this is in Christ Jesus *with eternal glory.* What does that mean? It means everlasting worship. We will forever be with the Lord. Our salvation is here and now, but we do not experience the full benefits of it till we get to glory. Paul will remind Timothy—and us—in verses 11 and 12, "This is a faithful saying: ... if we died with Him, we shall also live with Him. If we endure, we shall also reign with Him."

## Summary

Paul wants Timothy to remember the same things Paul himself has had to remember there in prison. Paul knew that he was not going to be around much longer, and he wanted to pass on three truths for young Timothy to cling to when he went through suffering and trouble for the gospel.

*Remember that God raised Jesus from the dead.* Do you believe God raised Jesus from the dead? During your last affliction, did you call to remembrance this wonderful truth? Jesus was raised from the dead, and you too will be raised on the last day! Death will have no sting. The troubles of this life do not compare to the glory revealed in us. If you have never considered the resurrection during a trial, I would urge you to remember that God raised Jesus from the dead.

*Remember that God's Word is not bound.* Do you think that the only time you can be effective for the Lord is when things are going well? During your last trial, did you call to remembrance that God's Word is not bound? Did you dwell on biblical truths to help you during your time of trouble? Did you seek to help those who were with you in the trial with the Word of God? Did you have gospel opportunities during your last trial? If you have never considered that God's Word is not bound during a difficulty, I would urge you to remember that God's Word is never bound.

*Remember that God provided salvation through Christ alone.* During your last difficulty, did you call to remembrance the saving grace of God, the gospel? Did you have opportunities to shine the light of Christ by your response to your trial? Did anyone ask you about the hope that is in you as they watched you respond with a Christ-like attitude? If you have never considered that God provided salvation through Christ alone during one of your difficulties, I would urge you to remember that God provided salvation through Christ alone.

Since I mentioned Joni Eareckson Tada earlier in this chapter, I want to close by encouraging you with something she said:

> Most people wish they could erase suffering out of the dictionary. Today's culture of comfort and instant gratification has no patience for suffering—most people want to drug it, escape it, divorce it; do anything but live with it. Yet suffering is arguably God's choicest tool in shaping the character of Christ in us. As I often say, "God permits what he hates, to accomplish what he loves." I can't think of a better answer to the ancient question of suffering. Even at the cross, God permitted what he hated—the unjust and agonizing death of his own precious Son—in order to accomplish something he prized above his own Son's cruel death; that is, salvation for a world of sinners. So the world's worst murder becomes the world's only salvation.[29]

And as Paul says, "Remember that Jesus Christ, of the seed of David, was raised from the dead according to my gospel, for which I suffer trouble as an evildoer, even to the point of chains; but the word of God is not chained. Therefore I endure all things for the sake of the elect, that they also may obtain the salvation which is in Christ Jesus with eternal glory" (2 Timothy 2:8-10).

---

29 Jonathan Petersen. "The Beyond Suffering Bible: An Interview with Joni Eareckson Tada." The Bible Gateway Blog, https://www.biblegateway.com/blog/2016/07/the-beyond-suffering-bible-an-interview-with-joni-eareckson-tada/. Accessed on February 13, 2024.

# QUESTIONS TO CONSIDER

1. (a) Read 2 Timothy 2:8-10. (b) What do you learn about Jesus from these verses? (c) What do you learn about Paul? (d) What encouragement do you find in these verses?

2. Memorize 2 Timothy 2:8.

3. (a) Why is the resurrection important, according to 1 Corinthians 15? (b) How does the truth of the resurrection encourage you during times of trouble? (c) What significance does the resurrection have to you personally? (d) Should we share about the resurrection when we are sharing the gospel? Why or why not?

4. (a) Read Genesis 39-41 and Jeremiah 33 and note who else was imprisoned and yet was not hindered from doing the work of the Lord. (b) What principles can you glean from these examples? (c) How do these examples encourage you?

5. (a) What do the following verses tell us about the Word of God? Psalm 19:7-11; 119:11, 50, 97-105; Proverbs 30:5; Luke 4:4; Ephesians 6:17; Hebrews 4:12; and 1 Peter 1:23. (b) How do these truths help you to understand what Paul says in 2 Timothy 2:9, when he writes that the Word of God is not bound or chained? (c) Why is it imperative for a believer to have a vital relationship with Scripture? (d) Do you see it as imperative to your daily walk?

6. (a) What things do you try to remember during difficult times? (b) What are some of the verses or passages that have aided you during times of trouble?

7. Reread 2 Timothy 2:8-10 and write a prayer for yourself or someone else who's going through a trial. Endeavor to use some of the truths that Paul mentions in these verses.

# Life to the Loyal! Death to the Disloyal!

*2 Timothy 2:11-14*

IN July of 2019, the Christian world was once again sobered by someone who at one time professed Christ as Lord and Savior but was now denying Him. That man's name is Josh Harris. Josh Harris had been well-known as a pastor and author, and especially for his book, *I Kissed Dating Goodbye*, which had a tremendous influence in the United States. But Josh Harris not only kissed dating goodbye; he also kissed his marriage goodbye and kissed his faith goodbye. The following are his own words from his Instagram account:

> My heart is full of gratitude. I wish you could see all the messages people sent me after the announcement of my divorce. They are expressions of love though they are saddened or even strongly disapprove of the decision.
>
> I am learning that no group has the market cornered on grace. This week I've received grace from Christians, atheists, evangelicals, exvangelicals, straight people, LGBTQ people, and everyone in-between. Of course there have also been strong words of rebuke from religious people. While not always pleasant, I know they are seeking to love me. (There have also been spiteful, hateful comments that angered and hurt me.)
>
> The information that was left out of our announcement is that I have undergone a massive shift in regard to my faith in Jesus. The popular phrase for this is "deconstruction," the biblical phrase is "falling away." By all the measurements that I have for defining a Christian, I am not a Christian. Many people tell me that there is a different way to practice faith and I want to remain open to this, but I'm not there now.
>
> Martin Luther said that the entire life of believers should be repentance. There's beauty in that sentiment regardless of your view of God. I have lived in repentance for the past several years—

> repenting of my self-righteousness, my fear-based approach to life, the teaching of my books, my views of women in the church, and my approach to parenting to name a few. But I specifically want to add to this list now: to the LGBTQ+ community, I want to say that I am sorry for the views that I taught in my books and as a pastor regarding sexuality. I regret standing against marriage equality, for not affirming you and your place in the church, and for any ways that my writing and speaking contributed to a culture of exclusion and bigotry. I hope you can forgive me.[30]

As believers, we read this and are saddened for Josh, for the testimony of our Lord, and for yet another who proves he was never really in the faith (1 John 2:19). But we should be greatly saddened by what God's Word says will happen to Josh in the end—unless he repents. Listen to Paul's words to Timothy in 2 Timothy 2:11-14:

> This is a faithful saying: for if we died with Him, we shall also live with Him. If we endure, we shall also reign with Him. If we deny Him, He also will deny us. If we are faithless, He remains faithful; He cannot deny Himself.
>
> Remind them of these things, charging them before the Lord not to strive about words to no profit, to the ruin of the hearers.

This portion of God's Word is one of several several New Testament passages that are known to have been hymns that were sung by the early church. Some believe this one, specifically, was quoted at believers' baptisms and was known as a cross-bearer's or Martyr's hymn. In our last chapter, we discovered three important things that we need to remember when we're going through affliction: We are to remember that God raised Jesus from the dead, that God's Word is not bound, and that God provided salvation through Christ alone. In the verses we'll study in this chapter, there are more truths that Paul wants Timothy, and all other believers, to remember. These truths are a tad bit more essential for us to remember, as they pertain to our eternal destination. We will see a vivid contrast between those who are loyal to the Lord and

30 Joshua Harris, @harrisjosh, *Instagram*, https://www.instagram.com/p/B0ZBrNLH2sl/. Accessed April 26, 2024.

those who are disloyal to Him. Our outline for these verses will include: *Life to the Loyal: Two Sweet Reminders* (vv 11-12b); *Death to the Disloyal: Two Sobering Reminders* (vv 12-13); and then Paul will end this section with *One Searching Reminder* (v 14). Let's consider the first reminder to the loyal, in verse 11.

## Life to the Loyal: Two Sweet Reminders *2 Timothy 2:11-12*

> This is a faithful saying: for if we died with Him, we shall also live with Him. (2 Timothy 2:11)

Paul begins by writing *this is a faithful saying*. The word *faithful* means trustworthy and true. In fact, it is translated as "trustworthy" in the LSB. This is a saying that you can bank on. There are a lot of sayings out there that are fabricated by men, but, my friend, you can bank on the sayings of our Lord. One popular fabricated statement by a man is: "Your time is limited, so don't waste it living someone else's life." Christ, however, would say, "Let each of you look out not only for his own interests, but also for the interests of others" (Philippians 2:4). So, Paul is clear that this saying is a faithful saying because it is written by Someone who is faithful; it is written by One who cannot lie. It is interesting that the word *saying* here is the Greek word *logos*, which is a term used in reference to the entire body of God's truth. So all of God's Word is faithful; we can count on it. But, specifically, what saying is Paul referring to here? Here it is: *If we died with Him, we shall also live with Him*. The question we have to answer is, "What does it mean to die with Him?" Paul is saying that if we want to *live with Him*, if we want to live with Christ, we must already *have died with Him*. The word *died* is in the aorist tense, meaning that it conveys the idea that we died once for all. When we became disciples of Christ, we took up the daily cross of death to self. Consider what Paul says in 2 Corinthians 4:10-11 (LSB), that we are "always carrying about in the body the dying of Jesus, so that the life of Jesus also may be manifested in our body. For we who live are constantly being delivered over to death for Jesus' sake, so that the life of Jesus also may be manifested in our mortal flesh." Also Mark 8:35-38 (LSB),

> For whoever wishes to save his life will lose it, but whoever loses his

> life for My sake and the gospel's will save it. For what does it profit a man to gain the whole world, and forfeit his soul? For what will a man give in exchange for his soul? For whoever is ashamed of Me and My words in this adulterous and sinful generation, the Son of Man will also be ashamed of him when He comes in the glory of His Father with the holy angels.

This means that I deny myself and live for others. I do whatever the Lord asks of me, even if it's difficult, even if it costs me my life. Some believers do lose their physical lives, like Paul did. Some are actually called to be killed for their faith. Even today, there are more than 90,000 people killed each year because they belong to the Lord. But, often, the harder death is the daily dying to ourselves for God and for others. Paul says in 1 Corinthians 15:31b, "I die daily," and he is not talking about a physical death—which would be impossible to do every day—but a death to himself. Paul's life, like Christ's, was one of continual sacrifice.

Does death-to-self describe your life? It should, when we consider what the next part of this faithful saying is: if we died with Him, *we shall also live with Him*. This is a reference to living with Him not only now, as His Spirit dwells within us, but eternally in glory. If we are not dying to ourselves daily, then we have no guarantee that we will live with Him forever in Heaven. Romans 6:8 reminds us, "Now if we died with Christ, we believe that we shall also live with Him." The first reminder to those who are loyal to Christ that, if they have died with Him, they will also live with Him. Let's continue with the second reminder to the loyal, in the first part of verse 12.

> If we endure, we shall also reign with Him. (2 Timothy 2:12a)

The second sweet reminder to those who are loyal to Christ is that *if we endure, we shall also reign with Him. Endure* means to persevere during suffering or affliction. We know that the Scriptures are replete with the warning that only those who endure to the end will be saved. Hebrews is especially filled with warnings that we would do well to heed. Consider Hebrews 3:6: "but Christ as a Son over His own house, whose house we are if we hold fast the confidence and the rejoicing of the hope firm to the end." And, again, in Hebrews 3:12-14,

> Beware, brethren, lest there be in any of you an evil heart of unbelief in departing from the living God; but exhort one another daily, while it is called "Today," lest any of you be hardened through the deceitfulness of sin. For we have become partakers of Christ if we hold the beginning of our confidence steadfast to the end.

So, if we endure, we shall also reign with Him. Paul explains this in Romans 8:16-17 (LSB), "The Spirit Himself testifies with our spirit that we are children of God, and if children, also heirs, heirs of God and fellow heirs with Christ, if indeed we suffer with Him so that we may also be glorified with Him." If we desire to reign with Him in glory and be joint heirs in glory, then we must be willing to endure suffering to the end, persevering in our faith to the end. If you want to wear the crown in the next life, you must bear the cross in this life. Are you enduring? How are you enduring? When suffering for Christ comes your way, do you run from it or do you embrace it? Tertullian once said, "The man who is afraid to suffer cannot belong to Him who suffered."

If we died with Him, we shall also live with Him. If we endure, we shall also reign with Him. These are Paul's two sweet reminders about the life of those who remain loyal to Christ. In the next part of verse 12, we find Paul's first sobering reminder of the death that awaits those who are disloyal to Christ.

## Death to the Disloyal: Two Sobering Reminders *2 Timothy 2:12-13*

> If we deny Him, He also will deny us. (2 Timothy 2:12b)

Paul now gives his first sobering reminder to those who would be disloyal to the One they claim. He puts it like this: *If we deny Him, He will deny us.* What does it mean to *deny Him*? It means we refuse Christ, we reject Him, we disavow Him. There are many ways in which we can do this. We might be as bold as Peter and curse and deny that we know Christ. We might be as brazen as Josh Harris and deny our Christianity on social media for the entire world to see. For some, it will be less obvious, as they remain silent when they should speak up about a doctrinal issue or the gospel. It might be embarrassing when praying in a public place, or reading your Bible in public. There are many ways in which we can deny the Lord. And Paul is crystal clear: if we deny Christ, *He will also deny us*. Matthew 10:32-33 (LSB) says, "Therefore everyone who confesses Me before men, I will also confess him before My Father who is in heaven. But whoever denies Me before men, I will also deny him before My Father who is in heaven." Another sobering passage, which is similar to what Paul is writing here in 2 Timothy, is Luke 9:23-26 (LSB),

> And He was saying to them all, "If anyone wishes to come after Me, let him deny himself, and take up his cross daily and follow Me. For whoever wishes to save his life will lose it, but whoever loses his life for My sake, he is the one who will save it. For what is a man profited if he gains the whole world, and loses or forfeits himself? For whoever is ashamed of Me and My words, the Son of Man will be ashamed of him when He comes in His glory, and the glory of the Father and of the holy angels."

It's important for us to know that denying the Lord was not as common in the biblical world as it is in ours. New Testament saints understood that holding fast to the gospel was a denial of themselves and a submission to Christ's Lordship. They understood that to bear the cross was to wear the crown. They understood that persecution and suffering were simply part of the cross. We, as western Christians, often shrink at the Lordship of Christ, at denial of ourselves, and at suffering for the name of Christ. But, no matter what our thinking is and how it may have shifted from the early church's way of thinking, God's thinking is the same and it has not shifted. He remains the same yesterday, today, and forever. Though the church has become a circus, though the church has compromised its views on the LGBTQ+ community, God's Word is clear on what He thinks about the LGBTQ+ community. God has not changed, nor will He—a truth that is foundational to Paul's second sobering reminder, in verse 13, to those who would be disloyal to Christ.

> If we are faithless, He remains faithful; He cannot deny Himself. (2 Timothy 2:13)

*If we are faithless, He remains faithful.* To be *faithless* means to not believe, to have an ongoing unbelief. So, if we prove to be unbelievers, if we prove to be faithless, it doesn't change the character of God. *He remains faithful.* He is always trustworthy. *He cannot deny Himself.* In fact, it is impossible for Him to deny Himself. Numbers 23:19 is clear: "God is not a man, that He should lie, nor a son of man, that He should repent. Has He said, and will He not do? Or has He spoken, and will He not make it good?" We must remember, then, His faithfulness includes not only the promises to the loyal but also the threats to the disloyal. If we deny Him, He will deny us. God is faithful. He cannot deny His nature. If we remain in unbelief and live a life of ongoing rebellion, then eternity in hell without Christ is our end. He will be faithful to cast all unbelievers into the lake of fire. He cannot deny Himself. This is the second sobering reminder to those who are disloyal. The great missionary, J. Hudson Taylor, often said, "It is not by trying to be faithful, but in looking to the Faithful One, that we win the victory."[31] It is in looking to the Faithful One that we remain faithful. Now, after this cross-bearer's hymn, Paul adds a searching reminder for Timothy that we would also do well to heed, in verse 14.

## One Searching Reminder *2 Timothy 2:14*

> Remind them of these things, charging them before the Lord not to strive about words to no profit, to the ruin of the hearers. (2 Timothy 2:14)

The question comes to mind, "What *things* is Timothy to remind them of?" It seems to be everything that Paul has said thus far in his letter to Timothy. We need to be reminded of the truths that Paul has already written about because our tendency is to move on and forget what we have been taught. I noticed many years ago that my husband, through

31 J. Hudson Taylor Excerpted from *The Bible Exposition Commentary on the New Testament* © 1989 Warren W. Wiersbe. Used by permission of David C Cook. May not be further reproduced. All rights reserved. 245.

the years and years that he preached, would spend ample time reviewing what he had been teaching from the pulpit, and it served to reinforce what we had learned so that we would not forget the truths that had been taught to us. In fact, Scripture is replete with commands that we are to remember certain truths. So, Paul tells Timothy to *remind them;* that is, keep on reminding the people in your church of *these things*. Remind them to stir up the gift that is in them; remind them that God has given them power and not fear as they use their gifts; remind them not to be ashamed of the testimony of Christ; remind them of their calling from God to salvation; remind them to hold fast to sound doctrine; remind them of the danger of turning from the faith like many have done; remind them of the importance of passing truths on to faithful men; remind them to endure hardship as a soldier, an athlete, and a farmer; remind them that the Word of God is never bound, no matter what suffering Christians may encounter; remind them to endure so that they can be with our Lord in eternal glory—remind them of these things, Timothy. Put them in remembrance!

And, as you're reminding your people of these things, Timothy, make sure you're *charging them before the Lord to not to strive about words to no profit*. The word *charge* means to attest earnestly. And Timothy was to do this *before*, or in the presence of, *the Lord*. This is a reminder to Timothy, and should be a reminder to all of us, that God is omnipresent. He is listening to the things that we speak, and teachers, especially, will be judged more strictly, according to James 3:1. Our words are important because we use our mouths to direct the lives of others. So, charge them in the presence of the Lord *not to strive about words to no profit*. When Paul says *strive about words to no profit*, he is communicating that these strivings over words are of no use. It is similar to what Paul wrote to Timothy in his first letter, in 1 Timothy 1:5-7 (LSB):

> But the goal of our command is love from a pure heart and a good conscience and an unhypocritical faith. For some, straying from these things, have turned aside to fruitless discussion, wanting to be teachers of the Law, even though they do not understand either what they are saying or the matters about which they make confident assertions.

It is also similar to what Paul wrote to another son in the faith, Titus, in Titus 3:9 (LSB): "But avoid foolish controversies and genealogies and strife and conflicts about the Law, for they are unprofitable and worthless."

You might be thinking, "Why can't I speak words of no profit? You're ruining my fun!" Paul says it is because such strivings are *to the ruin of the hearers*. Babblings, idle talk, foolish arguments—they're all unprofitable and worthless and can bring to ruin those who listen to them. *Ruin* refers to the idea that these strivings have the effect of causing others to be overthrown in their faith and even apostatize. Paul is clear in Ephesians 4:29 (LSB) regarding what our mouths are to be used for. He writes, "Let no unwholesome word proceed from your mouth, but only such a word as is good for building up what is needed, so that it will give grace to those who hear." Jesus even warns about what we hear in Mark 4:23-24 (LSB): "'If anyone has ears to hear, let him hear." And He was saying to them, 'Beware what you listen to. By your standard of measure it will be measured to you, and more will be given to you.'" So, you and I must be careful about what we speak, but we must also be careful about what we listen to.

This admonition should cause us to rethink the things going on in our world that were not going on in Paul's world. The social media of our day has lent itself to speaking words—written words—that are of no profit. We will be held accountable for everything we have said, good or bad, written or spoken. Many are being led astray by words of no profit on social media. When those who claim Christ as Lord and Savior diminish the creeds of our faith and make God's words mean something other than what they do, this can lead to the ruin of those who hear it. Many will turn from the faith and cast off Christianity as nonsense. In fact, when Josh Harris denounced the faith, my husband and I were conversing about the fact that this is happening more and more. He asked me why I thought it was happening so often. I picked up my cell phone and held it up and I said, "Because people are getting their theology and Christian ideas today from this. They have vacated the Word of God for the foolishness of men." (I also know that there is the prediction of a great falling away before the Son of Man comes and that those who defect were never in the faith to begin with. See 2 Thessalonians 2:1-3 and 1 John 2:19.)

## Summary

Are you loyal to the Lord or are you disloyal to Him? Have you died to yourself and all your earthly desires to be solely focused on serving God and others? If so, then you have the promise that you will one day live with Him. Are you enduring to the end? In what ways are you enduring, especially during periods of suffering and persecution? If you remain faithful to the end, you will also someday reign with Him.

In what ways might you be denying the Lord? Are you ashamed of the gospel or the fact that you are a Christian? Are you living as an unbeliever? If so, you are in grave danger because God is true, He cannot lie, and He will deny you, as He is faithful to keep His promises and His threats.

How are you using your mouth for that which is good and not for that which is evil? Be reminded next time you are tempted to speak words of no profit, that Matthew 12:36 tells us we will give account for every idle word which we speak.

I found it quite ironic that Josh Harris, while disowning Christ, had a strange boldness to quote Martin Luther, a man who stood firm in Christ to the end. Martin Luther, as we know, stood firm against the papal leaders of his day and their heresies. Consider a portion of his speech from April 1521, speaking to the German governing authorities:

> Since your most serene majesty and your lordships require of me a simple, clear and direct answer, I will give one, and it is this: I cannot submit my faith either to the pope or to the council, because it is as clear as noonday that they have fallen into error and even into glaring inconsistency with themselves. If, then, I am not convinced by proof from Holy Scripture, or by cogent reasons, if I am not satisfied by the very text I have cited, and if my judgment is not in this way brought into subjection to God's word, I neither can nor will retract

> anything; for it cannot be either safe or honest for a Christian to speak against his conscience. Here I stand; I cannot do otherwise; God help me! Amen.

For Josh Harris and all those who remain disloyal (without repenting), spiritual death awaits them; eternal destruction in hell. But for Martin Luther and all those who remain loyal, spiritual life awaits them; eternal delight in glory. Which describes you, loyal or disloyal?

# QUESTIONS TO CONSIDER

1. (a) Read 2 Timothy 2:11-14. What are the warnings in this passage? (b) What are the encouragements in this passage? (c) How could you use 2 Timothy 2:11-14 to encourage those who are loyal to Christ and admonish those who are disloyal to Him?

2. Memorize 2 Timothy 2:11-13.

3. (a) Paul writes in 2 Timothy 2:11 that if we died with Him, we will also live with Him. How do the following references help you to understand that saying? Romans 6:5; 2 Corinthians 4:10; Galatians 2:19-20; Philippians 3:10; Colossians 3:1-4. (b) Do you think it is possible for a professing believer to obtain a crown without enduring the cross? Prove your answer biblically.

4. (a) How does a believer endure sufferings to the end? Prove your answer from the Scriptures. (b) According to 1 Peter 4:13-19, what should be our attitudes when we suffer? (c) How are you remaining steadfast in your relationship with Christ?

5. (a) What are some of the ways believers deny the Lord, according to Proverbs 30:8-9; Matthew 26:69-75; Mark 8:38; 1 John 2:22-25; Jude 1:4? (b) What are some other ways in which believers deny the Lord? (c) According to what Paul says in 2 Timothy 2:12, what are the implications of denying the Lord?

6. (a) In 2 Timothy 2:14, Paul writes that we should avoid getting involved in words that are of no profit. What are some ways in which we engage ourselves in words of no profit? (b) How can we as women encourage other women to avoid meaningless chatter and encourage profitable conversation instead?

7. (a) Are you remaining faithful to the Lord in these trying days? (b) Are there ways in which you are denying the Lord? (c) Please come with a prayer request for yourself after considering this chapter.

# Rightly Divide the Truth or Stray from the Truth

*2 Timothy 2:15–18*

WHEN I enter the doors of my home church, I often notice a framed quote that hangs just to the left of the entryway. I have often stopped to read it and been deeply moved by its message. It reads:

> We preach Christ, who is the Eternal Son, one in nature with the Eternal Father and the Eternal Son—the triune God.
>
> Who is the Creator and life-giver, as well as the sustainer of the universe and all who live in it.
>
> Who is the virgin-born Son of God and Son of Man—fully divine and fully human.
>
> Who is the One whose life on earth perfectly pleased God and whose righteousness is given to all who by grace through faith become one with Him.
>
> Who is the only acceptable sacrifice for sin that pleases God and whose death under divine judgment paid in full the penalty for the sins of His people, providing for them forgiveness and eternal life.
>
> Who is alive, having been raised from the dead by the Father validating His work of atonement and providing resurrection for the sanctification and glorification of the elect to bring them safely into His heavenly presence.
>
> Who is at the Father's throne interceding for all believers.
>
> Who is God's chosen Prophet, Priest and King, proclaiming truth, mediating for His church and reigning over His kingdom forever.
>
> Who will return suddenly from heaven to rapture His church, unleash judgment on the wicked, bring promised salvation to the Jews and the nations and establish His millennial reign on earth.
>
> Who will, after that earthly reign, destroy the universe, finally judge all sinners and send them to hell, then create the New Heavens and the New Earth where He will dwell forever with His

> saints in glory, love and joy.
> This is the Christ we preach.[32]

I am ever so thankful to be in a church that preaches Christ and endeavors to rightly divide His Word. I am keenly aware, however, that I live in a city that is infiltrated with churches that do not rightly divide the Word of God, and I shudder to think of what will become of them in the end.

We come to another chapter in Paul's second letter to Timothy. In the verses we'll study in this chapter, Paul will admonish young Timothy regarding the importance of being diligent in his studies so that he can rightly divide the Word of God. If Timothy is not careful in this, Paul warns Timothy that danger is lurking around the corner, as evidenced by those who have left the faith. Let's listen in as Paul writes in 2 Timothy 2:15-18:

> Be diligent to present yourself approved to God, a worker who does not need to be ashamed, rightly dividing the word of truth. But shun profane and idle babblings, for they will increase to more ungodliness. And their message will spread like cancer. Hymenaeus and Philetus are of this sort, who have strayed concerning the truth, saying that the resurrection is already past; and they overthrow the faith of some.

Our outline for this chapter will show us what it means to rightly divide the truth or to stray from it. We will learn of: *The Requirements Needed to Rightly Divide the Word of Truth* (vv 15-16) and *The Risks of Straying from Truth* (vv 17-18). We considered, in our last chapter, that there are two sweet reminders to the loyal: If we die with Christ, we will live with Him; and if we endure, we will also reign with Him. We also saw two sobering reminders to the disloyal: If we deny Christ, He will deny us; and if we are faithless, we can be certain that He will remain faithful to His promises and to His threats. Paul also ended those verses with a charge to Timothy to remind the readers of this letter of all that Paul has

---

32 John MacArthur. "Bold Proclaimers of Gospel Truth." *Grace to You*, https://www.gty.org/library/sermons-library/81-104/bold-proclaimers-of-gospel-truth. Accessed February 22, 2024.

written since the beginning of his letter. Paul has just written that we are to beware of denying Christ, and one of the many ways we can deny Him is by denying the sufficiency and authority of His Word. Another way we can deny Him is by not being diligent to correctly divide the Word of Truth. Still another way we can deny Him is by cuddling up to those who teach error. So, let's consider the requirements necessary for rightly dividing the Word of Truth, from verses 15 and 16, and we will find two of them.

## The Requirements Needed to Rightly Divide the Word of Truth *2 Timothy 2:15-16*

> Be diligent to present yourself approved to God, a worker who does not need to be ashamed, rightly dividing the word of truth. (2 Timothy 2:15)

Paul has written several times already in 2 Timothy about the importance of not being ashamed of or denying the Lord. By now, perhaps, Timothy might be wondering how he is ever going to keep from denying the Lord or being ashamed of Him. Paul gives the answer right here in this verse. He writes *be diligent to present yourself approved to God, a worker who does not need to be ashamed.* The word *diligent* means to make every effort. The King James Version says to "study to show yourself approved." A good way to put it is this: give diligence to your study. There should be no such thing as a lazy Christian; we are to discipline ourselves unto godliness, and part of that involves studying the Word.

According to this verse, we are to be diligent in our study of God's Word for three reasons. The first reason is this: to *present yourself approved to God. Approved* means that we have been tried and found to be acceptable. This trying process is much like coins being tested in the fire to make sure that they are genuine, that they are approved.

The second reason we are to be diligent in our study is so that we *do not need to be ashamed.* Being *ashamed* is how we feel when we know that we have done something wrong. As a child, I remember often feeling ashamed when I was doing things I knew I shouldn't be doing.

As children of our heavenly Father, we should strive to please Him by diligently studying His truth, so that we do not misrepresent Him and, as a result of that misrepresentation, stand ashamed before Him someday. As God's workers, we have to stay the course. We are workers for God's field, for God's Kingdom. Paul writes of this in 1 Corinthians 3:9-10 (LSB): "For we are God's fellow workers; you are God's field, God's building. According to the grace of God which was given to me, like a wise master builder I laid a foundation, and another is building on it. But each man must be careful how he builds on it."

The third reason we are to be diligent in our pursuit of truth is so that we can be *rightly dividing the word of truth*. What does it mean to do this? To *rightly divide* means to cut straight, to be correct, accurate, precise. This term is only used in the New Testament in 2 Timothy 2:15 and in the Greek translation of the Old Testament in Proverbs 3:6 and 11:5. Proverbs 3:6 (LSB) states, "In all your ways acknowledge Him, and He will make your paths straight." Proverbs 11:5 (LSB) reads, "The righteousness of the blameless will make his way straight, but the wicked will fall by his own wickedness." Both of these Proverbs deal with staying on the straight path. So when we consider the use of this word in 2 Timothy, rightly dividing the word of truth would mean to cut it straight. Exposit it correctly. Stick with the Word, and do not ever veer off that path. It means "handling it accurately," as the LSB translates this phrase. Many in our day no longer cut straight the Word; rather, they have chopped it into pieces and turned it into a scrambled mess. The *word of truth* is a reference to the doctrine of God as contained in His Holy Scriptures. Even Jesus, the Son of God, taught the doctrine of God. Listen to John 7:16 (LSB), "So Jesus answered them and said, 'My teaching is not Mine, but from Him who sent Me.'" Jesus knew well that God's words have power, as the writer to the Hebrews states in Hebrews 4:12 (LSB), "For the word of God is living and active and sharper than any two-edged sword, and piercing as far as the division of soul and spirit, of both joints and marrow, and able to judge the thoughts and intentions of the heart."

Ladies, we must study and we must speak the words of God because they alone have the power to change lives. The words of false teachers only have power to ruin lives. We cannot cut and paste passages of Scripture for our own means, which is what many do today. We must study the Word in its context, endeavoring to discover what it was intended to mean to its original audience. We must be conscious that when we speak, especially when we are speaking God's Word, that it is correct—God is listening to us! If we are rightly dividing the word of truth, then when we are inspected by God, we will have no cause for shame. There is only one judge and it is God, and it is He to whom we will give an account. When I teach, I must be concerned not about pleasing my audience but about pleasing God, whose words I am representing. Likewise, when you open your mouth and you instruct others, whether it be formal teaching or informal, as with a child or friend or husband, you must not be concerned with pleasing them, but with pleasing God alone. In Galatians 1:10 (LSB), Paul reminds us, "For am I now seeking the favor of men, or of God? Or am I striving to please men? If I were still trying to please men, I would not be a slave of Christ."

Now, perhaps, some of you are under the delusion that diligent study is only for pastors. I assure you, it is not. Every one of us is commanded by God to grow in our relationship with Him. Peter makes this clear in 1 Peter 2:2 (LSB): "like newborn babies, long for the pure milk of the word, so that by it you may grow in respect to salvation." And, at the end of his second epistle, he writes, "but grow in the grace and knowledge of our Lord and Savior Jesus Christ" (2 Peter 3:18, LSB). As we study the Word and as we grow in the grace and knowledge of our Lord, we must make sure we are cutting His Word straight, studying it correctly. This takes time and diligence. We are to discipline ourselves unto godliness. *So, the first requirement needed to rightly divide the Word of Truth is: Diligence is needed to study the truth.* But there is also a second requirement, found in verse 16. Paul writes,

> But shun profane and idle babblings, for they will increase to more ungodliness. (2 Timothy 2:16)

Often the Greek word *de* (here translated *but*) is a word of contrast, but it can also be a word which means "and also," as is the case here.

As workers of God, not only do we need to be diligent in our study, but we also need to *shun profane and idle babblings. This is the second requirement needed to rightly divide truth: Desert the nonsense of false teachers.* One of the ways we rightly divide the truth is to shun profane and idle babblings. Now, perhaps you are wondering what these are. *Profane* means wicked, and *idle babblings* are fruitless discussions. *Babblings* is a word that refers to what we hear out of a child who is just learning to talk. They babble, and you don't understand what they are saying. It's meaningless. This was just recently illustrated to me as I was watching a friend's soon-to-be one-year-old. I watched this little baby talk to herself in a mirror and it was nothing but babbling. We are to keep away, which is what *shun* means, from the foolish talk of false teachers because it is in opposition to sound doctrine—it is nothing but babbling. Instead, we are to hold fast to the truth. Paul makes this clear in Romans 16:17-18. He says there,

> Now I urge you, brethren, note those who cause divisions and offenses, contrary to the doctrine which you learned, and avoid them. For those who are such do not serve our Lord Jesus Christ, but their own belly, and by smooth words and flattering speech deceive the hearts of the simple.

In that passage, Paul is coming to the end of his epistle to the Romans, which is laden with sound doctrine, and he tells the church at Rome to get away from these guys who are teaching doctrine that is contrary to what they had learned—to avoid them!

Now, you might be thinking to yourself, "Why can't I listen to them? I mean, they're kind of entertaining, and that way I can learn about all the nonsense out there." Granted, you do have to test the teachers, which means that, to at least some extent, you do have to listen to what they're saying. But once you discern that they are false, you don't make it your daily habit to tune in to their nonsense! Paul says we are to shun them, to get away from them, because *they will increase to more ungodliness. More* means greater, and *increase* means to advance or drive forward, and *ungodliness* is wickedness. Instead of advancing in godliness, false teachers are advancing in more ungodliness. And it's not just the false teachers themselves; it's the words they speak.

Through the years, as I've watched people veer off the straight path, I've seen that they start out with a little foolishness and then they become totally unhinged. They eventually make no sense. In fact, just a few days ago, I was reading something to my husband that was written by a false teacher, and he said the person had completely lost all rationale. The path onto which they had veered was heading them down a steep cliff to destruction. The words of false teachers are meaningless, empty, evil, fruitless, and a waste of time. Paul's desire was to speak the truth in order to be approved by God. Listen to what he writes to the church at Thessalonica in 1 Thessalonians 2:4-6:

> But as we have been approved by God to be entrusted with the gospel, even so we speak, not as pleasing men, but God who tests our hearts. For neither at any time did we use flattering words, as you know, nor a cloak for covetousness—God is witness. Nor did we seek glory from men, either from you or from others, when we might have made demands as apostles of Christ.

Since Paul says these people who talk like this are given to more ungodliness, the conclusion is that their ridiculous talk and ideas are like a rapidly spreading cancer. In fact, Paul goes on to name a couple of these guys in the next verse—unlike some in our day who are fearful to name false teachers. So we turn from the two requirements needed to rightly divide the word of truth to the risks of straying from the truth. There are also two of them. Let's read verse 17.

## The Risks of Straying from the Truth *2 Timothy 2:17-18*

> And their message will spread like cancer. Hymenaeus and Philetus are of this sort, (2 Timothy 2:17)

*Their message will spread like cancer*, or some translations say like gangrene. It's fascinating to me to watch the massive crowds who follow teachers like this. Peter tells us about this very thing happening, in 2 Peter 2:1-3 (LSB).

> But false prophets also arose among the people, just as there will also be false teachers among you, who will secretly introduce destructive heresies, even denying the Master who bought them, bringing swift destruction upon themselves. And many will follow their sensuality, and because of them the way of the truth will be maligned. And in their greed they will exploit you with false words, their judgment from long ago is not idle, and their destruction is not asleep.

Peter says many follow them; false teachers plant seeds of deceit and lies, and it spreads and infects many. The KJV renders Paul's words here in 2 Timothy 2:17 as "their word will eat as doth a canker," and the LSB renders it as "their word will spread like gangrene." Both of these translations convey the idea that these falsehoods have the ability to spread in the same way that gangrene or cancer naturally spreads to all the other healthy parts of a body. That's the way it is with false teaching; it corrupts the good parts, all the parts that are whole.

The term *cancer* that Paul uses here, or gangrene, comes from the Greek word *gangraina*, a word that doesn't occur anywhere else in the New Testament, and it refers to something that will corrode through the whole body. It's quite interesting that, in our day, we understand gangrene to be a condition that occurs when blood flow is cut off to the affected area. This causes the tissue to die. Often, the part of the body which is affected by the gangrene has to be cut off. I also find it interesting that people who are more likely to get gangrene are those whose immune systems are weakened. In the same way, people who are likely to be swept away by wrong teaching are those who are weak in the faith, precisely because they have not been rightly dividing the word of truth.

Paul will speak specifically, later on in this letter, in 2 Timothy 3:6, about women who were swept away in this very manner: "For of this sort are those who creep into households and make captives of gullible women loaded down with sins, led away by various lusts." In fact, we know that at least one of the guys Paul mentions here was cut off from the church, and they both have been cut off from the Kingdom. *Hymenaeus and Philetus* were teaching false ideas, and Paul also mentions *Hymenaeus* in his first letter to Timothy. Read what he writes in 1 Timothy 1:19-20: "having faith and a good conscience, which some having rejected, concerning the faith have suffered shipwreck, of whom are Hymenaeus and Alexander, whom I delivered to Satan that they may learn not to blaspheme." Hymenaeus was the one Paul had to put out of the church. He was probably the leader of the pairs of men who are mentioned in 1 Timothy and in 2 Timothy. The reason I say this is because his name is mentioned first, which in Greek typically indicates prominence. The Scriptures speak nothing else about *Philetus*, so we know nothing about him but what is written here. But it's sad enough that their names are recorded here in the Word of God for all to see—as reprobates!

*So, the first risk of straying from the truth is defection from the faith.* Paul finishes up with some more remarks about these two men, along with the second risk of straying from the truth.

> who have strayed concerning the truth, saying that the resurrection is already past; and they overthrow the faith of some. (2 Timothy 2:18)

Paul says these men *have strayed concerning the truth.* To say that they *have strayed* means they have swerved, they have departed from the truth. Evidently, they had heard the truth, but somewhere along the road, they had also dabbled with error. These guys claimed to be Christians and yet their error put them over the edge. No longer were they cutting it straight, no longer were they on the straight path, but they had swerved.

At least one of the errors we know these men believed was this: *that the resurrection is already past.* There were some in Paul's day who taught that the *resurrection* of believers took place at their baptism, that the Christian was buried with Christ in baptism and rose again to new life in Christ, and they denied that there would ever be a bodily resurrection. They believed that the resurrection was not a new physical body but a spiritual one. Others taught that the resurrection was lived on in one's children. These ideas were known and taught as part of the Gnostic heresies. These ideas, along with others, were some of the wrong teachings regarding the resurrection that were prominent in Paul's day. This is one of the reasons why it's imperative that we be like the Berean believers who daily checked to see if the things they were listening to were biblical (Acts 17:10-11).

The men who taught these things were so influential that they took others down the road of doctrinal error with them. Paul puts it like this: *they overthrow the faith of some*. To *overthrow* means to subvert. *Here, then, is the second risk of straying from the truth: It destroys the faith of others.* To deny the resurrection is to deny the gospel because the death and resurrection of Christ are essential aspects of the good news. Just as a cancer grows and affects the other parts of the body, just as gangrene grows and eats at the flesh, so one false idea can grow until it can affect the whole of a person's faith. Jesus has some strong words to say about those who lead others off the beaten path. Consider Matthew 23:15 (LSB), "Woe to you, scribes and Pharisees, hypocrites, because you travel around on sea and land to make one proselyte; and when he becomes one, you make him twice as much a son of hell as yourselves." Also consider Matthew 15:14 (LSB), "Let them alone; they are blind guides of the blind. And if a blind man guides a blind man, both will fall into a pit." Even Paul knew this would happen, telling the elders of the church at Ephesus, in Acts 20:29-30 (LSB), "I know that after my departure savage wolves will come in among you, not sparing the flock; and from among your own selves men will arise, speaking perverse things, to draw away the disciples after them." This is why it is imperative that we pass on to others the truth and not some mystical, made-up cute story we have fabricated in our minds. Causing others to stumble is serious; Jesus says in Matthew 18:6-7,

> Whoever causes one of these little ones who believe in Me to sin, it would be better for him if a millstone were hung around his neck, and he were drowned in the depth of the sea. Woe to the world because of offenses! For offenses must come, but woe to that man by whom the offense comes!

## Summary

What are the requirements needed to rightly divide the word of truth? Diligence is needed, as is deserting the nonsense of false teachers. What is the risk of straying from the truth? Defection from the faith and destroying the faith of others.

As we think about rightly dividing the Word, let me ask you: Are you diligent to study the Word? Do you make time for meaningful Bible study? Do you reject the teaching of false teachers? My friend, we must be careful because if we take in what they teach we risk defecting from the faith and possibly taking others with us down the path of destruction.

Before we close out this chapter, there may be some of you ladies who truly desire to have meaningful time in the Word but need some motivation. As we consider the importance of this passage, being diligent to rightly divide the word of truth, I think it imperative that we develop some discipline in our lives so that we can do that. I would like to leave you with some tips for how to be more diligent, and these tips are in the form of an acrostic: **DISCIPLINE**. (The following is actually only a portion of a larger message I wrote regarding being disciplined in the Word and in prayer.)

***D—D****esire the Word and Delight in the Word.* Do you have an appetite for the Word of God? If not, why not? What is taking away your appetite? Is your time in the Word and in prayer a delight or a dread? Do you pant for God like a deer pants for water? Can't wait to meet with Him? Again, if not, why not? Are you certain that you have a living relationship with the living God?

***I—I****dols must be put away.* What do you love, or whom do you love? Do you love that thing or that person more than you love God? What do you spend your day doing? Have you kept a time journal lately to see where your time goes? Your energy? Your monies? Many women get caught up in things which are passing when they could be spending time in the Word, which is eternal. Remember, my friend, God will have no other idols before Him. He is a jealous God when it comes to His time with you.

***S—Spend ample time.*** How much time do you spend in the Word and in prayer on a daily basis? Are you under the myth that a chapter a day will keep the devil away or that a popcorn call to God will keep you from becoming a fraud? Are you willing to miss sleep or even a meal to have more time with God? What are you willing to give up for Him? What is crowding your schedule that keeps you from having meaningful time with Him?

***C—Cultivate daily habits.*** What daily habits do you have in place right now? Brushing your teeth? Putting your make up on? Exercising? Eating? Working? Driving the kids to school or homeschooling them? Have you cultivated a meaningful daily discipline of time with God? Are you willing to put your apron over your head for two hours like Susanna Wesley to be with your Lord? (By the way, she did this while mothering 19 children! It was said of her that she had a thorough and profound knowledge of the Bible.)

***I—Important to understand proper hermeneutics.*** Do you know the proper rules of interpretation? If you don't, I would encourage you to find someone who does and let them help you. Do you involve yourself in serious Bible study, or are you sloppy in Bible study? What are you currently studying? What are you currently memorizing?

***P—Pray before, during, and after your study time and, of course, pray daily.*** Are you in the habit of praying when you read, study, or memorize? We cannot learn anything apart from the help of the Lord and His Spirit.

***L—Let the Holy Spirit be your teacher.*** Do you rush to other sources first to get help in answering your biblical questions, or do you pray and ask the dear Holy Spirit to help you as you study and read the Word?

***I—Increase in your knowledge.*** Do you know more about God this year than last year? How has it changed the way you live? Has your prayer life matured in the past year? Does God answer your prayers on a regular basis?

***N****—**N**ever think you have arrived.* Do you secretly think you are more mature than others when it comes to Bible knowledge and prayer? Do you come to the Word with humility and a desire to know more? Is there room for improvement when it comes to your time of prayer?

***E****—**E**ndeavor to use what you are learning.* Who have you passed biblical truths on to this week? Are you involved in a ladies Bible study or a discipling relationship where you can pass on the things God is teaching you?

Dear sister, I urge you to lay aside the trivialities of our age so that you can be diligent to study, so that you might one day be approved by God, a workman who needs not be ashamed, rightly dividing the word of truth. If not, you risk straying from the truth!

# QUESTIONS TO CONSIDER

1. (a) Read 2 Timothy 2:15-18. What commands do you notice in this passage? (b) What contrasts do you observe in this passage?

2. Memorize 2 Timothy 2:15.

3. (a) Look up the following verses and list the speech of genuine teachers and the speech of false teachers (you might want to make two columns in order to see the contrast): Jeremiah 23:16-17; Ezekiel 13:9-10; John 7:17-18; Romans 16:17-18; 1 Corinthians 2:1-5; 1 Timothy 6:3-5; 2 Timothy 4:3-4; 2 Peter 2:18-19; Jude 1:16. (b) How can these passages help you to discern truth from error?

4. (a) Hymenaeus and Philetus were teaching that the resurrection was past, according to 2 Timothy 2:17-18. Why is it essential that we believe in the resurrection, according to 1 Corinthians 15:12-19? (b) Who else was wrong about the resurrection, in Matthew 22:23-33? (c) Why were they in error about the resurrection, according to verse 29? (d) How does this relate to what Paul writes in 2 Timothy 2:15? (e) How should this motivate us as believers to make sure we know the Word of God? (f) What are some ways we can make sure we are rightly dividing God's Word?

5. (a) Why should we avoid foolish and godless chatter, according to the following verses? 1 Timothy 4:7-8; 6:20-21; 2 Timothy 2:14-18; Titus 1:14-16; 3:9. (b) What do these passages indicate that are we to do instead (if it is noted)? (c) How do you avoid meaningless chatter? (d) What are some ways in which we can elevate conversations from meaningless to meaningful?

6. (a) Do you know anyone who has veered into false ideas like Hymenaeus and Philetus did? (This does not have to be the false idea of the resurrection, as in their case.) (b) Are you willing to humbly confront the error of their way? Will you?

7. (a) Are you faithful to spend ample time in the Word of God? (b) Will you be able to stand unashamed as one who has rightly divided the Word of Truth? (c) Do you shun the idle chatter of our day?

8. After considering your answers from question 7, write a prayer request on how you can improve your Christian walk.

# Protecting the Purity of the Church

*2 Timothy 2:19-21*

RECENTLY, I have had a desire to get rid of things that are no longer useful to me—things like clothes, jewelry, kitchen items, etc. I've felt the urge to purge my home of unwanted items so that it can be more organized and functional, something I typically do about once a year. In fact, the week I was writing this chapter, I actually threw a couple items in the trash that are useless: an old dish rag and an old vacuum sweeper. You might be wondering, "Susan, what does your desire to rid your home of useless things have to do with a chapter that is entitled, *Protecting the Purity of the Church*?" Ridding our homes of unwanted and useless items is, in fact, a good analogy of what Paul writes to Timothy regarding the church. Paul has just mentioned two men who had defected from the faith and also persuaded others to do the same. Now, Paul warns Timothy of the need to cleanse himself from any vessels within the church that are no longer useful. Just as I desire a home that is functional and orderly and useful to my family, the Lord desires His church to be functional and orderly and useful to His family. Just as in one's home, in order for this to take place in the church, there are a few things that need to happen. Let's listen in as Paul writes to Timothy regarding the purity of the church in 2 Timothy 2:19-21.

> Nevertheless the solid foundation of God stands, having this seal: "The Lord knows those who are His," and, "Let everyone who names the name of Christ depart from iniquity." But in a great house there are not only vessels of gold and silver, but also of wood and clay, some for honor and some for dishonor. Therefore if anyone cleanses himself from the latter, he will be a vessel for honor, sanctified and useful for the Master, prepared for every good work.

As we consider what it looks like to protect the purity of the church, we will consider three important truths. We will see *The Foundation of the*

*Church* (v 19); *The Furniture in the Church* (v 20); and *The Function of the Church* (v 21). In our last chapter, we looked at the requirements needed to rightly divide the Word of Truth as well as the risks of straying from the truth. We finished up that chapter with some practical ways to develop a disciplined time in the Word of God; I trust you have begun to implement some of those in your life. We also discovered that Hymenaeus and Philetus strayed from the truth and were even able to overthrow the faith of some. But Timothy must not be shaken because of those who have defected from the faith. Why? Because he has a solid foundation of God that stands and is sealed. Let's consider verse 19 together as we look at the foundation of the church.

## The Foundation of the Church *2 Timothy 2:19*

> Nevertheless the solid foundation of God stands, having this seal: "The Lord knows those who are His," and, "Let everyone who names the name of Christ depart from iniquity." (2 Timothy 2:19)

*Nevertheless*, even though some have strayed from the truth and have overthrown the faith of some, *the solid foundation of God stands*. That foundation is solid and it stands. The word *solid* means steadfast; steady; sure; stable. The foundation of God is sure because it has God's name on it. It has His seal on it, and in the biblical world no one would break a seal of ownership. God's true church is solid, Timothy, and don't listen to those who will tell you otherwise. Don't let this disrupt your faith in God! God isn't wringing His hands in Heaven; He knows those who are His. In fact, we have a sobering account in Matthew 7:23, where Jesus tells some to depart from Him and that He never knew them. These were those who claimed to have done wonderful works in His name, but they'd never known Him and He knew they hadn't! (See also what Jesus says in John 2:23-25.) In contrast to some who profess the faith, whose foundation is built on sinking sand, true Christians have a foundation that *stands* because it is built on a solid rock. Their *foundation* is Christ. As Paul writes in 1 Corinthians 3:10-11, "According to the grace of God which was given to me, as a wise master builder I have laid the foundation, and another builds on it. But let each one take heed how he builds on it. For no other foundation can anyone lay than that which is laid, which is Jesus Christ." Timothy needed to remind himself of what his spiritual father Paul wrote in his first letter to Timothy in 1 Timothy 3:15: "but if I am delayed, I write so that you may know how you ought to conduct yourself in the house of God, which is the church of the living God, the pillar and ground of the truth." The church of the living God is the pillar and ground of the truth!

But Paul goes on to write that not only is the church's foundation solid; it also has God's *seal.* As I already mentioned, a seal would be a symbol of ownership which no one could break. Two parts to this seal are mentioned in this text, and those two parts represent the church's security and purity. The church's security is communicated in the words *"the Lord knows who are His"* and the church's purity is communicated in the words *"let everyone who names the name of Christ depart from iniquity."* One man has written of this, "Here are two inscriptions on the foundation stone, the one guaranteeing the 'security,' the other the 'purity,' of the church. The two go together. The purity of the church is indispensable to its security."[33] Our Lord wants His people to not be threatened by wolves in the church and He wants His church to be a pure bride. And this requires that we have shepherds who watch over the purity of their flock so that the flock can be secure. I am perplexed by churches where the pastors don't guard against those false intruders aiming to harm the flock, and I am puzzled by the true sheep who remain in those churches. We must also have shepherds who are courageous when it comes to removing those who would affect the purity of the church.

Now, the terminology regarding the two parts of the seal appears to come from Numbers 16:1-40 (LSB). Let's read it together:

> Now Korah the son of Izhar, the son of Kohath, the son of Levi, with Dathan and Abiram, the sons of Eliab, and On the son of Peleth, sons of Reuben, took others, and they rose up before Moses, together with some of the sons of Israel, 250 leaders of the congregation, those

33 Marvin Vincent, *Word Studies in the New Testament* (Peabody: Hendrickson, 1985), Biblesoft.

called upon by the assembly, men of renown. Then they assembled together against Moses and Aaron, and said to them, "You have gone far enough, for all the congregation are holy, every one of them, and Yahweh is in their midst; so why do you exalt yourselves above the assembly of Yahweh?"

And Moses heard this and fell on his face; and he spoke to Korah and all his congregation, saying, "Tomorrow morning Yahweh will show who is His, and who is holy, and will bring him near to Himself; even the one whom He will choose, He will bring near to Himself. Do this: take censers for yourselves, Korah and all your congregation, and put fire in them, and lay incense upon them in the presence of Yahweh tomorrow; and the man whom Yahweh chooses shall be the one who is holy. You have gone far enough, you sons of Levi!"

Then Moses said to Korah, "Hear now, you sons of Levi, is it not enough for you that the God of Israel has separated you from the rest of the congregation of Israel, to bring you near to Himself, to perform the service of the tabernacle of Yahweh, and to stand before the congregation to minister to them; and that He has brought you near, Korah, and all your brothers, sons of Levi, with you? And are you seeking for the priesthood also? Therefore you and all your congregation are gathered together against Yahweh; but as for Aaron, who is he that you grumble against him?"

Then Moses sent a summons to Dathan and Abiram, the sons of Eliab; but they said, "We will not come up. Is it not enough that you have brought us up out of a land flowing with milk and honey to put us to death in the wilderness, but you would also lord it over us? Indeed, you have not brought us into a land flowing with milk and honey, nor have you given us an inheritance of fields and vineyards. Would you put out the eyes of these men? We will not come up!"

Then Moses became very angry and said to Yahweh, "Do not regard their offering! I have not taken a single donkey from them, nor have I done harm to any of them." And Moses said to Korah, "You and all your congregation be present before Yahweh tomorrow, both you and they along with Aaron. And each of you take his firepan and put incense on it, and each of you bring his censer near before Yahweh, 250 firepans; also you and Aaron shall each bring his firepan." So they each took his own censer and put fire on it, and laid incense on it; and they stood at the doorway of the tent of meeting, with Moses and Aaron. Thus Korah assembled all the congregation against them at the doorway of the tent of meeting. And the glory of Yahweh appeared to all the congregation.

Then Yahweh spoke to Moses and Aaron, saying, "Separate yourselves from among this congregation, that I may consume them instantly." But they fell on their faces and said, "O God, God of the spirits of all flesh, when one man sins, will You be angry with the entire congregation?"

Then Yahweh spoke to Moses, saying, "Speak to the congregation, saying, 'Get back from around the dwellings of Korah, Dathan and Abiram.'"

Then Moses arose and went to Dathan and Abiram, with the elders of Israel following him, and he spoke to the congregation, saying, "Turn aside now from the tents of these wicked men, and touch nothing that belongs to them, lest you be swept away in all their sin." So they got back from around the dwellings of Korah, Dathan and Abiram; but Dathan and Abiram came out and stood at the doorway of their tents, along with their wives and their sons and their little ones. And Moses said, "By this you shall know that Yahweh has sent me to do all these deeds; for this is not from my heart. If these men die the death of all men or if they suffer the fate of all men, then Yahweh has not sent me. But if Yahweh creates an entirely new thing and the ground opens its mouth and swallows them up with all that is theirs, and they go down to Sheol alive, then you will know that these men have spurned Yahweh."

And it happened that as he finished speaking all these words, the ground that was under them split open; and the earth opened its mouth and swallowed them up, and their households, and all the men who belonged to Korah with their possessions. So they and all that belonged to them went down to Sheol alive; and the earth closed over them, and they perished from the midst of the assembly. Then all Israel who were around them fled at their outcry, for they said, "Lest the earth swallow us up!" Fire also came forth from Yahweh and consumed the 250 men who were bringing near the incense.

Then Yahweh spoke to Moses, saying, "Say to Eleazar, the son of

> Aaron the priest, that he shall take up the censers out of the midst of the blaze, and you scatter the burning coals abroad; for they are holy. As for the censers of these men who have sinned at the cost of their lives, make them into hammered sheets for a plating of the altar, since they brought them near before Yahweh, and they are holy; and they shall be for a sign to the sons of Israel." So Eleazar the priest took the bronze censers which the men who were burned had brought near, and they hammered them out as a plating for the altar, as a memorial to the sons of Israel that no outsider who is not of the seed of Aaron should come near to burn incense before Yahweh; so that he will not become like Korah and his congregation—just as Yahweh had spoken to him by the hand of Moses.

Korah and his companions were challenging the authority of Moses and Aaron and were leading others astray, just as in Timothy's church Hymenaeus and Philetus were overthrowing the faith of some. Moses is clear that *the Lord knows those who are His*; false teachers and false men will always cause problems, but the Lord knows those who belong to Him. The unbelief of Korah and his companions led to rebellion and apostasy, and the earth opened up and swallowed them. Also note, in verses 21-26 above, that the Israelites were commanded to separate themselves from these men. That's exactly what Paul tells Timothy to do, that is, *let everyone who names the name of Christ depart from iniquity*, that *iniquity* in this context refers to false teaching. That's why we don't tolerate evil in the church! It is a spiritual cancer that the church must be rid of, as Paul has already warned about in verse 17.

Paul would have been very familiar with this portion of the Old Testament and probably would have had it memorized. This is a good time to pause and remind ourselves of the importance of the Old Testament. Paul reminds us in Romans 15:4 (LSB), "For whatever was written in earlier times was written for our instruction, so that through the perseverance and the encouragement of the Scriptures we might have hope." In fact, did you know that there are at least 283 direct quotations in the New Testament that are from the Old Testament? It behooves us to be familiar with all 66 books of the Bible; what a treasure we miss out on when we don't read the whole counsel of God!

What is the foundation of the church? It is solid, and it has a twofold seal, security and purity. Maybe you are also wondering what is in the church. In verse 20, Paul moves from teaching us about the foundation of the church to teaching us about the furniture in the church.

## The Furniture in the Church *2 Timothy 2:20*

> But in a great house there are not only vessels of gold and silver, but also of wood and clay, some for honor and some for dishonor. (2 Timothy 2:20)

In a great house, there are different kinds of *vessels*. We understand this as women. We have items, like furniture or dishes, that we hold dear. They are precious to us, like gold or silver, which are used to convey honor. In other words, we put them out for our honored guests. Not long ago, my husband and I had a group of 10 for dinner, and I set the table in the formal dining room; I used my Mom's china and other nice utensils. But you know what? This week, my husband and I will eat on my everyday dishes, and when the grandkids or other casual company come over, we often use paper plates and plastic cups that we then toss in the trash.

This *great house* Paul mentions is an analogy of the church. The church is often called a building and even a house. Hebrews 3:6 (LSB, emphasis mine) states, "but Christ was faithful as a Son over His *house*—whose house we are, if we hold fast our confidence and the boast of our hope." And Peter writes in 1 Peter 2:5 (LSB, emphasis mine), "you also, as living stones, are being built up as a *spiritual house* for a holy priesthood, to offer up spiritual sacrifices acceptable to God through Jesus Christ." And later on in Peter's epistle, he warns, in 1 Peter 4:17 (LSB, emphasis mine), "For it is time for judgment to begin with the *house of God*; and if it begins with us first, what will be the outcome for those who do not obey the gospel of God?"

Paul is telling Timothy that not everyone who gathers with the church is the same. In fact, there are those who profess the faith who do not possess the faith. Those who possess genuine faith are like *vessels of gold and silver*, vessels of *honor*. Then there are those who only profess faith who are likened to *wood and clay*, vessels of *dishonor*. The former are more useful, like the things in our home we display or use when guests come. These vessels would be the ones we value the most, as they have sentimental value or lasting usefulness to us, and we treat those vessels with honor. The latter we might use temporarily, like paper plates and plastic utensils, but eventually we throw them out because they have little value or usefulness to us, like I just did with the old vacuum and dishrag just recently; we don't treat those vessels with honor, but with dishonor. You might be thinking that all should be treated equally. I mean, why would we get rid of anyone in the church? Aren't we to be kind to all and love all people, even our enemies? Yes, of course, we are to love even our enemies, but they don't belong in the church when they are falsely professing the faith or false teachers. Paul talks about these different types of vessels in Romans 9:19-24 (LSB):

> You will say to me then, "Why does He still find fault? For who resists His will?" On the contrary, who are you, O man, who answers back to God? Will the thing molded say to the molder, "Why did you make me like this"? Or does not the potter have authority over the clay, to make from the same lump one vessel for honorable use and another for dishonorable use? And what if God, wanting to demonstrate His wrath and to make His power known, endured with much patience vessels of wrath having been prepared for destruction, and in order that He might make known the riches of His glory upon vessels of mercy, which He prepared beforehand for glory—even us, whom He also called, not from among Jews only, but also from among Gentiles?

God has the right to make some vessels for destruction, and, yes, sometimes they end up in our churches unawares. They are like the tares that grow up with the wheat, and we won't know who they are until the judgment (see Matthew 13). Sometimes, we know before then, and that is when it is our responsibility to get away from them, lest they influence us. One man writes, "False teachers are not valuable; they are like wood and clay. They are utensils to dishonor, no matter how popular they may be today. Wood and clay will not survive the test of fire."[34]

Like Timothy, we should not be discouraged by this. As it was in the days of Noah, so it is now; as it was in the days of Korah, so it is now. Just like there are corrupt politicians who give a bad name to good politicians who are trying to better our country, there are corrupt "believers" who give a bad name to those who are trying to live out real Christianity. Just like there are arrogant doctors who give a bad name to those doctors who really care about their patients, so there are arrogant "believers" who give a bad name to those who are endeavoring to walk humbly with their God. Just as a wise person gets away from corrupt politicians and arrogant doctors, genuine believers get away from those who are false believers and are harming the church, as Paul will write in the next verse.

What is the furniture in the church? There are two types. There are vessels of honor and vessels of dishonor. Some will stand the test of fire; they are gold and silver. Some will not stand the test of fire; they are made of clay and wood. We now end our study of this portion of 2 Timothy by considering the function of the church. What is she to be about? Paul mentions four functions here. (These are certainly not all the functions of the church; they are simply the four Paul mentions in this text.)

## The Function of the Church *2 Timothy 2:21*

> Therefore if anyone cleanses himself from the latter, he will be a vessel for honor, sanctified and useful for the Master, prepared for every good work. (2 Timothy 2:21)

*Therefore*, because of these various types of vessels in this great house, those that are called by His name, the gold and silver vessels, *cleanse [themselves] from the latter*, the wood and clay vessels. The *latter*, those

34 Excerpted from The Bible Exposition Commentary on the New Testament © 1989 Warren W. Wiersbe. Used by permission of David C Cook. May not be further reproduced. All rights reserved. 248.

vessels of wood and clay, are those like Hymenaeus and Philetus. The word *cleanse* means to purge oneself. We are commanded not only here but also in other passages to get away from false teachers. *This is the first function of those in the church, according to this verse: Get away from false teachers and false teaching.* A true child of God gets away from these types of people and their teaching. We do not give them a platform, and we do not listen to their teaching. Instead, we are to cleanse ourselves from them. The bride of Christ is to be pure and not taint herself with unwholesome doctrine or those who would teach it. I am shocked at those who will listen to false teachers, justifying them because, they claim, "Not all that they say is wrong. They have some good things to say." That is dangerous! A little leaven leavens the whole lump. A frog that sits in water that is slowly boiling doesn't realize it until it's too late and he's cooked. Once we determine that someone does not teach the pure milk of the Word, once they have become aberrant in their theology, we get away from them. The very morning that I was getting ready to open my computer to prepare this chapter, I received a text from someone in another state asking me what I thought of a certain teacher. I quickly responded to her with what I knew to be factual, and it wasn't good. She texted me back, saying, "Thank you, Susan. I thought something wasn't right." Before we go on to the second function of the church, notice that we don't cleanse ourselves of the house itself; the house is the church, God's building. (Hebrews 10:25 is clear that we are not to forsake the assembling of ourselves with the gathered church.) Rather, we are to cleanse His house of those who don't belong there.

*The second function of those in the body, the church, is that we are to be sanctified.* And isn't it interesting that sanctification is listed here after we have gotten rid of the evil in our midst? To be *sanctified* means to be set apart for His glory and His service. We are to be holy as He is holy. We are to be so like our Lord that we put Him on display, not only in the church but also in the world.

*The third job or function of those who belong in this building, this house, the church, is that we are to be useful to the Master.* Remember, Paul has already written that we are to be like a soldier who has enlisted in God's army, like an athlete who competes by the rules, and like a farmer who works hard (2 Timothy 2:3-6). We are employed by God and, therefore, we are to be useful to our Master, our Owner, our Lord. And this means we should be using our gifts for the good of the body of Christ and for His glory.

*Our fourth and final function is that we are to be prepared for every good work.* (As I already mentioned, this passage does not delineate all of our responsibilities as part of this great house, but simply the ones mentioned in this text.) The order of responsibilities is appropriate: We first have to cleanse ourselves from all evil, including false teachers, then make sure that we are set apart and useful to the Master, and then we will be prepared and ready for all He asks of us, *for every good work*. When we are willing and ready to be used for His Kingdom, then we will be ready for every good work. Paul reminds us of this in several passages. In Ephesians 2:10 (LSB), he writes, "For we are His workmanship, created in Christ Jesus for good works, which God prepared beforehand so that we would walk in them." In Titus, he speaks of this twice. First, in Titus 3:1 (LSB), he says, "Remind them to be subject to rulers, to authorities, to be obedient, to be ready for every good work." And again, in Titus 3:14 (LSB), "And our people must also learn to lead in good works to meet pressing needs, so that they will not be unfruitful." Later on in 2 Timothy, Paul will give us a hint about how we can be prepared for these good works; consider 2 Timothy 3:16-17, "All Scripture is given by inspiration of God, and is profitable for doctrine, for reproof, for correction, for instruction in righteousness, that the man of God may be complete, thoroughly equipped for every good work." We equip ourselves for all these good works by the Holy Scriptures, which are sufficient for all that God has called us to do.

## Summary

What is the foundation of the church? It is solid, and it has a twofold seal: security and purity. Are you in a church that is solidly built on the foundation of Christ alone? Is your pastor protecting you from the false teachers and false teaching that are prevalent today? Does your church practice church discipline (as described in Matthew 18:15-18)? Are you doing your part to protect the purity of your church by shunning all evil, including false teaching?

What is the furniture in the church? Vessels of honor, like gold and silver, and vessels of dishonor, like wood and clay. Which category do you fall under—a vessel of honor or a vessel of dishonor? When others think of you as one of God's vessels, do they see you as shining gold or silver or as wood or clay? How are you excelling in your spiritual walk?

What are the functions of the church? To be vessels of honor, by cleansing ourselves of all who are false; by being sanctified; by being useful for the Master; and by being prepared for every good work. Do you get away from all spiritual falsehood? This would include teaching and teachers and even well-meaning friends who try to persuade you toward that which is false. Are you growing in sanctification, that is, are you growing more and more into the image of Christ? Is your life more Christlike this year than it was last year? And what about being useful for the Master? Of what use were you this week to Him? How about today? And, finally, are you prepared for those good works He has called you to do? Is there something you could be doing that would aid you in being more prepared for what He has called you to do?

As important as it is for us as women to have our homes in order so that things run smoothly and efficiently, it is far more important for us to have our hearts in order so that the church of Jesus Christ remains secure and pure! Let's endeavor by the grace of God to do our part!

## QUESTIONS TO CONSIDER

1. (a) Read 2 Timothy 2:19-21. (b) What are our responsibilities, according to these verses? (c) What does each of these mean?

2. Memorize 2 Timothy 2:21.

3. (a) What do false teachers do, according to 2 Peter 2:1-3 and Jude 1:16-19? (b) What is our responsibility toward false teachers, according to Romans 16:17; 2 Thessalonians 3:6, 14; 2 Timothy 3:5; Titus 3:10; and 2 John 10-11? (c) Why is it essential that pastors protect their flocks from false teaching?

4. (a) How does getting away from false teachers and false teaching help us to be sanctified, useful for the Master, and prepared for every good work? (b) How do you protect yourself from false teaching?

5. (a) According to Proverbs 3:7, what must happen before we can depart from evil? (b) Why is it essential that we depart from all evil, according to Job 28:28; 1 Corinthians 3:16-17; 2 Corinthians 7:1? (c) Do you think departing from evil would include departing from false teaching and false teachers? (Use Scripture to back your answer.)

6. (a) How can God's people do their part to protect the purity of the church? (b) Besides getting away from evil (including false teaching), what other ways can we be more sanctified, useful for the Master, and prepared for every good work?

7. Are you a vessel that is useful for the Master (private question)? Come prepared to share a prayer request on how you might be more useful for His glory.

# What to Flee From and What to Follow After

*2 Timothy 2:22-26*

ONE of the challenges we face in our walk with the Lord is learning how to put off wrong thinking and actions and to replace them with right thinking and right actions. Often, when I am meeting with a woman for counseling or discipleship, I will give her a journaling assignment to help her in this area. For example, if she struggles with anxiety, I have her list in a week's time all the thoughts that go through her mind when she is anxious about something. I also have her list the circumstances or people around which she finds herself tempted to be anxious. Then, we go through the list together and I endeavor to help her biblically with what she should be thinking and how she should be acting. With the Holy Spirit's help and her cooperation, she can learn how to put off anxiety and put on peace and contentment. It's that way with any sin we face. The Scriptures are replete with commands to put off sin and put on obedience, and when we do what the Scriptures command, the results are fruitful. Some familiar passages that deal with this put-off/put-on dynamic include Colossians 3:1-17; Ephesians 4:17-32; and Philippians 4:6-9. We have come to one such passage in our study in 2 Timothy. Let's read it together.

> Flee also youthful lusts; but pursue righteousness, faith, love, peace with those who call on the Lord out of a pure heart. But avoid foolish and ignorant disputes, knowing that they generate strife. And a servant of the Lord must not quarrel but be gentle to all, able to teach, patient, in humility correcting those who are in opposition, if God perhaps will grant them repentance, so that they may know the truth, and that they may come to their senses and escape the snare of the devil, having been taken captive by him to do his will. (2 Timothy 2:22-26)

As we examine this text, we'll discover the things Paul tells us we need to flee from, the things we need to follow after, and the fruit that comes as a result of doing both. These will all fall into three categories that are addressed all throughout the text: *What Do I Flee From?* (we'll discover three of these); *What Do I Follow After?* (we'll discover eight of these); and *What Fruit will Come as a Result?* (we'll discover six of these). In our last chapter, we learned three truths about the church that pertain to protecting its purity. Its foundation is solid, and it has a twofold seal: security and purity. We also learned that the furniture in the church includes vessels of honor: gold and silver, and vessels of dishonor: wood and clay. Lastly, we saw the function of the church: that its members are to be vessels of honor by cleansing themselves from all that is false, by being sanctified, by being useful for the Master, and by being prepared for every good work.

The transition from the verses we examined in our last chapter to the verses we'll examine in this chapter is simple to see. Those who desire to be vessels of honor cleanse themselves from all that is false because they desire to be useful for the One who chose them. In order to do that, they must put off certain things and put on certain things and the result will be fruits of righteousness. And, by the way, the words written here by the apostle Paul are not for Timothy only but for the entire church at Ephesus and the church universal. Those who know the Lord are His servants. And there are certain things that His servants must flee from and certain things that they must follow after. Let's consider the first thing we must flee from and the first four things we must follow after, in verse 22.

> Flee also youthful lusts; but pursue righteousness, faith, love, peace with those who call on the Lord out of a pure heart. (2 Timothy 2:22)

*The first thing Timothy must flee from is youthful lusts.* No one can call on the Lord with a pure heart, as Paul mentions at the end of this verse, while maintaining a lustful heart. The word *flee* means to run away from, and it has the idea of escaping so as not to be captured. This is a serious fleeing, as if running to save your life. It is what we see Joseph doing when he runs out of the house when pressed by Potiphar's wife, in Genesis 39:12. And Jesus addresses this very thing when He instructs us, in the Sermon on the Mount, to gouge out an eye or cut off an arm, if need be, to keep ourselves from sinning (Matthew 5:27-30). In a sense, that's what we do when we put off sin; our spiritual life is at stake, and so we do whatever it takes to fling off the things that adhere to us, that hinder or harm us spiritually.

Now, the question might come to mind, "What is a *youthful lust*?" *Youthful* refers to being young in age, one who is a young person. And Timothy was between 30 and 40 years old at this point; in our day, we would call him a young adult. *Lust* is a longing for something that is forbidden. This would not only include sexual lusts, but also the lusts for power, wealth, health, or anything that would be idolatrous. One man sums up lusts in three categories; he says they are "Pleasure, which is the inordinate craving for the satisfaction of the physical appetites. Power, which is the ungoverned passion to be Number 1, the lust to 'shine' or be dominant. Possessions, which is the uncontrolled yearning for material possessions and for the 'glory' that goes with them."[35] The first thing that Timothy, the church of Ephesus, and the church universal are to flee from is youthful lusts, or we might say anything you long for that is forbidden. And, the only way to know what is forbidden is to know what God says is forbidden.

Instead of longing for what is wrong, we are to long for what is right. Paul tells Timothy to follow four things. He uses the word *pursue*, which means to follow, hunt, and chase after. This is a strenuous effort, and not one that is half-hearted. A person pursuing these virtues hunts them down until they have been found. In this pursuit, there is a great determination to catch one's prey. *The first thing Timothy—and we—must pursue is righteousness. Righteousness* refers to the doing of what is right, just, and holy. I often think of and remind myself of what one precious woman said to me years ago: "Susan, you will never regret doing what is right, but you will always regret doing what is wrong." Now, the only way to pursue righteousness is to know what God says is righteous in His Word. The Psalmist says in Psalm 11:7 (LSB), "For Yahweh is righteous, He loves righteousness; the upright will behold His face." Also, Jesus says, in Matthew 5:6 (LSB), "Blessed are those who hunger and thirst for righteousness, for they shall be satisfied." A true

35 William Hendriksen, *Pastoral Epistles*, 272, paraphrase.

child of God hungers and thirsts for not a little righteousness, but all the righteousness there is, so much so that, later on in Matthew 5:10 (LSB), Jesus says persecution can come because of it: "Blessed are those who have been persecuted for the sake of righteousness, for theirs is the kingdom of heaven."

*The second thing we must chase after is faithfulness.* This would be *faithfulness* to God, faithfulness to others, and faithfulness to what He has called us to do. Paul began this chapter by commanding Timothy to pass truth on to faithful men, men who not only possess genuine faith but who will be faithful. This is a much needed virtue in our day, as it seems there are few who are faithful, few you can count on. Proverbs 20:6 puts it well: "Most men will proclaim each his own goodness, but who can find a faithful man?" A vessel of honor must be faithful and must chase after faithfulness.

*The third virtue to pursue is love.* The word for *love* in Greek here is *agape.* Not a love that is mushy-gushy and feeling-oriented, but a love that is an act of your will. You may not feel like loving someone, but you are commanded to love. (Just like a woman may not feel like submitting to her husband, but she is commanded to do so, whether she feels like it or not.) Love seeks to meet the needs of others like God met our need for salvation by providing Jesus as a substitute for our sin. Paul states in Romans 13:10 (LSB), "Love does not work evil against a neighbor; therefore love is the fulfillment of the Law."

*The fourth thing to follow after is peace. Peace* is quietness and rest. It is not a feeling but a condition of your soul, which makes every effort to be at peace with God and with others. It's interesting that the writer to the Hebrews says, "Pursue peace with all people, and holiness, without which no one will see the Lord" (Hebrews 12:14). Servants of the Lord pursue peace, not strife. They prefer to settle things rather than to stir up things. And note that a pursuit of these things is not just for Timothy; Paul adds *with all those who call on the Lord with a pure heart.* These virtues are for *all* those who name the name of Christ. We call on Him with purity of *heart*, which indicates that this purity relates to our minds or our emotions. To be *pure* is to be clean, and Jesus is clear that it is only the pure in heart who will see God. In Matthew 5:8 (LSB), He says, "Blessed are the pure in heart, for they shall see God."

So, according to verse 22, we are to flee youthful lusts, anything that is forbidden. But we are also to follow after righteousness, faithfulness, love, and peace. *And what will be the fruit of this? The first fruit we see is purity of heart.* Paul now continues with another thing we are to flee from, in verse 23.

> But avoid foolish and ignorant disputes, knowing that they generate strife. (2 Timothy 2:23)

*The second thing Timothy and the church must flee from is foolish and ignorant disputes.* The word *avoid* means to refuse, to get away from. We get away from *foolish* and *ignorant disputes. Foolish* means stupid or absurd, and *ignorant* means uninstructed. Often, people want to argue about things because they haven't done the hard work of studying to know the facts. This is often true in the church. People have preconceived ideas without having studied those ideas theologically. There are some issues that are just not worth debating about, while others are worth fighting for. We need to be cautious about those who want to get us distracted from what we are to be about. I often receive emails in which people just want to argue with me about something I believe or have said in my teaching. Often, it is foolish and a waste of time. Many, however, have genuine questions or concerns and I welcome those. The social media of our day has become a conduit of foolish and ignorant disputes, and I hope and pray that you don't waste your time on such worthless striving. The enemy loves to distract us from time spent in meaningful study of God's Word and from working with our hands on what is profitable. In fact, a recent statistic states that suicide rates among teens and young adults have reached their highest point in nearly two decades, and I do believe that a great contributor to the depression which often results in suicide is the internet. It not only is a huge generator of what Paul is talking about here, but it leads to a purposeless life, with so much time being wasted on social networking. It also furthers our culture's propensities toward narcissism. God has created us for His glory and to be fruitful for His Kingdom; not to get side-tracked by things of no eternal value, like foolish and ignorant disputes.

If you choose to involve yourself in foolish and ignorant disputes, you will bear fruit, but it will not be good fruit. It will be bad fruit. Not all the fruit we produce is good, unfortunately. What fruit comes from foolish and ignorant disputes? *Paul says it generates strife. This is the second fruit that will come.* When Paul says foolish and ignorant disputes *generate strife*, he means that these disputes lead to more fighting and more controversy. This kind of talk promotes ungodliness, instead of godliness. Paul is very clear about this when he writes to Titus, another one of his spiritual sons, in Titus 3:9-11 (LSB): "But avoid foolish controversies and genealogies and strife and conflicts about the Law, for they are unprofitable and worthless. Reject a factious man after a first and second warning, knowing that such a man is perverted and is sinning, being self-condemned." If you choose to continue in this type of talk, it proves that you are warped, in sin, and self-condemned. James 3:14-16 (LSB) is also clear about this awful sin of strife: "But if you have bitter jealousy and selfish ambition in your heart, do not be arrogant and so lie against the truth. This wisdom is not coming down from above, but is earthly, natural, demonic. For where jealousy and selfish ambition exist, there is disorder and every evil practice." A better avenue for each of us is found in the wisdom of Proverbs 15:1-2 (LSB): "A gentle answer turns away wrath, but a harsh word stirs up anger. The tongue of the wise makes knowledge look good, but the mouth of fools pours forth folly." Instead of using your mouth for arguing and foolish talk, use it wisely and rightly, and when you discern that an argument is about to take place where there is ignorance over the issues, try answering back with a soft and wise answer. We must flee from foolish arguments and, if we don't, it will only produce the bad fruit of more strife. Instead of being involved in this nonsense, we are to do something a tad different, as Paul mentions in the next verse.

> And a servant of the Lord must not quarrel but be gentle to all, able to teach, patient, (2 Timothy 2:24)

*Paul is very clear here that a servant of the Lord must not quarrel; we must flee this type of behavior. This is the third thing that we must flee from.* This is a command from our Lord. Timothy is *a servant of the Lord* and so are all who call upon His name with a pure heart. The term *servant* simply means slave, which is how it is translated in the LSB. Being a slave of Christ involves hard work, as we've seen. We labor like a farmer; we endure like an athlete; and we fight like a soldier. There is suffering involved. And there are battles to be won, and part of that involves fighting for the truth—but as we do so, we *must not quarrel.* The words *must not* communicate that this is our moral obligation. It is our moral obligation to not *quarrel*, which means to dispute or fight with others. You can read all through the pages of the New Testament, and you will not find our Lord quarreling. You will see Him speak the truth in love and sometimes in righteous anger, but He does not quarrel and neither should we. We must contend for the faith but we must not strive and argue. We must speak truth in love.

Now, we do have examples of some heated disagreements that are recorded for us in the Word of God. Paul writes in Galatians 2 about reproving Peter to his face, but Paul explains that it was necessary for him to do so because Peter was to be blamed. Peter was fearful to eat with the Gentiles because of what the Jews might think of him, and Paul knew that was wrong. Barnabas and Paul also had a contention, recorded in Acts 15, over whether to take Mark on a missionary journey. Paul would not agree to do so, because Mark had not done the work he should have done. So, Paul and Barnabas departed from one another, and Barnabas took Mark, and Paul took Silas.

Euodia and Syntyche were also at odds with one another over something, as mentioned in Philippians 4:2-3, and Paul calls on others in the church to get involved and help them. I bring these examples out as illustrations of people in the Scriptures who had issues with one another, but they dealt with them or someone else came alongside them to help them. Christians are not immune from conflict, but we must do what Paul tells the church at Colossae to do in Colossians 3:13 (LSB): "bearing with one another, and graciously forgiving each other, whoever has a complaint against anyone, just as the Lord graciously forgave you, so also should you." The word *complaint*, in that verse, is the same word Paul uses here in 2 Timothy for quarrel. We must forgive and we must endeavor to maintain peace.

*Instead of quarreling, we must be gentle. This is yet another virtue we must follow after, and the fifth in our list. Gentle* means to be mild or kind. It's the same Greek word that Paul uses in 1 Thessalonians 2:7 (LSB) when describing his care for the church at Thessalonica. He puts it like this: "But we proved to be gentle among you, as a nursing mother tenderly cares for her own children." Nursing mothers ought to be kind and mild toward their babies; they don't quarrel with them. In fact, it would be foolish for them to do so! Babies are not fully aware of much of what their mothers are saying. Gentleness is the virtue we must put on when dealing with others. This does not mean we enable, but it does mean we are gentle in our dealings with them.

*The sixth virtue we are to follow after is "able to teach," which starts with being teachable (cf. Proverbs 9:8; 10:8).* It is very difficult to be around someone who thinks they know everything and have no need to learn anything. We must be humble and we must be willing to learn. We need humility when we're dealing with others, but we also need a teachable spirit when we're dealing with others—we need to consider that we may not have considered certain aspects of this person or their ideas. I am not advocating compromising or coddling others, but I am encouraging us to be patient and to take time to listen. We might just learn something. Over the years, I have changed a lot of my theological views as I have grown in grace and in knowledge of God and His Word.

*The seventh quality we ought to chase after is patience.* For us to be *patient* means we are to be forbearing, to bear with others even when we are at the end of our rope. My husband used to say to me years ago, "Susan, in *patience* possess your soul," which is a quote from Jesus in Luke 21:19. We must be patient both in difficult circumstances and with difficult people. We must remember that God is sovereign and He fully knows what we are going through. Often it is a test for us to see what is in our hearts.

There is yet one more virtue to follow after; it is found in verse 25, and we all would do well to pursue a good dose of it, especially when dealing with those who oppose us.

> in humility correcting those who are in opposition, if God perhaps will grant them repentance, so that they may know the truth, (2 Timothy 2:25)

*The eighth virtue that servants of the Lord must follow after is humility. Humility* can also be translated as meekness (KJV) or gentleness (LSB and NASB); it means to have strength under control. It is the same quality that we as women are commanded to have before our husbands in 1 Peter 3, and the context there has to do with how we ought to behave toward unbelieving spouses. Your husband doesn't want weakness, but he does desire meekness. Now, the context here in 2 Timothy is not in dealing with an unbelieving husband but with *those who are in opposition*. This would include false teachers and false teaching. We must make an effort at *correcting* them, but we must do so in humility. It's interesting that Paul uses the word humility here because we saw in our last chapter that Korah and his companions had set themselves up in opposition against Moses. And remember what the Scripture says about Moses? In Numbers 12:3 (LSB) it says, "(Now the man Moses was very humble, more than any man who was on the face of the earth)." Perhaps we should review Moses' life and learn how to deal with people. He not only faced Korah and his companions in their rebellion, but he also dealt with Pharaoh and his opposition numerous times and the rebellious Israelites in the wilderness for forty years. We can learn a lot from Moses' example.

Now, there is good fruit that can come from being humble when we're exhorting those who oppose the truth. What is the fruit? There are four listed in this verse and the next, which will bring our total to six. *The first fruit mentioned in this verse is repentance.* What great fruit can come from confronting others with humility! Paul says *if God will perhaps grant them repentance*. In this context, *repentance* would imply a reversal of the issues for which they are in opposition; it would mean that they have turned from their heretical teachings. It also could result in their salvation, especially when we consider that false teachers are lost.

*In fact, Paul goes on to say so that they might know the truth. This would be the second fruit mentioned here. The truth* would be whatever is true to what God says. For example, if those who are in opposition are in error about the gospel, in that they think the gospel is health, wealth, and prosperity, for them to come to *know the truth*, they would need to embrace the truth of the Lordship of Christ and the denial of themselves. If they are in error about baptism, as Apollos was in Acts 18, they would be brought into the truth regarding baptism. If they are in error about women preaching to men, they would be brought into the truth about that. If they are in error about women being submissive to their husbands, they would be brought into the truth about that. These are just a few examples of how one might move from opposition to the truth to knowing the truth.

We want those who are in opposition to know the truth for the glory of God and His name and the reputation of His church. These are the things that are at stake. The importance of this has been made clear to me again just recently, as I have had several people who have challenged me on issues—people I've never met. It's been interesting that a couple have responded back to me, not necessarily in agreement with my answers, but thanking me for responding and for doing it graciously. Argumentative people shut doors for helpful dialogue. If we speak the truth in love, it opens doors for helpful dialogue and by it some will come to repentance and the knowledge of the truth.

Paul ends this section in verse 26 with yet two more fruits that might follow if we do things the way we should when dealing with those who are caught up in error.

> and that they may come to their senses and escape the snare of the devil, having been taken captive by him to do his will. (2 Timothy 2:26)

*The third fruit that could come as a result is that they may come to their senses.* To *come to their senses* means they will regain their senses as one awakened out of a deep sleep. It's as if they were intoxicated in error or in a deep sleep and they need to be awakened to their senses. It's possible that Paul had this in mind when he wrote to the church at Ephesus in Ephesians 5:14 (LSB). "For this reason it says, 'Awake, sleeper, and arise from the dead, and Christ will shine on you.'"

*The fourth probable fruit that can come from correcting others with humility is that they may escape the snare of the devil. The snare of the devil* would be a reference to the devil's tricks. We must not forget that he is like a roaring lion seeking whom he may devour (1 Peter 5:8). He is like a lion that wants to hunt and kill his prey. He especially wants to kill, to steal, and to destroy. He is behind all lies and all that is false. So he certainly doesn't want those who have been duped by his tactics to be awakened out of their slumber. In fact, Paul ends this verse by describing those Satan has deceived as *having been taken captive by him to do his will.* They have been held *captive* by him, ensnared by his pleasure *to do his will.* They were in such a stupor that they did not realize they were being held captive by the evil one. We must, as servants of Christ and good soldiers of His, do battle with the evil one for the minds of the many who are being held captive by him.

## Summary

*What does a servant of the Lord flee from?* We flee from all youthful lusts, any longing for anything forbidden. Do you know what is forbidden? Adam and Eve knew that the tree of the knowledge of good and evil was forbidden, and yet they disobeyed the Lord in eating of it, and mankind is still reeling from their sin. What are you doing to run away from things that you know are forbidden? We are also to flee from foolish and ignorant disputes and quarreling. Are you known as a woman who stirs up trouble? Are you always looking for an argument? Do people run when they see you coming because they know you are a troublemaker?

*What does a servant of the Lord follow after?* We follow after righteousness, faith, love, peace, gentleness, teachability, patience, and humility. Would others describe you as righteous in your dealings or as unrighteous? Faithful or unfaithful? Loving or unloving? Someone who endeavors to be at peace with others or someone who stirs up trouble with others? Are you gentle with others or harsh? Are you teachable or do you think you have a handle on all truth? Are you patient or impatient with others, especially those who oppose the truth? Would others describe you as a woman who is meek, who has her strength under control? Or would they describe you as a woman who is always out of control?

*What fruit will come as we do the right thing?* For us, purity of heart. For those who oppose the truth: some will be granted repentance, come to the truth, come to their senses, and escape the snare of the devil. As we seek to help others with a heart that is pure, it may be that we will see some repent and come to the truth, come to their senses, and escape the snare of the devil. Is the Lord using you to help others to come to a knowledge of the truth? If not, have you asked yourself why? Could the fault lie with you, in the sense that you are not a clean vessel that is fleeing certain things and following after certain things? If you are producing the bad fruit of strife in your dealings with others, perhaps self-examination of your own heart and repentance should be the first thing you do before you endeavor to help others (Matthew 7:3-5).

We have now completed chapter two of Paul's second letter to Timothy, and one man sums it up in a way that should help us all. He says,

> Looking back over the chapter, we are now able to picture in our minds the composite portrait of the ideal Christian minister or worker which Paul has been painting with a variety of words and images. As good soldiers, law-abiding athletes and hard-working farmers, we must be utterly dedicated to our work. As unashamed workmen we must be accurate and clear in our exposition. As vessels for noble use we must be righteous in our character and conduct. And as the Lord's servants we must be courteous and gentle in our manner. Thus each metaphor concentrates on a particular characteristic which contributes to the portrait as a whole, and in fact lays down a condition of usefulness. Only if we give ourselves without reserve to our soldiering, running and farming can we expect results. Only if we cut the truth straight

and do not swerve from it shall we be approved by God and have no need to be ashamed. Only if we purify ourselves from what is ignoble, from all sin and error, shall we be vessels for noble use, serviceable to the Master of the house. Only if we are gentle and not quarrelsome, as the Lord's true servants, will God grant our adversaries repentance, knowledge of the truth and deliverance from the devil. Such is our heavy responsibility to labour and suffer for the gospel. No wonder the chapter began with an exhortation to "be strong in the grace that is in Christ Jesus"[36]

36 John R. W. Stott, *The Message of 2 Timothy*, 80.

# QUESTIONS TO CONSIDER

1. (a) Read 2 Timothy 2:22-26 and list all the commands that Paul mentions. (b) What are the reasons given for obeying these commands?

2. Memorize 2 Timothy 2:22.

3. (a) What do you learn about gentleness from the following passages? Isaiah 40:10-11; Galatians 5:22-23; 1 Thessalonians 2:7; Titus 3:1-2; James 3:17-18. (b) What example of gentleness can you recall in Scripture and what do you learn from it? (c) Why should Christians endeavor to be gentle when dealing with others?

4. (a) What happens when one chooses to involve themselves in foolish questions and arguments, according to 1 Timothy 1:4; 6:3-5; 2 Timothy 2:14-18; Titus 3:9? (b) Who in Scripture comes to mind as one who was argumentative or involved in foolish disputes and what do you learn from their negative example?

5. (a) In 2 Timothy 2:26, Paul mentions that some have been snared by the devil. What else does Paul tell us about the devil in 2 Corinthians 2:11 and 2 Thessalonians 2:9-12? (b) What does Peter tell us about the devil in 1 Peter 5:8? (c) How do you avoid being duped by the evil one?

6. (a) How could you use 2 Timothy 2:22-26 to help someone who is being held captive by the evil one? (b) How does one flee passionate desires that are evil? (c) How does one pursue righteous desires? (Use Scripture, when you are able, to back up your answers.)

7. (a) Does "gentle" or "argumentative" describe you when you're dealing with others? (b) How can one put off being argumentative?

8. Come with a request for yourself based on our chapter or for someone whom you know is under the influence of the evil one.

# Nineteen Descriptions of the Disobedient During the Dangerous Last Days

*2 Timothy 3:1-5*

I WAS privileged to grow up in a minister's home where the Word of God was taught faithfully each week. My dad was a good expositor of Scripture, and his love was studying Bible prophecy. In fact, he was on television for many years and had a program, called "Thy Kingdom Come," that dealt with prophetic issues. He began his telecast with these words: "Maranatha! Our Lord is coming!" And, indeed, my Daddy talked often about the Lord's coming and about the last days. My father passed away several years ago at the age of 96 and yet still I hear people say frequently that we are living in the last days. What are the last days, and how will we know that we are in them? In the verses we'll cover in this chapter, Paul will give Timothy a glimpse of what the last days will look like. As we begin chapter three of 2 Timothy, Paul writes,

> But know this, that in the last days perilous times will come: For men will be lovers of themselves, lovers of money, boasters, proud, blasphemers, disobedient to parents, unthankful, unholy, unloving, unforgiving, slanderers, without self-control, brutal, despisers of good, traitors, headstrong, haughty, lovers of pleasure rather than lovers of God, having a form of godliness but denying its power. And from such people turn away! (2 Timothy 3:1-5)

In these verses, Paul gives us nineteen descriptions of the disobedient during the dangerous last days. Our outline will include: *The Descriptions of the Disobedient* (vv 1-5a) and *Our Duty to the Disobedient* (v 5b). As we ended chapter two of this letter in our last chapter, we learned that we are to flee youthful lusts, disputes, and quarrels. And, as we put off those things, we are then to follow after righteousness, faith, love, peace, gentleness, teachability, patience, and humility. The good fruit of that will be purity of heart and, for those who are in opposition, some will be granted repentance, come to know the truth, come to their senses, and escape the snare of the devil. The bad fruit of our involvement in continual disputes and quarrels is more strife.

Paul has been writing regarding the purity of the church and those who are within the church. Unfortunately, there are those among us who are within the church building who have a form of godliness but who are not actually in the church of Jesus Christ. As we look to these sober warnings from Paul, we need to remember that he is getting ready to leave this earth; the time of his departure is at hand. He has warned Timothy that there will be vessels in the church that are not genuine; they are made of wood and clay. There will be some who want to argue over foolish issues, and they will exhibit some characteristics that don't match up to genuine faith in the Lord. So, as Paul begins chapter three, he gives Timothy 19 descriptions that Timothy can look for to help him (and us) discern those who claim they know God but whose lives deny the power of God. Paul will also write about our responsibility toward those who profess Christ but don't possess Him.

## The Descriptions of the Disobedient *2 Timothy 3:1-5*

> But know this, that in the last days perilous times will come: (2 Timothy 3:1)

Paul begins with these words: *know this.* In addition to everything else I have written to you young Timothy, know this, be aware of this. What does Paul want Timothy to be aware of? *In the last days perilous times will come.* Paul has already mentioned the latter times in his first letter to young Timothy. In 1 Timothy 4:1-3 (LSB), Paul writes,

> But the Spirit explicitly says that in later times some will fall away from the faith, paying attention to deceitful spirits and doctrines of demons, by the hypocrisy of liars, who have been seared in their own conscience, who forbid marriage and advocate abstaining from foods which God created to be shared in with thanksgiving by those who believe and know the truth.

So Timothy has already been instructed in the first letter he received from Paul that doctrines of demons would creep into the church during the last days. Paul now writes, in this second letter to Timothy, some more information regarding those last days.

Now, what are *the last days*? The words mean the latter end. It could refer to a time near or distant. In fact, every generation has thought that they were in the last days. My dad thought that he would not die but would be taken up in the Rapture. The early church was no different; they expected the Lord to come at any time. Peter even writes about some who will scoff about the last days. In 2 Peter 3:3-4 (LSB), he says, "knowing this first of all, that in the last days mockers will come with their mocking, following after their own lusts, and saying, 'Where is the promise of His coming? For since the fathers fell asleep, all continues just as it was from the beginning of creation.'" The last days began with the ascension of Christ into Heaven, and they will end when He comes to take us home. Timothy would naturally think that he was in the last days, and there would be evidence of that in his day just like there is evidence of it in our day. This doesn't mean that things aren't worse today, because they are, and Paul will make that clear in verse 13 of our text: "But evil men and impostors will grow worse and worse, deceiving and being deceived." So, when people tell you that they don't know how it can get any worse, just let them know that it can and it will. It is certainly not going to get any better in this life, even though some might tell you otherwise.

Paul writes that in these last days *perilous times will come. Perilous* means dangerous, difficult, and fierce, words that were used to describe savage beasts. These will be difficult times to bear. And, indeed, we cannot deny that some days, even now, it's hard to wrap our heads around what is happening in our world. How does Paul describe what these last days will look like? What will be the signs that tell us that we are in the last days? He begins describing them in verse 2.

> For men will be lovers of themselves, lovers of money, boasters, proud, blasphemers, disobedient to parents, unthankful, unholy, (2 Timothy 3:2)

*Here, Paul begins to give us 19 descriptions of the disobedient in these dangerous times. The first one is that men will be lovers of themselves.* The word *men* just means mankind. So this is not referring to just males but to males and females alike. What does it mean to be *lovers of themselves*? It means to be fond of themselves.

We certainly are living in an age of narcissism, a time in which we can witness this before our very eyes. This is one of the reasons that it is so dangerous in our age to buy into the psychology of the self-esteem movement—it only furthers the narcissist ideas of our age. We are never commanded in Scripture to love ourselves, but we are commanded to love our neighbors as ourselves (Matthew 22:39). The idea in that verse is that we already love ourselves—which is a problem! So Jesus is saying, "The way you love yourself—instinctively—that is the way you should love others!" We are completely selfish for the most part, aren't we? We wake up thinking about ourselves, and we go to bed thinking about ourselves. I mean, how many of you woke up this morning thinking that you needed to tend to your kids or your husband, rather than thinking, "I need to go get me some coffee so I can wake up!" Or, "I sure am hungry; I need some food." Or, "I wonder who has texted me or emailed me during the night." Paul put it well in Philippians 2:21 (LSB): "For they all seek after their own interests, not those of Christ Jesus." Now, *lovers of themselves* is the first characteristic in this list, but it is also the heading to the entire list—or, as I once heard it put, the sewer out of which the rest come out. We can understand it this way: lovers of themselves are lovers of money; lovers of themselves are boasters and proud; lovers of themselves are disobedient to parents; lovers of themselves are unthankful and unholy, etc. This concept of lovers of themselves being the heading to the entire list and the summarizing description of the entire list is similar to the list of fruit of the Spirit, found in Galatians 5:22-23. There, Paul lists love first because it is the heading to the entire list, and out of love flows joy, peace, longsuffering, etc.

*The second description of those in the last days is that they are lovers of money, or covetous, as one translation puts it.* Lovers of themselves are fond of *money*. This is dangerous, as Paul wrote to Timothy in 1 Timothy 6:10 (LSB), "For the love of money is a root of all sorts of evils, and some by aspiring to it have wandered away from the faith and pierced themselves with many griefs." These people just want to accumulate more and more wealth, and their desire is to lay up treasure here on earth and not in Heaven.

*Lovers of themselves are also boasters, which is the third characteristic of the disobedient.* The term *boaster* means a braggart, and the root idea of the Greek word *alazon* means to wander about. In the biblical world, it often referred to a wandering quack, a phony doctor who would wander from town to town bragging about all the medicine and the spells he had to cure all kinds of sicknesses. It was a term used to describe a person who thinks and claims that they can do more than they can do. They value themselves more than anything else. We see this today among politicians, in the medical field, in the workplace, and, I'm afraid, even in the church. But there is no room in the church of Jesus Christ for a boaster.

*Number four on Paul's description of the disobedient is proud. Proud* people are those who are haughty and think they are above others. They like to make it known how great they are. I recall meeting a woman for the first time in the lobby of our church, and the first words out of her mouth after I introduced myself were, "I can't wait for you to get to know me!" I immediately took that as a red flag and, believe me, that's the way it was for many years to follow. I certainly got to know her! Peter tells us, in 1 Peter 5:5 (LSB), that we are to be clothed with humility and then he gives us the reason why: "God is opposed to the proud, but gives grace to the humble."

*The fifth description of those in the last days is that they are blasphemers, which means they are revilers, and especially toward God.* This certainly describes the beast mentioned in Revelation 13:6 (LSB), where John writes, "And he opened his mouth in blasphemies against God, to blaspheme His name and His tabernacle, that is, those who dwell in heaven." Paul mentions, in his first letter to Timothy, two men who were blasphemers and later apostatized; in 1 Timothy 1:20 (LSB), Paul says, "Among these are Hymenaeus and Alexander, whom I have handed over to Satan, so that they will be taught not to blaspheme."

*Number six on the list is certainly prevalent in our age—disobedient to parents.* Traveling has given me numerous opportunities to witness such *disobedience* in airports, airplanes, and the general public. I have witnessed things that have been shocking and would not have been tolerated by parents when I was growing up. Children are commanded to obey their *parents* (Ephesians 6:1). They are commanded to obey the spoken word of their parents. If, as a parent, you are not requiring obedience of your child, you are teaching your child to not only disrespect all earthly authority, but also training them to disobey God, who is their ultimate and final authority.

*The seventh characteristic is yet another we see prevalent in our society—unthankfulness.* Someone who is *unthankful* thinks they have a right to everything without showing gratitude. I recall a time when I was speaking at a retreat, and there was an announcement made by one of the women that no longer would ladies who were getting married or having a baby need to write thank you notes for the gifts they received. I was saddened by what I heard, and on the way to the airport, I lovingly told the woman who invited me to speak there that that announcement sent the wrong message—the message that we don't have to be thankful. We used to teach our kids to say "please" and "thank-you," but I guess common courtesies are out the window now. My friend, this should not be for God's children. Unthankfulness is a serious sin. Christians, of all people, should be grateful to God and to man. It baffles me when I am in a group where we are asked to give praises for things that God has done and it is dead silent. How can that be? Paul says in 1 Thessalonians 5:18 (LSB), "in everything give thanks, for this is God's will for you in Christ Jesus."

*Those who are disobedient also possess the quality of being unholy. This is the eighth description on Paul's list. Unholy* is a strong word which was used to describe someone who had committed incest or refused to bury a dead body. So, it is a person with no decency to do the right thing. Those who are unholy have no reverence for God and certainly no fear of God. Peter tells us that as God's children we are to be holy as He is holy (1 Peter 1:15).

Paul continues in verse 3 with six more ways we can discern those who profess Christ but not genuinely.

> unloving, unforgiving, slanderers, without self-control, brutal, despisers of good, (2 Timothy 3:3)

*The ninth character quality of these people is that they are unloving, or your translation may say without natural affection.* This is a reference to family relationships: parents toward children and children toward parents. Rarely, does a day go by when we don't hear of an unthinkable act of a parent toward their child. And it isn't uncommon for us to hear of children killing their own parents.

*Unforgiving or trucebreakers is the tenth description on Paul's list.* Those who are *unforgiving* don't care about how their actions affect others. They don't forgive others, they don't care about being reconciled to others, and, because of that, they live lives of self-destruction.

*Number 11 on the list is certainly one that most politicians are guilty of: slanderers. Slanderers* are false accusers whose desire is to ruin other people. They make stuff up for the sole purpose of ruining another person's reputation. We would be wise, as God's daughters, to remember Proverbs 10:18-19, "Whoever hides hatred has lying lips, and whoever spreads slander is a fool. In the multitude of words sin is not lacking, but he who restrains his lips is wise." Titus 2:3 reminds us, "the older women likewise, that they be reverent in behavior, not slanderers, not given to much wine, teachers of good things."

*Also prevalent in this age is number 12—without self-control, or your translation may read incontinent.* Someone who lacks self-control is given over to appetites of uncleanness. Those unclean or unholy appetites could be sexual or physical, could be in your thoughts or speech or any area of your life that is out of control.

*Brutal, or fierce, is the thirteenth description of those who are disobedient to what they profess.* To be brutal means to behave like savages in one's treatment of others. Harsh and severe would describe such behavior. Sometimes, the brutal things people do to one another are so gross that we ought not even mention them. These people are willing to do the unthinkable.

*Number fourteen I think we are seeing more and more of in the church in our day. It is despisers of those who are good.* A *despiser of those who are good* is someone who is hostile toward those who desire to be virtuous. They think you're a "goody-two-shoes" or "holier than-thou." We saw this when Vice President Mike Pence stated that it is his practice to never be alone with another woman who is not his wife. He was made fun of for it. I recently talked to a young lady whose pastor's wife was almost shaming her for her righteous living. Much of our persecution comes from within the church, from those who mock those who desire to live godly in Christ Jesus. Isaiah 5:20 (LSB) is a good reminder for us: "Woe to those who call evil good and good evil, who substitute darkness for light and light for darkness, who substitute bitter for sweet and sweet for bitter!"

Let's move on to verse 4, where Paul gives us four more character qualities of those who say that they follow Christ but in essence do not.

> traitors, headstrong, haughty, lovers of pleasure rather than lovers of God, (2 Timothy 3:4)

*The fifteenth on our list is traitors or betrayers.* A *traitor* is someone who delivers to the enemy. This term was used to describe a soldier who would betray his country or a friend who would betray another. In Luke 21:16 (LSB), Jesus warns His disciples, "But you will be betrayed even by parents and brothers and relatives and friends, and they will put some of you to death." Betrayal by someone you thought was your friend is devastating. David was betrayed by his son, Absalom, and even by his close friend, Ahithophel. David even wrote a Psalm regarding this betrayal by Ahithophel; he says, in Psalm 55:12-14 (LSB),

> For it is not an enemy who reproaches me, then I could bear it; nor is it one who hates me who has magnified himself against me, then I could hide myself from him. But it is you, a man my equal, my close companion and my familiar friend; we who had sweet counsel together walked in the house of God in the throng.

This word, traitor, appropriately describes the betrayal of the faith one claims to possess.

*Number sixteen is headstrong or heady.* To be *headstrong* has the idea of doing things that are inconsiderate with no thought as to the consequences of those actions. Not long ago, it was reported in the news that a woman in my town was hit head-on by a drunk driver and killed. Sadder even than that news, was the news that this man had just hit another car a few minutes before and had fled that scene. When he was arrested, police discovered that this man had been convicted of numerous DUI's. These things are heartbreaking and senseless; they are the actions of one who is headstrong.

*Haughty, or high-minded, is number 17. Haughty* describes the person who is so puffed up with pride it's as if smoke has blinded them. They are full of themselves. They are conceited. And they have no place in the church of the living God. This attitude reminds me of Satan, in Isaiah 14:13-15 (LSB),

> But you said in your heart, "I will ascend to heaven; I will raise my throne above the stars of God, and I will sit on the mount of assembly in the recesses of the north. I will ascend above the heights of the clouds; I will make myself like the Most High." Nevertheless you will be brought down to Sheol, to the recesses of the pit.

*The description found at the end of verse 4 and the eighteenth one Paul gives is lovers of pleasure more than lovers of God.* God is not their pleasure; rather, their *pleasure* is their god. This doesn't just have to be the pleasures of entertainment or sports. It could be the pleasure of sin. Perhaps they find pleasure in slandering others, betraying others, or dishonoring their parents.

In verse 5, we finish up with the last description of those living during the last days. Paul says,

> having a form of godliness but denying its power. (2 Timothy 3:5a)

*The final ungodly trait Paul mentions is number 19: having a form of godliness but denying its power.* These individuals have an appearance of holiness, but they refuse the power of it. We would say they go to church, they come to ladies' Bible study, they know the religious talk, they put money in the offering plate—they look just like the real deal. They are like the Pharisees, who outwardly were like white-washed tombs, which look good on the outside and appear righteous before others, but inwardly are full of dead men's bones and hypocrisy and lawlessness (Matthew 23:27-28). Paul says they *have a form of godliness.* In other words, they look like their lives are marked by godliness, but they *deny its power,* which means they shut it off. The power of godliness is totally absent from their lives. They have resisted the Holy Spirit. They have blasphemed Him, committing the unpardonable sin, and therefore do not possess His power to be overcomers of evil.

You might be thinking, "Wow! These are awful descriptions of people!" And, indeed, they are. What is more shocking is that some of these people are in the church! In fact, did you know that the Bible has sold over 6 billion copies and still remains the bestselling book of all time? Even the kinds of people about whom Paul has been writing in 2 Timothy 3:1-5 own copies of the Bible! Religion is rampant today, but godliness is not. Our churches are filled with these types of people. So what are we to do with these people? What is our duty to them?

> And from such people turn away! (2 Timothy 3:5b)

Paul says *from such people turn away!* Get away from them! Certainly don't imitate them—they are dangerous people! They do not belong in the church because they will weaken the resolve of everyone in it to live holy lives. It's very similar to what he says in Ephesians 5:3-7.

> But fornication and all uncleanness or covetousness, let it not even be named among you, as is fitting for saints; neither filthiness, nor foolish talking, nor coarse jesting, which are not fitting, but rather giving of thanks. For this you know, that no fornicator, unclean person, nor covetous man, who is an idolater, has any inheritance in the kingdom of Christ and God. Let no one deceive you with empty words, for because of these things the wrath of God comes upon the sons of disobedience. Therefore do not be partakers with them.

And, again, in 2 Thessalonians 3:6, "Now we command you, brothers, in the name of our Lord Jesus Christ, that you keep away from every brother who walks in an unruly manner and not according to the tradition which they received from us." If and when we know of people like this in the church, it behooves us to speak the truth to them in love, following the principles set forth in Matthew 18:15-19. These people do not belong in the church. A little leaven leavens the whole lump.

## Summary

As we think about this chapter, sobering as it is, we must not close without self-examination because, more than likely, some of you possess an outward form of godliness but are not genuine in your faith. So, let's consider some probing questions before we close out this chapter.

◊ Are you a lover of yourself? This can manifest itself in so many ways, and, unfortunately, many well-meaning people will feed your desire to love yourself. Do you spend your days thinking about how you might better serve others and serve God, or do you spend your days praising and admiring yourself?

◊ What about loving money? What is your reason for wanting money? So you can spend more on yourself or impress others with what you have? Or do you look at money as the means you need to provide for your family and to help others who are in need?

◊ And what about boasting and pride? Do you secretly think you're better than others? Do you like to promote yourself and talk about yourself? Or do you take a genuine interest in the needs of others and see them as more important than you are?

◊ Is there any way in which you are blaspheming God with your mouth or with your life?

◊ If you have parents whose authority you are under, are you obeying them? If you are older, are you honoring your parents? Are you training your children to obey you?

◊ When people do things for you, do you thank them? Are you training your children to be thankful?

◊ Is there any form of uncleanness or unholiness that you are not repenting of?

◊ Are you in any way behaving in an unloving manner toward anyone?

◊ Is there anyone you refuse to forgive?

◊ Is there anyone you have slandered?

◊ Are you out of control in any area of your life?

◊ Is treating others harshly or brutally a habit of your life?

◊ Do you look down on others who are endeavoring to live good and holy lives?

◊ Is there any form of betrayal in your life? Toward God? Toward your husband? Toward friends? Toward anyone?

◊ Are you reckless in your daily living, not giving thought to how your rash decisions affect others?

◊ Are you haughty in how you think of yourself or in how you treat others?

◊ And, lastly, do you enjoy the pleasures of this life and of this world more than you enjoy God? Is there anything or anyone you love more than you love God?

My prayer is that none of us have only a form of godliness in these dangerous days in which we live. We are in the final days, and each day that passes will become worse and worse, just like Jesus said it would. Don't lose heart in these evil days, but do make sure your life is not exhibiting any of these 19 descriptions that Paul has given us. And do make sure that you are not tolerating those who practice these things in the church of Jesus Christ!

May God help each of us, as the time draws near, to walk in a manner that pleases Him. *Maranatha*! Our Lord *is* coming!

# QUESTIONS TO CONSIDER

1. (a) As you read 2 Timothy 3:1-5, what is the first thing that comes into your mind? (b) Would you say that these descriptions describe the day in which we live? (c) Do you think these descriptions described the day in which Timothy lived? (Prove your answer from the Bible.)

2. Memorize 2 Timothy 3:1.

3. (a) Choose three of the nineteen characteristics Paul mentions in 2 Timothy 3:1-5, and find someone in the Word of God who exhibited those characteristics. (b) What do you learn by their negative example?

4. (a) What are the opposite qualities of those three characteristics you chose in Question 3? (b) Find three people in the Word of God who exhibited those good qualities and write down what you learn from their positive example.

5. (a) Compare Paul's list of sins in 2 Timothy 3:1-5 with those he mentions in Romans 1:21-32. Which ones are similar? (b) What does Paul say in Romans 1:32 and 2 Timothy 3:5 about these individuals? (c) Do you know someone who professes Christ and yet is living in a manner similar to what Paul says in these passages? (d) Will you love them enough to warn them?

6. (a) In what ways can we help children to obey and honor their parents? (b) In what ways can adults honor their parents who are still living? (c) How can we avoid being guilty of any of the characteristics Paul lists in 2 Timothy 3:1-5? (d) How should we be living in light of the last days, according to Romans 13:11-14, Ephesians 5:15-16; 1 Peter 4:7-11? (e) Are you living this way?

7. These verses from 2 Timothy 3:1-5 should cause us all to pause and make sure that we are not guilty of any of these sins. After considering the list prayerfully, write a prayer request for yourself to share with your group.

# The Prey and Ploy of False Teachers

*2 Timothy 3:6–9*

A DAILY paper recently revealed that a well-known TV evangelist wrote a letter to a widow in a nursing home asking for $200. His appeal was that if she did not have the money, she should borrow it and then send it to him. The letter was called to the attention of a reporter who published it in the newspaper. The evangelist defended his action by claiming that God had instructed him to send this letter to the widow. Unfortunately, the lady had been dead for three months.[37]

If that is not appalling enough,

> Some years ago, an incident of solicitation by intimidation, which was reported to the police in Canada, was exposed in *Christianity Today*. The Executive Director of the New Brunswick Senior Citizens Federation charged that a popular evangelist in the United States took financial advantage of the sensitivity of seniors and preyed on them at a time in their lives when they are most susceptible. In his solicitation letter the evangelist warned the senior citizens that if they neglected to pay attention to what He (God) was saying, then Satan would take advantage and hit them with "bad things" and they would "wish they had never been born." On the other hand, the evangelist stated, through the gift of prophecy he had been told that recipients could expect creative miracles: things seemingly dead in their body, their spirit, their mind, and their finances would come alive again. These tactics may be legal but they are far from Christian.[38]

---

37 James Matheny. "They Devour Widow's Houses." *Bible.org*, https://bible.org/article/they-devour-widows-houses. Accessed November 6, 2023.

38 Ibid.

We read things like this and, as awful as they are, they are only a smidgen of the stories that we could tell about false teachers and those on whom they prey. One group of people that is a primary target of false teachers is women, and Paul writes about this reality in the verses we'll cover in this chapter in 2 Timothy. 3:6-9. He says,

> For of this sort are those who creep into households and make captives of gullible women loaded down with sins, led away by various lusts, always learning and never able to come to the knowledge of the truth. Now as Jannes and Jambres resisted Moses, so do these also resist the truth: men of corrupt minds, disapproved concerning the faith; but they will progress no further, for their folly will be manifest to all, as theirs also was.

As we consider the prey and ploy of false teachers, we will learn of: *The False Teachers' Ploy* (v 6a); *The False Teachers' Prey* (vv 6b-7); *The False Teachers' Problem* (v 8a); and *The False Teachers' Punishment* (vv 8b-9). As we began chapter three of 2 Timothy in our last chapter, we discovered nineteen descriptions of the disobedient during the dangerous last days. The disobedient are: lovers of money, boasters, proud, blasphemers, disobedient to parents, unthankful, unholy, unloving, unforgiving, slanderers, without self-control, brutal, despisers of good, traitors, headstrong, haughty, lovers of pleasure rather than lovers of God, having a form of godliness but denying its power. These people might profess Christ, but they are dangerous because they are not in Christ. We also learned that it is our responsibility to get away from people like this. If we don't, we risk the danger of being led away by them and being taken captive by their lies. Paul writes of this danger in the verses that follow, and in verse 6 he specifically writes regarding the prey and the ploy of false teachers. Who do they prey on the most?

## The False Teachers' Ploy *2 Timothy 3:6*

> For of this sort are those who creep into households and make captives of gullible women (2 Timothy 3:6a)

*For of this sort* is a reference to those whose lives are defined by the nineteen characteristics we learned of in our last chapter. These types of people are false teachers, no matter what they might profess from their mouths. You will know who they truly are by their fruits. These people also have a desire to spread their false teaching and draw disciples into their clan. So, they *creep into households*, which means they sneak in by worming their way in like a crafty snake. It is interesting that the word for *creep* means cunning, like a serpent, and it is interesting that they go after *women*. The reason I say it is interesting is because, if you will recall from Genesis, when Satan was doing his creepy business in the Garden of Eden, it was Eve that Satan went after, not Adam!

What is the ploy of false teachers? To make women *captives*, which means they are like prisoners of war; they cannot be released. It's like what Paul said about Satan in 2 Timothy 2:26, when he was giving us reasons why we must not quarrel but should be gentle with those who oppose us. He said there, "that they may come to their senses and escape the snare of the devil, having been taken captive by him to do his will." *The ploy of false teachers is to take women captive.*

## The False Teachers' Prey *2 Timothy 3:6-7*

> For of this sort are those who creep into households and make captives of gullible women loaded down with sins, led away by various lusts, (2 Timothy 3:6)

False teachers do the work of the evil one, and they, like their father the devil, capture their prey to do his will. And it is *gullible women* on whom these false teachers prey. Now, perhaps you're wondering how they *creep into households*. To understand how false teachers would do this, it helps us to consider the time in which Paul's words were written. During biblical times, women were usually separated from men in that they were not allowed to be seen on the street with men and they ate separately from men. For the most part, women were also at home because there were no opportunities for employment outside the home. Also, women were not educated like they are today, and that lack of education would make them easy prey for false teachers and false teaching. Husbands would typically be out working and not at home, so false teachers would know these women to be easy victims. There would also be many widows at home, and they too would fall victim to these false teachers. In fact, Jesus rebukes the false teachers of His day for this very thing, in Matthew 23:14 (LSB), when He says, "Woe to you, scribes and Pharisees, hypocrites, because you devour widows' houses, and for a pretense you make long prayers; therefore you will receive greater condemnation." Jude also mentions this in verse 4 of his letter: "For certain men have crept in unnoticed, who long ago were marked out for this condemnation, ungodly men, who turn the grace of our God into lewdness and deny the only Lord God and our Lord Jesus Christ." When you think about it, this creeping into houses by false teachers is so much easier today because we don't have to open our doors for them; instead, we just turn on the television and "let them in," or "let them in" on our computer or smartphones. And, my friend, they are creeping everywhere. In fact, there are over 4,200 false religions—that is downright creepy in itself!

You might wonder why false teachers do this. The answer is that they want to make merchandise of their prey. It is all for money. (Remember the examples in the introduction to this chapter?) Several passages deal with this reality. In Titus 1:11 (LSB), Paul writes, "who must be silenced because they are upsetting whole families, teaching things they should not teach for the sake of dishonest gain." Peter also writes of this in 2 Peter 2:1-3 (LSB):

> But false prophets also arose among the people, just as there will also be false teachers among you, who will secretly introduce destructive heresies, even denying the Master who bought them, bringing swift destruction upon themselves. And many will follow their sensuality, and because of them the way of the truth will be maligned. And in their greed they will exploit you with false words, their judgment from long ago is not idle, and their destruction is not asleep.

And Jude writes in verse 16 of his letter, "These are grumblers, complainers, walking according to their own lusts; and they mouth great swelling words, flattering people to gain advantage."

I do want to clarify before we go on that not all women are *gullible*, but unfortunately many are. Today things have changed a lot, and women in a huge portion of the world are given the freedom to study and learn, but I say with all sincerity, humility, and love that women are still the perfect prey for false teachers. I have met quite a few women on my journeys who are biblically illiterate and possess no discernment. When you see a false teacher and the massive audiences they attract, you will notice that most of the people in the audience are women. I sometimes stand in awe of the massive number of women I see drinking the lies of false teachers like water and eating their poison like it was the finest of chocolates. We need men—whether it's a husband or a leader in the church. They are given to us for our protection and headship. I could not even begin to write of all the ways my husband had helped me through the many years of our marriage by helping me see things in a more biblical way. But, again, we women must know the Word of God, as Paul has admonished throughout this letter, so that we won't be prey for false teachers.

So what does it mean that these women are *loaded down with sins* and *led away by various lusts*? *Loaded down with sins* means they are piled up with sins. It might be sexual sins, sins of pride, idleness, gossip, slander, anxiety, or jealousy. These are just some of the common sins that women commit and, if not repented of, can be a pretty heavy load. Not only are they loaded with sins, Paul says, but they are also *led away by various lusts*. *Lust* is a longing for what is forbidden. We had this word back in 2 Timothy 2:22, where Paul commanded Timothy to flee youthful lusts. It could be that Paul is referring to sexual lusts here in 2 Timothy 3:6, but I think it's more likely that he is referring to what we learned about when we took a look at 2 Timothy 2:22. These lusts would include things like pride, vanity, and flattery. John mentions this in 1 John 2:16, where he calls these the lusts of the flesh, the lusts of the eyes, and the pride of life. Let me say with all seriousness that once we allow sin to go unchecked and we become engrossed in it, we open ourselves up to be taken captive by false teaching and false teachers. You will be setting yourself up to be held captive and be in bondage to the evil one. A woman who is idle at home can be tempted with many sins, and the teacher who flatters her and lures her is a tool of Satan. 2 Peter 2:18-19 has some sobering reminders for us regarding this truth: "For when they speak great swelling words of emptiness, they allure through the lusts of the flesh, through lewdness, the ones who have actually escaped from those who live in error. While they promise them liberty, they themselves are slaves of corruption; for by whom a person is overcome, by him also he is brought into bondage."

Now, before we move on to the next verse, here's a friendly reminder: Instead of opening our doors to these rascals, we must shut the door. John writes in 2 John 10-11 (LSB), "If anyone comes to you and does not bring this teaching, do not receive him into your house, and do not give him a greeting, for the one who gives him a greeting participates in his evil deeds." Did you catch what John is saying? If you let them in your home, either literally or through your television or computer or smartphone, you are sharing in their evil deeds. Again, as I've mentioned in previous chapters, this does not mean that we don't check out teachers. John tells us in his first letter that we are to test the spirits to see if they are of God; 1 John 4:1 (LSB) reminds us, "Beloved, do not believe every spirit, but test the spirits to see whether they are from God, because many false prophets have gone out into the world." But once we have tested them and determined that they are false teachers, we don't go on listening to them for the purpose of learning spiritual truth. They are dangerous! I often receive links from ladies who want me to check out a teacher or listen to a sermon, and it isn't uncommon for me to be 15 minutes or less into it and have to stop. I will have heard or seen enough by then to know that this person is off their rocker!

In verse 7, Paul goes on to write some more sad truths about these silly women. He says they are:

> always learning and never able to come to the knowledge of the truth.
> (2 Timothy 3:7)

These gullible women are *always learning* but are *never able to come to the knowledge of the truth*. This makes sense because what they would be *always learning* are false and novel ideas, but those things only lead to more ungodliness, as we saw when we studied chapter two of this letter. The admonition in 2 Timothy 2:16-17 is to "shun profane and idle babblings, for they will increase to more ungodliness. And their message will spread like cancer." The warning is to shun this type of talk because it will spread like cancer or like gangrene. It will go on to affect the whole of the person until they have become fully engulfed in falsehood. I have seen this often, even among those who teach; it starts with one compromise and then they fall prey to more and more falsehood until they are engulfed in foolishness. They apostatize and they take others down that road with them.

These women that Paul mentions are learning, but they are learning wrong doctrine, which is why they can *never come to the knowledge of the truth.* These gullible women are feeding themselves foolish and novel ideas, which keeps them from knowing truth. They are being taken captive by these false teachers. These are sobering words by the apostle Paul. False teachers infect their pupils with ridiculous ideas and the students are taken captive and become just like their teachers and pass those ridiculous ideas on to others. Jesus mentions this in Luke 6:39-40 (LSB): "And He also spoke a parable to them: 'Can a blind man guide a blind man? Will they not both fall into a pit? A student is not above his teacher; but everyone, after he has been fully trained, will be like his teacher.'" If you will carefully observe the false teachers of our day, you will note that those who follow them become just like them. Wise women will feed themselves the pure milk of the Word, and that will enable them to come *to the knowledge of the truth. So, who are the false teachers' prey? It is gullible women loaded down with sins and lusts, who are always learning but never able to come to the knowledge of the truth.*

Now, perhaps you're wondering why false teachers would prey on these women. Well, these false teachers have a problem, which Paul writes about next, in verse 8.

## The False Teachers' Problem *2 Timothy 3:8*

> Now as Jannes and Jambres resisted Moses, so do these also resist the truth: men of corrupt minds, (2 Timothy 3:8a)

By the way, before we consider this verse, this is the second reference Paul makes, in this letter, regarding Moses. When we examined 2 Timothy 2:19, we looked at resemblances between Paul's words there and the account in Numbers 16 regarding Korah and his companions. Now, you may have read verse 8 here and wondered who these men were. Their names are of Egyptian origin, and they are not mentioned anywhere else in Scripture. *Jannes* might mean one who seduces, and *Jambres* might mean he who makes rebellion. These men are thought to have been the magicians mentioned in Exodus 7-9 and their names had been handed down by tradition. The apostle Paul was well taught at the feet of his teacher Gamaliel and would more than likely have learned these men's names along with the story about them in Exodus. In Acts 22:3 (LSB), while Paul is making a defense for himself, he says, "I am a Jew, born in Tarsus of Cilicia, but having been brought up in this city, having been instructed at the feet of Gamaliel according to the strictness of the law of our fathers, being zealous for God just as you all are today." These two men, Paul writes, *resisted Moses*, which means they opposed him. Exodus 7:11-12 (LSB) says, "Then Pharaoh also called for the wise men and the sorcerers, and they also, the magicians of Egypt, did the same with their secret arts. And each one threw down his staff, and they became serpents. But Aaron's staff swallowed up their staffs." And then in Exodus 9:11 (LSB), "And the magicians could not stand before Moses because of the boils, for the boils were on the magicians as well as on all the Egyptians." These men opposed, or *resisted*, Moses by imitating what he did. We know that, eventually, they were unable to imitate all the plagues the Lord sent; when it came to the plague of the lice, they could not imitate Moses. They could no longer oppose him.

It is important for us to keep in mind that magic was forbidden in the Old Testament. Moses writes in Deuteronomy 18:10-14 (LSB),

> There shall not be found among you anyone who makes his son or his daughter pass through the fire, one who uses divination, one who practices soothsaying or one who interprets omens or a sorcerer, or one who is an enchanter or a medium or a spiritist or one who inquires of the dead. For whoever does these things is an abomination

> to Yahweh; and because of these abominations Yahweh your God will dispossess them from before you. You shall be blameless before Yahweh your God. For those nations, which you shall dispossess, listen to those who practice soothsaying and to diviners, but as for you, Yahweh your God has not allowed you to do so.

In fact, we read of this encounter with an evil spirit that took place when Paul was preaching and doing miracles, in Acts 19:15-20 (LSB),

> And the evil spirit answered and said to them, "I recognize Jesus, and I know about Paul, but who are you?" And the man, in whom was the evil spirit, leaped on them, subdued all of them, and utterly prevailed against them, so that they fled out of that house naked and wounded. And this became known to all, both Jews and Greeks, who lived in Ephesus; and fear fell upon them all and the name of the Lord Jesus was being magnified. Also, many of those who had believed kept coming, confessing and disclosing their practices. And many of those who practiced magic brought their books together and were burning them in the sight of everyone; and they counted up the price of them and found it fifty thousand pieces of silver. So the word of the Lord was growing mightily and prevailing.

Magic was associated with evil, with the devil himself. And so is all false teaching: it is of the devil and not of God. Just as Jannes and Jambres resisted Moses and endeavored to imitate what he was able to do, so do Satan and his followers, which would include false teachers. They do the same thing in the sense that they resist God and endeavor to imitate what He does. Paul warns of this in 2 Corinthians 11:13-15 (LSB). He says, "For such men are false apostles, deceitful workers, disguising themselves as apostles of Christ. And no wonder, for even Satan disguises himself as an angel of light. Therefore it is not surprising if his ministers also disguise themselves as ministers of righteousness, whose end will be according to their deeds."

Paul goes on to say that these are *men of corrupt minds*. This is in reference not only to the magicians but also to the false teachers who prey on silly women. *Corrupt* means their *minds* are depraved, and it is a settled and permanent condition. A person who has a *corrupt mind* brings forth corrupt words. Didn't Jesus say, in Matthew 12:34, that out of the abundance of the heart the mouth speaks? *So, the false teachers' problem is that they are men who resist the truth and have corrupt minds.*

## The False Teachers' Punishment *2 Timothy 3:8-9*

> disapproved concerning the faith; (2 Timothy 3:8b)

What is the punishment of these pretenders? Paul ends this verse with one aspect of their punishment. And then, in verse 9, he mentions two more aspects of their punishment. The first form of punishment is that they are *disapproved concerning the faith*. To be *disapproved* means they are cast away as worthless. They have been tested in regard to their faith, like coins are tested, but they have been found worthless, needing to be thrown out. And not only that, but Paul also says,

> but they will progress no further, for their folly will be manifest to all, as theirs also was. (2 Timothy 3:9)

The second punishment of these pretenders is that *they will progress no further*. This means they will not be able to increase or advance with their false teaching. They cannot proceed any further and they can only go as far as a sovereign God permits.

The third punishment these false teachers will receive is that *their folly will be manifest to all*. (Like those mentioned in the introduction.) *Folly* indicates their madness and stupidity. At some point, people will realize that these false teachers are nothing but a sham. Eventually, their scams will be uncovered. Because these types of individuals get worse and worse, they eventually are discovered as foolish and false. We have seen many in our day whose folly has been uncovered and revealed for all to see. And, of course, we have television and social media as a means to let everyone know how foolish these false teachers are. They eventually prove to be who they were all along. They can't mask it anymore.

Paul says the false teachers of his day will be revealed just like Jannes and Jambres were revealed. He uses the words *as theirs also was*, which is a reference to Jannes and Jambres. When the magicians could no longer do what Moses could do, when it came to the boils and the lice, their folly became known, just like these false teachers' folly will become known. One man says of these false teachers, "Jannes and Jambres were finally exposed and made fools of by the judgments of God. This will also happen to the leaders of false religions in the last days. When God's judgments fall, the true character of these counterfeits will be revealed to everyone."[39] *So, what is the false teachers' punishment? They are disapproved, they progress no further, and their folly will be known to all.*

## Summary

What do we learn about false teachers from this passage? We learn that their ploy is to capture others and hold them in bondage. Are you on the alert regarding the false teachers of our day? Do you lovingly warn others, especially women, who have fallen prey to false teachers and are held captive by them? Are you willing to suffer for speaking out against false teachers?

We also learn from this passage of Scripture that the false teachers' prey are silly women piled up with sins and various lusts, always learning and yet never able to come to the knowledge of the truth. Are you gullible? Do you believe everything you hear? Have you been seduced by wrong teaching? Are you piling up sins, or are you confessing and forsaking them? Do you struggle with pride, vanity, or worldliness of any form? These are some of the various lusts that women struggle with. Are you fulfilling your duties as a wife and mom, so that you don't give Satan an opportunity to worm his way into your house by way of false teaching? Paul reminds us, in his first letter to Timothy, of some of our responsibilities. In 1 Timothy 5:11-15, Paul is writing about women who are to be put on the list of widows who are to receive financial aid from the church, and he says,

39 Excerpted from *The Bible Exposition Commentary on the New Testament* © 1989 Warren W. Wiersbe. Used by permission of David C Cook. May not be further reproduced. All rights reserved. 251.

> But refuse the younger widows; for when they have begun to grow wanton against Christ, they desire to marry, having condemnation because they have cast off their first faith. And besides they learn to be idle, wandering about from house to house, and not only idle but also gossips and busybodies, saying things which they ought not. Therefore I desire that the younger widows marry, bear children, manage the house, give no opportunity to the adversary to speak reproachfully. For some have already turned aside after Satan.

We women should not be wasting precious time with trivial pursuits but should spend our days serving God and others. Idle hands are indeed the devil's workshop.

Yet another thing we learn about false teachers from this passage is that they have a problem. In fact, they have many problems. But here, in the text, we learn that their problems are twofold: they resist the truth and their minds are corrupt. Do you resist the truth? When you hear a sermon and you are pricked in your heart, do you resist what is being said? When you read the Word and you know you need to make some changes in your life, are you stubborn in doing so? James is clear regarding what our response to the Word of God is to be. These verses are often taken out of context but the context is our response to Scripture.[40] James writes, in James 1:19-25 (LSB),

> Know this, my beloved brothers. But everyone must be quick to hear, slow to speak and slow to anger; for the anger of man does not achieve the righteousness of God. Therefore, laying aside all filthiness and all that remains of wickedness, in gentleness receive the implanted word, which is able to save your souls. But become doers of the word, and not merely hearers who delude themselves. For if anyone is a hearer of the word and not a doer, he is like a man who looks at his natural face in a mirror; for once he looked at himself and has gone away, he immediately forgot what kind of person he was. But one who looks intently at the perfect law, the law of freedom, and abides by it, not having become a forgetful

---

40 For more details, see: Susan J. Heck, *With the Master In the Fiery Furnace* (Irvine, Three Sixteen Publishing), 316Publishing.com.

> hearer but a doer of the work, this man will be blessed in what he does.

We are not to get angry at what we hear or read in the Word of God, but we are to lay aside all wickedness so that we can receive the Word of God and we can be more than merely hearers of it—so that we can be actual doers of it. And the result of that kind of reception of the Word of God, James says, is being blessed.

We also learned that the false teachers have corrupt minds. We all are sinners, yes, but do you protect your mind from corruption? What types of things do you allow to go into your mind? Remember that false teachers resist the truth and have corrupt minds.

The last thing we learn about false teachers in this passage is about their punishment: they are disapproved (thrown out and worthless), they will progress no further, and their folly will be known to all. Do you know men and women who are teachers who are veering off the path? Do you love them enough to warn them? Do you know people who have been duped by them? Do you love those people enough to warn them? Are you distressed about false teachers and puzzled by the massive crowds who follow them? Remember that God knows, that nothing is escaping His notice, and that they will only progress as far as He allows and soon their folly will be known to all—if not in this life, certainly in the next, which is a terrifying thought. Jude says for them is reserved the blackness of darkness forever (Jude 13).

# QUESTIONS TO CONSIDER

1. (a) Read 2 Timothy 3:6-9. What things do you notice about the false teachers in these verses? (b) What type of women do these false teachers prey on? (c) What sins and lusts could these women be involved in?

2. Memorize 2 Timothy 3:6.

3. (a) How is it possible for someone to be learning but never be able to come to the knowledge of the truth? See Ezekiel 12:1-2; Matthew 13:13-15; John 8:31-32. (b) How can we make sure our learning is producing more than mere knowledge?

4. (a) In 2 Timothy 3:8-9, Paul mentions two men, named Jannes and Jambres. What does Paul say about these two men in these verses? (b) According to Jewish tradition, these men are the magicians mentioned in Exodus 7-9. Read those chapters and write down any observations you see which give further insight into what Paul writes in 2 Timothy 3:8-9.

5. (a) How can we as women avoid the error of false teachers? (b) What can we do to protect ourselves? (c) If someone were to try to entice you with their false ideas, what would you do?

6. (a) What do you do to ensure that false teaching doesn't creep into your home and into your heart? (b) Are you studying the Word diligently so that you can be discerning of error?

7. (a) How has this chapter helped you or convicted you? Please come with a request to share regarding your need(s).

# What Does a Godly Life Look Like?

*2 Timothy 3:10-12*

HAVE you ever wondered what a godly life really looks like? Does godliness mean we go to church, read our Bibles, pray, memorize some Scripture, evangelize, tithe, fellowship with other believers, use our spiritual gifts, and the like? What is genuine godliness? There is nothing wrong with any of the above things that I mentioned, and we should all be involved in all of them and more. But godly living, according to the apostle Paul, as he was inspired by the Holy Spirit to write in 2 Timothy, is defined a bit differently, and it may come as a surprise to some of you. Let's read the text together.

> But you have carefully followed my doctrine, manner of life, purpose, faith, longsuffering, love, perseverance, persecutions, afflictions, which happened to me at Antioch, at Iconium, at Lystra—what persecutions I endured. And out of them all the Lord delivered me. Yes, and all who desire to live godly in Christ Jesus will suffer persecution. (2 Timothy 3:10-12)

As we consider what these verses tell us regarding what a godly life looks like, our outline of this passage will include: *The Examination of a Godly Life* (vv 10-11), and we'll see nine traits in this examination; *The Effects of a Godly Life* (vv 11-12); and *The Encouragement of a Godly Life* (v 12). In our last chapter, we learned that: the ploy of false teachers is to take people captive; the prey of false teachers is silly women loaded with sins and laden with lusts, ever learning but never able to come to the knowledge of the truth; the problem of false teachers is that they resist the truth and have corrupt minds; and the punishment of false teachers is that they are disapproved, they progress no further, and their folly will be known to all.

Paul will now contrast the ungodly people he has just mentioned—the ones who are false and who teach lies—with those who are godly and who teach truth. And Paul will use himself as an example for young Timothy. Paul is not being egotistical here but is reiterating to Timothy the importance of godly living. Because Paul has lived a godly life before Timothy, Paul is able to set himself forth as an example for Timothy to emulate. Paul is soon to leave this earth, and he wants to pass on to Timothy a living example of someone to follow. So, Paul begins in verse 10 with the examination of a godly life and lists the first 7 of 9 traits that Timothy—and we—should follow.

## The Examination of a Godly Life *2 Timothy 3:10-11*

> But you have carefully followed my doctrine, manner of life, purpose, faith, longsuffering, love, perseverance, (2 Timothy 3:10)

Paul is saying to Timothy, "But you, Timothy, in contrast to the false teachers who have not carefully followed godly men—you follow godly men!" Some might read these words and assume that Paul is tooting his own horn, but we must remember that the time of his death is around the corner, and he has some pressing last words for his son in the faith. Paul is passing the baton on to Timothy, as he has mentioned in 2 Timothy 2:1-2. This isn't anything new; Paul wrote to the church at Corinth, a church that was a mess, "Be imitators of me, just as I also am of Christ" (1 Corinthians 11:1, LSB). And, again, in 1 Corinthians 4:16 (LSB), Paul says, "Therefore I exhort you, be imitators of me." Even to the church at Philippi, which wasn't a mess, but was one that Paul deeply loved and longed for, he writes, "Brothers, join in following my example, and look for those who walk according to the pattern you have in us" (Philippians 3:17 LSB). To the church at Thessalonica, Paul writes something similar, in 2 Thessalonians 3:9 (LSB), "not because we do not have the authority, but in order to offer ourselves as a model for you, so that you would imitate us." And the writer to the Hebrews states in Hebrews 6:12 (LSB), "so that you may not become dull, but imitators of those who through faith and patience inherit the promises." We would all do well to follow living examples of godliness. God has given us godly men and women we can follow and, like Timothy, we should find one and stick to them like glue. Unfortunately, in our society, people isolate themselves and, in doing so, we forfeit the benefit and joy of seeing how godly people live. We'd rather gain more "friends" on social media than gain godliness by actually spending time with those friends. We'd rather entertain ourselves to death than encourage one another in matters of eternal significance. But not Timothy. He had been carefully following and examining these traits in Paul, and now Paul is reiterating to Timothy just how important those traits really are.

Now, what does Paul mean when he says that Timothy *carefully followed* him? The Greek word *parakoloutheo*, translated as *carefully followed*, carries the idea of tracing something—to examine it and, because of that examination, to fully know it. It's like tracing a pattern on material so your garment turns out exactly like the pattern! Timothy had been with Paul on many journeys and had watched his life and examined these traits in him. Timothy had seen Paul in plenty and in want, in prison and in the synagogue teaching, healing the sick and raising the dead, weeping over the churches and longing to see them and impart truth to them. Timothy had seen it all. He knew Paul was the real deal.

*The foremost trait that Timothy is to examine and follow in Paul is his doctrine.* This is the heading to all the other qualities in this list. Without correct doctrine, you will not have the other things Paul mentions. Godly doctrine that is obeyed results in godly living. It is sad to say, but in most pulpits today we have psychology, personality, and two points and a poem, but very little sound doctrine. Perhaps the word *doctrine* is scary to you—but it should not be. Doctrine is simply sound teaching, teaching that is wholesome, that is based on God's truth in His Word. So, Paul is saying, "You, Timothy, in contrast to the false teachers who teach corrupt doctrine, you follow the pattern I have set by teaching sound doctrine." Paul's teaching was a far cry from the false teachers who were involved in foolish babbling and preying on silly women. He mentions this in 1 Corinthians 2:4-5, "And my speech and my preaching were not with persuasive words of human wisdom, but in demonstration of the Spirit and of power, that your faith should not be in the wisdom of men but in the power of God." Paul's preaching was not full of convincing human wisdom, but it was in the Spirit and power of God. Paul was interested in the spiritual welfare of those he taught, and was not concerned at all about gaining an audience for fame or fortune.

One's manner of life or conduct flows from right doctrine. *Right doctrine results in right behavior. So, the second trait that Timothy is to follow in Paul is his manner of life. Manner of life* means how I live, how I conduct myself. Doctrine that is heeded results in a life that is holy. If you have wrong doctrine, your life will reflect that. If you have correct doctrine, your life will reflect that. Paul's life was not perfect, but he endeavored to live a godly life. In Acts 20:18-20 (LSB), Luke writes regarding Paul,

> And when they had come to him, he said to them, "You yourselves know, from the first day that I set foot in Asia, how I was with you the whole time, serving the Lord with all humility and with tears and with trials which came upon me through the plots of the Jews; how I did not shrink from declaring to you anything that was profitable, and teaching you publicly and from house to house."

Paul's manner of life was serving the Lord with humility, not with haughtiness. Paul's manner of living was certainly a far cry from the false teachers. Listen to how Peter describes the conduct of false teachers, in 2 Peter 2:12-14 (LSB).

> But these, like unreasoning animals, born as creatures of instinct to be captured and killed, blaspheming where they have no knowledge, will in the destruction of those creatures also be destroyed, suffering unrighteousness as the wages of their unrighteousness, considering it a pleasure to revel in the daytime—they are stains and blemishes, reveling in their deceptions, as they feast with you, having eyes full of adultery and unceasing sin, enticing unstable souls, having a heart trained in greed—they are accursed children.

*Correct doctrine also gives one purpose in life. This is the third trait of a godly life that Timothy is to follow.* The word *purpose* means a plan or design. Paul's life was purposeful. He wanted his life to count for the Kingdom. He knew that to be a servant of Christ meant serving the Kingdom. Generally speaking, people today have no purpose in life, which is why I think we are seeing an alarming increase in depression and suicide. When God saves us, He gives us purpose, and that purpose is to glorify Him by loving Him with all our heart and loving our neighbor as ourselves. That's a lifetime job, isn't it? It's like what we see in Barnabas, one of Paul's traveling companions, in Acts 11:23, "When he came and had seen the grace of God, he was glad, and encouraged them all that with purpose of heart they should continue with the Lord." Timothy traveled with Paul; Timothy knew that Paul was serious about his calling as a servant of the gospel. If Paul were alive today, I imagine that he would be appalled at the trivial pursuits that Christian men and women involve themselves in. Paul was purposeful with his time and Timothy saw that, day in and day out. Paul's life certainly was a contrast to the false teachers who crept into houses to lead people away with their false ideas, as we saw in our last chapter.

*The fourth trait that Timothy carefully examined in Paul and followed was Paul's faith.* This would not only mean Paul's *faith* in God but his faithfulness to God. Paul set forth his faith in God in the beginning of this letter, in 2 Timothy 1:12, where he wrote, "For this reason I also suffer these things; nevertheless I am not ashamed, for I know whom I have believed and am persuaded that He is able to keep what I have committed to Him until that Day." Paul was saying there, "I know, Timothy, in whom I have believed. I was a persecutor, a blasphemer, a murderer, but I obtained mercy from the Lord." Paul also set forth his faithfulness to the Lord in the beginning of this letter, when he wrote in 2 Timothy 1:3, "I thank God, whom I serve with a pure conscience, as my forefathers did, as without ceasing I remember you in my prayers night and day." Paul served God with a pure conscience. Paul was a faithful servant, not a flattering celebrity like the false teachers. What a contrast to the false teachers, who were servants alright, but servants of corruption! Peter writes about them in 2 Peter 2:19 (LSB), "promising them freedom while they themselves are slaves of corruption; for by what a man is overcome, by this he is enslaved." Jude says in Jude 12 that false teachers serve themselves: "These are spots in your love feasts, while they feast with you without fear, serving only themselves."

*Timothy is also admonished by Paul to closely follow his example of longsuffering. This is the fifth quality of a godly life that Paul lists. Longsuffering* is patience with others, and in this context, Paul is specifically thinking of those who wanted to persecute him. He's already written to Timothy in 1 Timothy 6:11 (LSB) about the importance of this quality: "But you, O man of God, flee from these things, and pursue righteousness, godliness, faith, love, perseverance, gentleness." And Paul will write to Timothy in the next chapter of 2 Timothy regarding the importance of this quality: "Preach the word! Be ready in season and out of season. Convince, rebuke, exhort, with all longsuffering and teaching" (2 Timothy 4:2). Timothy saw longsuffering modeled in his spiritual father Paul, and this will help him to do the same as he ministers to others in the future. Again, what a contrast this is to the false teachers who were far from being longsuffering! Listen to Jude 16 (LSB): "These are grumblers, finding fault, following after their own lusts; and their mouth speaks arrogantly, flattering people for the sake of their own benefit."

*The sixth quality that, no doubt, Timothy witnessed in Paul over and over again was love.* The word for *love* here is *agape*; in the Bible, this is a love that considers not what the person wants but what they need. Paul loved people. He did not coddle them, but he loved them. He gave them what they needed, which was sound doctrine. He also ministered by preaching the Word for hours at a time. In one account, in Acts 20, we find Paul preaching and it's midnight, and some guy falls asleep and falls out of a third story window. Paul stops his preaching long enough to go and heal the guy (or raise him from the dead, we are not told which), and then Paul goes on preaching till daybreak. As a teacher of the Word of God, I can tell you that teaching or preaching that long is definitely loving others. Some experts have claimed that teaching for 45 minutes can be equivalent to an 8-hour work day. In that account in Acts 20, Paul must have taught at least 8-10 hours. He did not consider his life dear to himself. In fact, later on in that very same chapter, in Acts 20:22-24 (LSB), he says,

> And now, behold, bound by the Spirit, I am on my way to Jerusalem, not knowing what will happen to me there, except that the Holy Spirit solemnly testifies to me in every city, saying that chains and afflictions await me. But I do not make my life of any account nor dear to myself, so that I may finish my course and the ministry which I received from the Lord Jesus, to testify solemnly of the gospel of the grace of God.

In contrast to false teachers who walked in ungodly lusts, Paul walked in godly love. Consider Jude 18-19 (LSB): "[the apostles] were saying to you, 'In the last time there will be mockers, following after their own ungodly lusts.' These are the ones who cause divisions, worldly-minded, not having the Spirit."

*The seventh trait that Paul urges Timothy to carefully follow is perseverance. Perseverance* is patience that continually waits with a calm temper. Paul admonishes the church at Thessalonica about the importance of this quality in 1 Thessalonians 5:14: "Now we exhort you, brethren, warn those who are unruly, comfort the fainthearted, uphold the weak, be patient with all." Timothy had examined Paul's patience with the unruly, his patience with those who were fainthearted, and his patience with those who were weak. We too, as God's children, must exhibit patience. In fact, in 2 Corinthians 6:3-10, Paul writes this long list of things he encountered in ministry, and the first quality on his list is the need for patience.

> We give no offense in anything, that our ministry may not be blamed. But in all things we commend ourselves as ministers of God: in much patience, in tribulations, in needs, in distresses, in stripes, in imprisonments, in tumults, in labors, in sleeplessness, in fastings; by purity, by knowledge, by longsuffering, by kindness, by the Holy Spirit, by sincere love, by the word of truth, by the power of God, by the armor of righteousness on the right hand and on the left, by honor and dishonor, by evil report and good report; as deceivers, and yet true; as unknown, and yet well known; as dying, and behold we live; as chastened, and yet not killed; as sorrowful, yet always rejoicing; as poor, yet making many rich; as having nothing, and yet possessing all things.

Jesus said, in Luke 21:19 (LSB), "By your perseverance you will gain your lives." The patience of Paul was certainly a far cry from that of the false teachers. Peter writes of these false teachers in 2 Peter 2:10, "And especially those who walk according to the flesh in the lust of uncleanness and despise authority. They are presumptuous, self-willed. They are not afraid to speak evil of dignitaries." Presumptuous and self-willed is certainly the opposite of patient.

The last two qualities that Timothy needs to be reminded to emulate are, perhaps, foreign to our modern way of thinking about a godly life. These also are the two effects of a godly life. Paul writes,

## The Effects of a Godly Life *2 Timothy 3:11-12*

> persecutions, afflictions, which happened to me at Antioch, at Iconium, at Lystra—what persecutions I endured. And out of them all the Lord delivered me. (2 Timothy 3:11)

*The eighth quality Paul wrote of a godly man or woman is persecution.* Now, maybe you're saying to yourself, "Wait a minute! What?! I thought Jesus loved me and had a wonderful plan for my life!" He does! If you will peek into the next verse, you will see that, indeed, persecution is a part of God's plan for your life if you are godly. The next verse says, "Yes, and all who desire to live godly in Christ Jesus will suffer persecution." *Persecution* actually means to drive away. It would include hatred, affliction, and hostile treatment. Paul *endured* many persecutions, some of which he mentions in 2 Corinthians 11:24-25 (LSB): "Five times I received from the Jews forty lashes less one. Three times I was beaten with rods, once I was stoned, three times I was shipwrecked—a night and a day I have spent in the deep." The godly man or woman will suffer persecution; Paul suffered many persecutions. But false teachers recoil from such suffering. In fact, Peter writes that false teachers promise freedom, not persecution, in 2 Peter 2:19 (LSB); he says, "promising them freedom while they themselves are slaves of corruption; for by what a man is overcome, by this he is enslaved."

*The ninth trait of a godly man or woman is afflictions.* Paul writes that he not only went through persecutions but also afflictions. *Afflictions* are the trials, hardship, or pain that come as a result of persecutions. Paul knew this would be a part of his life, as evidenced by what he says in Acts 20:22-24 (LSB):

> And now, behold, bound by the Spirit, I am on my way to Jerusalem, not knowing what will happen to me there, except that the Holy Spirit solemnly testifies to me in every city, saying that chains and afflictions

> await me. But I do not make my life of any account nor dear to myself, so that I may finish my course and the ministry which I received from the Lord Jesus, to testify solemnly of the gospel of the grace of God.

Paul even lists the places where these persecutions and afflictions happened: *at Antioch, at Iconium, and at Lystra. Antioch* is in Syria. *Iconium* and *Lystra* are both in Asia Minor. In fact, Lystra would have been Timothy's hometown, as we learned from Acts 16:1-2 (LSB): "Now Paul also arrived at Derbe and at Lystra. And behold, a disciple was there, named Timothy, the son of a Jewish woman who was a believer, but his father was a Greek, and he was well spoken of by the brothers who were in Lystra and Iconium." It is needful to say that the people in this area tried to kill him. Acts 14:19-20 (LSB) states, "But Jews came from Antioch and Iconium, and after winning over the crowds and stoning Paul, they were dragging him out of the city, supposing him to be dead. But while the disciples stood around him, he rose up and entered the city. The next day he went away with Barnabas to Derbe." I doubt any of us have ever been stoned and left for dead!

*Godly living will produce persecutions and afflictions, both of which Paul endured. These are the effects of a godly life.* And they are quite a contrast from what Jesus says about false teachers in Luke 6:26 (LSB): "Woe to you when all men speak well of you, for their fathers were doing the same things to the false prophets." After Paul mentions enduring these persecutions and afflictions, he writes *and out of them all the Lord delivered me*. This means the Lord rescued me. And, indeed, the Lord did rescue Paul, even though Paul endured things that should have killed him. He will write later on in this letter, in 2 Timothy 4:17-18, "But the Lord stood with me and strengthened me, so that the message might be preached fully through me, and that all the Gentiles might hear. Also I was delivered out of the mouth of the lion. And the Lord will deliver me from every evil work and preserve me for His heavenly Kingdom. To Him be glory forever and ever. Amen!" The Lord delivered Paul from every difficulty, and his final deliverance is soon to come when he will be beheaded by Nero and delivered up to glory. We cannot take from these verses the principle that we are all going to be delivered *in this life* out of all our afflictions and persecutions. In Paul's case, he was still living when he wrote this letter to Timothy and thus he had been delivered from all his persecutions thus far. But he also knows that the time of his departure is at hand. Soon he will be delivered, in the ultimate sense, into the hands of Jesus. Paul knew that to live is Christ and to die is gain. Paul knew the words of his Lord in Luke 12:4-5 (LSB): "But I say to you, My friends, do not fear those who kill the body and after that have no more that they can do. But I will show you whom to fear: fear the One who, after He has killed, has authority to cast into hell; yes, I tell you, fear Him!" Paul wrote and knew the joy of Romans 8:35-39 (LSB):

> Who will separate us from the love of Christ? Will affliction, or turmoil, or persecution, or famine, or nakedness, or peril, or sword? Just as it is written, "For Your sake we are being put to death all day long; We were counted as sheep for the slaughter." But in all these things we overwhelmingly conquer through Him who loved us. For I am convinced that neither death, nor life, nor angels, nor rulers, nor things present, nor things to come, nor powers, nor height, nor depth, nor any other created thing, will be able to separate us from the love of God, which is in Christ Jesus our Lord.

Would that we all had the heart of Shadrach, Meshach, and Abed-Nego, who said to King Nebuchadnezzar, in Daniel 3:17-18 (LSB), "If it be so, our God whom we serve is able to save us from the furnace of blazing fire; and He will save us out of your hand, O king. But if not, let it be known to you, O king, that we are not going to serve your gods, and we will not worship the golden image that you have set up." So, is there any encouragement when you live a godly life? Of course, there is! And Paul ends with these words in verse 12:

## The Encouragement of a Godly Life *2 Timothy 3:12*

> Yes, and all who desire to live godly in Christ Jesus will suffer persecution. (2 Timothy 3:12)

Perhaps you're thinking, "*This* is an *encouragement*?!" *Yes, the encouragement is that if you are godly, you will suffer.* This statement is not a possibility but an absolute. If you haven't been persecuted for your faith yet, no worries, you will! It's a promise. But, also, if you have never suffered persecution at all, then you might need to examine whether you are walking in a holy manner. Paul knew that suffering for Christ was not a curse but a gift. Consider what he writes to the church at Philippi, in Philippians 1:29 (LSB): "For to you it has been granted for Christ's sake, not only to believe in Him, but also to suffer for His sake," With the suffering, there is also the encouragement of being delivered. That deliverance might come in this life, like it had so many times for the apostle Paul, or it might come in being delivered into glory—which is a far better deal!

So Paul writes to Timothy, *yes, and all who desire to live godly in Christ Jesus will suffer persecution*. Timothy, evidently, needed to be reminded of this truth, even though he had examined the persecutions Paul had endured. Paul would be leaving soon, and Timothy must not give way to fear and timidity but, instead, be fearless and courageous. If it pleases you to *live godly*, if this is how you love to live, then suffering will come to you. But note that living godly is *in Christ Jesus*. We live for Him, and He is the one who helps us during times of persecution. Jesus Himself gives us great encouragement, in John 15:18-21 (LSB).

> If the world hates you, know that it has hated Me before it hated you. If you were of the world, the world would love its own; but because you are not of the world, but I chose you out of the world, because of this the world hates you. Remember the word that I said to you, "A slave is not greater than his master." If they persecuted Me, they will also persecute you; if they kept My word, they will keep yours also. But all these things they will do to you for My name's sake, because they do not know the One who sent Me.

Some people flee from persecution and do everything they can do to avoid it. But godly men and women know that persecution will come and they can embrace it, knowing that their Lord suffered too and He has promised to deliver them.

## Summary

What are the things Timothy examined in Paul's life of godly living? His doctrine, manner of life, purpose, faith, longsuffering, love, perseverance, persecutions, and afflictions. Consider the following areas of your life:

◊ Doctrine: If someone were to examine your life of faith, would they see that sound doctrine governs your living or your false doctrine?

◊ Manner of life: Would they see your conduct as holy or questionable?

◊ Purpose: What about your purpose for living? Would they examine your life and see that your days are full of purpose and meaning, or that your days are full of idle talk and lounging around wasting time?

◊ Faith: Would they see you living out your faith in God by being faithful to Him and to what He requires of you? Or would they wonder about your faith in God and your faithfulness to your commitments?

◊ Longsuffering: Do others see you exhibit longsuffering with others who are trying in your life or do they see you as irritable and impatient and even angry at times?

◊ Love: Do others examine your life and see one who loves others, who is willing to sacrifice time, energy, and money, if need be, for them? Or as one who is stingy with her time, energy, and money, and basically living for self?

◊ Perseverance: Can others watch you in difficult times and with difficult people and see one who is persevering? Or do they examine your life and see that you are despairing and wanting to give up during times of trouble?

◊ Persecutions and afflictions: And what about the persecutions and afflictions you incur because of your faith? Do those around you examine your life and see that you recoil from those times and resent them, or that you embrace the suffering as part of the cross, as part of the course you enrolled in when you became a Christ-follower?

What are the effects of a godly life? Persecution and affliction. Do you shy away from controversy or speaking up when there is incorrect doctrine being taught or wrong behavior being exhibited? Do you fear the persecution you may receive because of it? Do not be afraid, my friend! These are wonderful opportunities to prove your loyalty to the Lord and to draw ever so close to Him.

What is the encouragement of a godly life? First, that you will suffer persecution and that persecution will be an evidence that you are living a godly life. Second, that you will be delivered either in this life or in the life to come. When you suffer for the Lord, be encouraged. He suffered too. Come boldly to His throne of grace to find help in your time of need. Be encouraged that you can know a bit of what He went through as He suffered afflictions and persecutions while on earth. He may deliver you in this life, or He may deliver you in the life to come.

Just as Timothy had the privilege of examining Paul's life and carefully following his example, I too have had the privilege of examining others and following their examples. One of my mentors, whose life exhibited the qualities of Paul, whose life was full of suffering and persecution, who considered it a joy to suffer for her Lord, was Elisabeth Elliot. She once wrote, "The deepest things that I have learned in my own life have come from the deepest suffering. And out of the deepest waters and the hottest fires have come the deepest things I know about God."[41]

41 Elisabeth Elliot. "About Elisabeth Elliot." https://elisabethelliot.org/about/. Accessed April 30, 2024.

# QUESTIONS TO CONSIDER

1. (a) Read 2 Timothy 3:10-12. What word is repeated in these three verses? (b) Why does godly living produce persecution?

2. Memorize 2 Timothy 3:12.

3. (a) What are the results of following sound doctrine, according to the following Scriptures? Acts 2:42-47; Romans 16:17-19; Ephesians 4:11-16; 2 Timothy 3:16-17; Titus 2:6-8; 2 John 9-11? (b) What are the results of following false doctrine, according to the following Scriptures? Romans 16:17-19; Ephesians 4:11-16; 1 Timothy 1:3-4; 2 Timothy 4:3-4; Hebrews 13:7-9; 2 John 9-11? (c) Are you in a church that is teaching sound doctrine? (You should be able to evaluate its fruits from the verses above.) (d) How can you use the above verses to help others who are sitting under wrong doctrine?

4. (a) Paul mentions, in 2 Timothy 3:11, the persecutions and afflictions that happened to him at Antioch, Iconium, and Lystra. Read Acts 13-14 to discover what these persecutions and afflictions were. (b) Why will godly men and women suffer persecution, according to Matthew 5:11-12; 10:17-23; 24:9-11; Mark 13:9-13; John 15:20-25; 2 Timothy 3:12? (c) How does this encourage you or discourage you? (d) What should be our attitude when we are persecuted for Christ, according to Matthew 5:12 and 1 Peter 4:14?

5. (a) From what we see in 2 Corinthians 11:22-33, what are some of the other afflictions Paul went through? (b) What is Paul's attitude about his afflictions, according to 2 Corinthians 12:7-10? (c) How can we develop these same attitudes when going through persecution?

6. Read Psalm 34 and write down at least five ways this Psalm could comfort someone who is facing persecution and affliction?

7. Come with a request for yourself or someone else who is suffering for the cause of Christ.

# The Importance of the Holy Scriptures

*2 Timothy 3:13–15*

Holy Bible, Book divine,
Precious treasure, thou art mine:
Mine to tell me whence I came;
Mine to teach me what I am.

Mine to chide me when I rove,
Mine to show a Savior's love;
Mine thou art to guide and guard;
Mine to punish or reward.

Mine to comfort in distress,
Suffering in this wilderness;
Mine to show by living faith,
We can triumph over death.

Mine to tell of joys to come,
And the rebel sinner's doom:
O thou holy Book divine,
Precious treasure thou art mine.[42]

THE words of this hymn were written by John Burton, an English Sunday School teacher who was born in 1773. Burton had a passion and a burden for children to be taught the Word of God and the spiritual truths that come from it. This particular hymn was part of a book entitled *Incentives for Early Piety.* I hope that each of us has a burden like John Burton, not only for our own children, but also for children around the world, that they be instructed with the Holy Scriptures. Timothy, the young pastor to whom Paul has been writing

42 John Burton, "Holy Bible, Book Divine", Public Domain, 1803.

in 2 Timothy, was blessed to have a grandmother and mother who wanted him to know the Scriptures and who began teaching him in his infancy. Let's listen in as Paul reminds his son in the faith of this truth.

> But evil men and impostors will grow worse and worse, deceiving and being deceived. But you must continue in the things which you have learned and been assured of, knowing from whom you have learned them, and that from childhood you have known the Holy Scriptures, which are able to make you wise for salvation through faith which is in Christ Jesus. (2 Timothy 3:13-15)

Our previous chapter flows nicely into this one. In that chapter, we examined what a godly life looks like, and we discovered nine qualities that mark a godly life. We also discovered the effects of a godly life, which are persecution and affliction. Finally, we discovered the encouragement of a godly life, which is suffering and deliverance. Paul has been instructing young Timothy regarding the example he has to follow from Paul's life. But Timothy didn't only have Paul's example to follow; he also had the examples of his mother and grandmother who had taught him the Holy Scriptures from his childhood. And, in addition to Paul's example and the examples of his mother and grandmother, Timothy also had the negative example of evil men and seducers whom he would not want to emulate. Our outline for this chapter on the importance of the Holy Scriptures will include: *The Rejection of Scripture and Its Results* (v 13) and *The Receiving of Scripture and Its Results* (vv 14-15). Let's consider the rejection of Scripture and its results, in verse 13.

## The Rejection of Scripture and Its Results *2 Timothy 3:13*

> But evil men and impostors will grow worse and worse, deceiving and being deceived. (2 Timothy 3:13)

We turn from the godly example of Paul to the ungodly example of evil men. In contrast to Paul, the apostle, we have the evil men, the apostates. This is why Paul uses the word *but* as a contrast. *Evil men and imposters will grow worse and worse. Evil men* are those who are malicious. This has not so much to do with mankind, as we are all evil apart from Christ, but *evil* in the sense of those who profess Christ but do not possess Christ. They are hypocrites, and they become *worse and worse*. They are much like the ones who creep into houses and lead people into captivity. I have lived long enough to see that once a professing believer compromises, and especially if they are a teacher, if they will not repent, they will grow worse and worse. One man describes this phrase, worse and worse, as "Shall cut forward to the worse stage."[43] Our brother Peter talks of this as well in his second epistle. Consider his words in 2 Peter 2:18-22 (LSB):

> For speaking out arrogant words of vanity, they entice by sensual lusts of the flesh, those who barely escape from the ones who conducted themselves in error, promising them freedom while they themselves are slaves of corruption; for by what a man is overcome, by this he is enslaved. For if they are overcome, having both escaped the defilements of the world by the knowledge of the Lord and Savior Jesus Christ and having again been entangled in them, then the last state has become worse for them than the first. For it would be better for them not to have known the way of righteousness, than having known it, to turn away from the holy commandment handed on to them. The message of the true proverb has happened to them, "A dog returns to its own vomit," and, "A sow, after washing, returns to wallowing in the mire."

Do you hear what Peter is saying? It would have been better for them to have never known the truth at all than to have known it and turned away from it. What a tragedy, indeed!

Paul writes that it is not only evil men who become worse and worse but also *imposters*. An imposter is a seducer or a wizard, like Jannes and Jambres, of whom we learned of back in verse 8, the supposed magicians who resisted Moses. Imposters would be those who practice so-called magical arts or, in our day, false miracles. I do believe that these will be the ones whom Jesus mentions in Matthew 7:21-23 (LSB), when He says,

---

43 A. T. Robertson, *Robertson's Word Pictures in the New Testament* (Des Moines: Broadman Press, 1985), Biblesoft.

> Not everyone who says to Me, "Lord, Lord," will enter the kingdom of heaven, but he who does the will of My Father who is in heaven will enter. Many will say to Me on that day, "Lord, Lord, in Your name did we not prophesy, and in Your name cast out demons, and in Your name do many miracles?" And then I will declare to them, "I never knew you; depart from Me, you who practice lawlessness."

These people are imposters, seducers, and, my friend, we have a multitude of them today! Just turn your TV on to the "religious" channel and observe it for yourself! Most of these men and women are imposters.

Paul says evil men and imposters will grow worse and worse, *deceiving and being deceived. Being deceived* means to go astray, to wander, to be out of the way. These people actually believe their own lies. We've seen that in our government in the impeachment processes that have gone on in recent years between the Democrats and Republicans. Both sides cannot be telling the truth, and the ones who are lying actually believe their own lies, or so it appears.

Notice that Paul says these imposters are not only deceived themselves, but they are *deceiving* others as well. It's like Hymenaeus and Philetus, who were deceived themselves and then went on to deceive others. We saw this back in 2 Timothy 2:17-18: "And their message will spread like cancer. Hymenaeus and Philetus are of this sort, who have strayed concerning the truth, saying that the resurrection is already past; and they overthrow the faith of some." Error breeds more error, my friend, and that is why the truth of God's Word must be heeded. Jesus predicted the same thing Paul does here, which is probably how Paul knew this would take place. Consider Jesus' words in Matthew 24:24-25 (LSB): "For false christs and false prophets will arise and will show great signs and wonders, so as to deceive, if possible, even the elect. Behold, I have told you in advance." So, the next time someone tells you that things are getting worse, you can tell them that, indeed, they are—and the good news is (or bad news, however you view it) that it's going to get worse! *According to this verse, then, those who reject Scripture grow worse and worse, they are deceived, and they deceive others.* Perhaps some of you think that you can pick and choose what you obey or believe about the Bible. My friend, you are toying with disaster if you do so! Those who choose to reject any part of Scripture are heading for disaster. It's like the hundreds of people now who have died unnecessarily by taking selfies because they simply won't follow the rules, which say, "No Selfie Zone." If we don't follow the rules in the Holy Scriptures, we too are heading for disaster.

Paul now contrasts the evil men who rejected the Scriptures with young Timothy who received the Holy Scriptures. So, we turn from those who reject the Word and the results that come from that rejection to those who receive the Word of God and the results that come from that reception, in verses 14-15.

## The Receiving of Scripture and Its Results *2 Timothy 3:14-15*

> But you must continue in the things which you have learned and been assured of, knowing from whom you have learned them, (2 Timothy 3:14)

Paul is saying, "*But you*, Timothy, in contrast to the ones I've mentioned in verse 13, instead of being deceived by lies, you *must continue* in the truth." In Paul's first letter to Timothy, he also wrote about the importance of continuing in the truth. Listen to 1 Timothy 4:16: "Take heed to yourself and to the doctrine. Continue in them, for in doing this you will save both yourself and those who hear you." The word *continue* means to endure or remain. Instead of departing from truth, we are to continue in the truth. Jesus spoke of this in John 8:31-32 (KJV): "Then said Jesus to those Jews which believed on him, If ye continue in my word, then are ye my disciples indeed; And ye shall know the truth, and the truth shall make you free." Right after Paul was stoned in Lystra and left for dead, he got up and starting preaching again, this time in Derbe. And it says in Acts 14:21-22 (LSB), "And after they had proclaimed the gospel to [Derbe] and had made many disciples, they returned to Lystra and to Iconium and to Antioch, strengthening the souls of the disciples, encouraging them to continue in the faith, and saying, Through many afflictions we must enter the kingdom of God.'" No matter how tempting it might be to get caught up in the trivialities of our day, we must continue in the things of Christ. And we must remember that no one is above being tempted to veer off the beaten path. The evil one is always luring us with his schemes. *So, the first result of those who receive the Scriptures is that they continue in the faith.*

Paul mentions the things Timothy is to continue in are the things, he says, *which you have learned.* The word *learned* means to acquire knowledge by studying or being taught. We must remember that learning alone will not save a person. The people mentioned in verse 7 were always learning but never able to come to the knowledge of the truth. Learning must be followed by obedience. Just like those who are obsessed with taking selfies—they have knowledge that they are in a no-selfie-zone, they know of others who have died doing what they are getting ready to do, but the knowledge they have learned has done them no good. They disobey the very thing they have learned.

With Timothy, however, we know that the things he learned bore fruit because Paul goes on to say that not only did Timothy learn these things but he was also *assured of* them. *These would be the second and third results of those who receive the Scriptures: they learn them and they are assured of them.* To be *assured of* these things means that Timothy was persuaded of what he had been taught. He was not in doubt about what the Scriptures said. Paul made a similar statement in the beginning of this letter to Timothy. In 2 Timothy 1:12, Paul wrote, "For this reason I also suffer these things; nevertheless I am not ashamed, for I know whom I have believed and am persuaded that He is able to keep what I have committed to Him until that Day." This should motivate us to pray for our children and grandchildren that as they learn the Word of God they would be assured of it, that it is indeed true. Knowledge alone will produce nothing. Knowledge of God without obedience to His Holy Word is like those about whom Paul wrote in Romans 1:28 (LSB): "And just as they did not see fit to acknowledge God, God gave them over to an unfit mind, to do those things which are not proper."

Paul ends this verse by writing *knowing from whom you have learned them.* Timothy would have *learned* from Paul, and back in verses 10-11, Paul has already written regarding the things Timothy had learned from him. Also, in 2 Timothy 2:1-2, Paul exhorted Timothy to pass on to faithful men the truths he had learned from Paul. Timothy also learned the truth from two other individuals in his family, whom Paul also has mentioned in 2 Timothy 1:5: "when I call to remembrance the genuine faith that is in you, which dwelt first in your grandmother Lois and your mother Eunice, and I am persuaded is in you also." And, since we are on this topic, I will tell you from experience that learning the Word of God from parents is of great importance, but it is also of great importance to have others who come alongside and reinforce biblical truth to your children. I will be forever grateful for those who have poured into my children when they were young and even now as they are adults. And I am thankful for those who pour into my life even now!

Before we finish up this chapter by looking at the final verse in this passage, we should note that Paul has mentioned the word "learn" twice in these verses. Anytime anything is repeated in Scripture, it is of great importance. Learning the Bible is important. The Psalmist says in Psalm 119:7 (LSB), "I shall give thanks to You with uprightness of heart, when I learn Your righteous judgments." And, again, in Psalm 119:73 (LSB), "Your hands made me and established me; give me understanding, that I may learn Your commandments." Oh, that we would have a desire to learn the Word!

*So, for those who will receive the word, they continue in the faith, they learn the Word, and they are assured of the Word.* Paul goes on to mention another very important result for those who receive the word—and this one is a matter of spiritual life or death! He says,

> and that from childhood you have known the Holy Scriptures, which are able to make you wise for salvation through faith which is in Christ Jesus. (2 Timothy 3:15)

Paul says that *from childhood* Timothy has known the Holy Scriptures. *Childhood*, or child, as your translation might say, refers to one who is a baby or young infant. This would mean that from the time he was a baby, before he even fully understood it, Timothy was being taught the Scriptures. The Jews are known to have said that children learned the

Scriptures while still in their swaddling clothes and from the breast. We also have these interesting words, recorded in Luke 11:27-28 (LSB), from a woman who was listening to and observing Christ's teachings:

> Now it happened that while Jesus was saying these things, one of the women in the crowd raised her voice and said to Him, "Blessed is the womb that bore You and the breasts at which You nursed." But He said, "On the contrary, blessed are those who hear the word of God and keep it."

This woman knew that from His infancy Jesus had known the Scriptures. Jews also claimed that children would be more likely to forget their name than to forget the Holy Scriptures. *The Holy Scriptures*, at the time in which Paul is penning these words to Timothy, would have included the books of Genesis to Malachi. We have mentioned before the importance of the Old Testament, and here we see that Timothy was brought up with the Old Testament alone, whereas you and I often leave out the Old Testament when instructing our children and mainly instruct them from the New Testament. What great truths we are missing out on when we do that! One man helps us here:

> The mother of Timothy was a pious Hebrewess, and regarded it as one of the duties of her religion to train her son in the careful knowledge of the word of God. This was regarded by the Hebrews as an important duty of religion, and there is reason to believe that it was commonly faithfully performed. The Jewish writings abound with lessons on this subject. Rabbi Judah says, "The boy of five years of age ought to apply to the study of the sacred Scriptures." Rabbi Solomon, on Deut 11:19, says, "When the boy begins to talk, his father ought to converse with him in the sacred language, and to teach him the law; if he does not do that, he seems to bury him."[44]

Timothy must have felt like the Psalmist, who wrote in Psalm 71:17 (LSB), "O God, You have taught me from my youth, and I still declare

---

44 Albert Barnes, "Barnes' Notes," *CCEL*, https://ccel.org/ccel/barnes/ntnotes/ntnotes.xix.i.xvii.html. Accessed February 27, 2024.

Your wondrous deeds." I am thankful for a Father who taught me the Word from my childhood and for a husband who taught our children. I am also thankful to be in a church where the children's Sunday School class teaches them the Bible from Genesis all the way through Revelation. And, in the worship service, the children are encouraged to take notes from the pastor's sermon, and then they return at night to be instructed once again as to what they learned in the morning. What a sad state many of our churches are in when they think the church and Sunday School need to be entertainment!

And please note that Paul says these Scriptures are *Holy*. This means they are consecrated for sacred use. They are holy writings! Dear one, your Bible is not like any other book, nor should it be treated like any other book. It is sacred, it is holy, and it was inspired by the Holy Spirit. It is God-breathed, the very words of God Himself. Peter makes this clear in 2 Peter 1:20-21 (LSB): "Know this first of all, that no prophecy of Scripture comes by one's own interpretation. For no prophecy was ever made by the will of man, but men being moved by the Holy Spirit spoke from God." In fact, when Jesus was walking on the Emmaus road after His resurrection, He met up with some men and began to converse with them regarding the Scriptures. Luke records for us that, after Jesus left, they said to one another, "Were not our hearts burning within us while He was speaking to us on the road, while He was opening the Scriptures to us?" (Luke 24:32, LSB). It is alarming today the number of men and women who claim that God is speaking to them, and they are writing down in a book what He supposedly said to them, for the purpose of making money off of it. I fear for them because God's Holy Word is clear that those who add or take away from the Holy Scriptures are in trouble. Listen to what John writes in Revelation 22:18-19 (LSB):

> I bear witness to everyone who hears the words of the prophecy of this book: If anyone adds to them, God will add to him the plagues which are written in this book. And if anyone takes away from the words of the book of this prophecy, God will take away his part from the tree of life and from the holy city, which are written in this book.

These Holy Scriptures have power; Paul tells Timothy they are *able to make you wise for salvation.* But, please note that Paul doesn't stop with this, because the Scriptures alone cannot bring salvation; they do, however, contain the truths within them that are necessary and *able* to *make* us *wise for salvation*, which comes only by faith in Christ. You can know the Bible and not be saved. Satan is a good example of that. He believes, but he only trembles. The scribes and the Pharisees are also good examples of that. They rejected the Messiah and were counting on the oracles of God and their own adherence to those oracles to save them. But Paul makes it clear that salvation comes by grace alone through faith alone in Christ alone. The Scriptures are able to make you wise for salvation *through faith which is in Christ Jesus.* So, instead of rejecting Scripture and becoming worse in your sin, like those mentioned in verse 13, you can receive the Scriptures and become wise unto salvation in Jesus. *This is the fourth result of those who receive the Holy Scriptures—it will make them wise unto salvation, but only through faith in Christ alone.* Acts 4:12 (LSB) is clear: "And there is salvation in no one else, for there is no other name under heaven that has been given among men by which we must be saved." The Psalmist writes, in Psalm 19:7 (LSB), "The law of Yahweh is perfect, restoring the soul; the testimony of Yahweh is sure, making wise the simple."

It was the Word of God that changed the heart of Martin Luther, who the Lord used to begin the Reformation and the recovery of the biblical gospel. He was a brilliant professor who knew the Bible, but he had not been saved until he realized justification is by grace through faith alone. As he wrestled with what the Bible talks about in Romans 1:16-17, he wrote,

> Night and day I pondered until I saw the connection between the righteousness of God and the statement that "the righteous shall live by his faith." Then I realized that the righteousness of God is the righteousness by which, through grace and mercy, God justifies us through faith. From there I felt I was reborn as if I had gone through open doors into Paradise. All of Scripture seemed to take on a new meaning and whereas before the "righteousness of God" had filled me

> with hate, now this phrase became to me inexpressibly sweet in great love. This passage of Paul became to me a gate to heaven.

It is Scripture that brings salvation and anyone looking to know God cannot ignore it. Whether an unsaved Bible scholar or an atheist who knows nothing about it, the Word is the only way to be made *wise for salvation*. This is why Luther would go on to say, speaking about the world-changing movement of the Reformation, "I did nothing: the Word did it all."

The Scriptures are of utmost importance. In fact, in our next chapter we will finish up chapter three of 2 Timothy with these words from Paul: "All Scripture is given by inspiration of God, and is profitable for doctrine, for reproof, for correction, for instruction in righteousness, that the man of God may be complete, thoroughly equipped for every good work" (2 Timothy 3:16-17).

## Summary

If we reject the Scriptures, we run the risk of becoming worse and worse, deceiving and being deceived. Are there any portions of God's Word which you are rejecting as unimportant? Submitting to your husband? Forsaking the assembling of yourself with the church for worship? Praying without ceasing? Honoring your parents? Loving the brethren? Praying for your enemies? Putting off anger, anxiety, worry, sexual sins, lying, and the like? Bringing your children up in the nurture and admonition of the Lord? Loving your neighbor as yourself? Considering your trials with joy? Rejoicing in persecution?

Well, you get the idea. There are more than 600 commands in the Holy Scriptures and I have only listed a few of them. Is there any portion of Scripture that you are purposefully rejecting? Beware, my friend, if you are, because you are in a danger zone and are risking straying even more from the truth.

If we receive the Scriptures, we have the joy of hopefully continuing in them, learning more of them, being more assured of them, and, most important, being saved by believing the truths contained in them. Are you continuing daily in the Word of God? Is reading your Bible a dreaded duty for you or a daily delight? How are you continuing in the Word?

What about learning? Are you more knowledgeable about the Scriptures today than you were a few years ago, a few months ago, a few days ago? Recently, in a book I read, it was suggested that you shouldn't stop reading your Bible each day until you have learned at least one new fact. I found that to be very intriguing. And, since we are talking about learning, remember that Timothy learned from his mother and grandmother. If I were to ask your children or grandchildren if you instructed them more from the Bible than any other book, what would they say? Would it be *Peter Rabbit* or 1 Peter? *Dr. Seuss* or Dr. Luke? A science book or the book of Genesis? Books on learning their numbers or the book of Numbers? *Finding Nemo* or the book of Jonah? *War of the Worlds* or the book of the Revelation? To be clear, I am not deprecating children's books, if they are of good quality, but our children should be learning the Bible foremost, and they should be learning it from their parents.

And what about being more assured of what you are learning in the Scriptures? Are you more convinced today about God's Word and what it says than you were a few years ago, or are you doubting the things that you read or learn? Do you think Jonah was *actually* in the belly of the fish? Do you think God *in fact* parted the Red Sea? Do you think the earth *really* opened up and swallowed Korah and his companions? Do you think that Jesus *truly* rose on the third day? Hopefully, you are becoming more and more assured of these truths as you grow and learn the Holy Scriptures and fall more in love with the author of them.

And, lastly, but certainly not least, the last result—in fact, this is the most important of the results of receiving the Word. Have you been saved by faith alone in Christ alone? Are you certain that you are not depending on following rules or works for salvation?

Is the Bible a precious treasure to you? A book divine? I pray that we would all have the heart of John Wesley, who once said, "I want to know one thing, the way to heaven: how to land safe on that happy shore. God himself has condescended to teach the way; for this very end he came from Heaven. He has written it down in a book! Oh, give me that book! At any price, give me the book of God! I have it: here is knowledge enough for me. Let me be: 'A man of one book.'"[45]

45 John Wesley, quoted in "Sermons on Several Occasions", *CCEL*, https://ccel.org/ccel/wesley/sermons/sermons.iv.html. Accessed February 22, 2024.

# QUESTIONS TO CONSIDER

1. (a) Read 2 Timothy 3:13-15 and make note of any contrasts you observe. (b) What is the importance of the Scriptures, according to these verses?

2. Memorize 2 Timothy 3:15.

3. (a) Why is it important that children listen to the instruction of their parents, according to Proverbs 4:1-27; 5:1-2; Proverbs 6:20-24? (b) What does Proverbs 30:17 say regarding children who don't listen to their parents? (c) How can we train our children to listen to and heed our instructions, especially those which pertain to spiritual truth?

4. (a) What child can you think of in Scripture who heeded the instruction of their parent(s), and what was the result? (b) What child can you think of in Scripture who did not heed the voice of the parent(s), and what was the result?

5. (a) Timothy learned the Scriptures as a young child. According to the following verses, what value do the Scriptures have, not only for the young, but for all ages? Psalm 119:9, 11, 50, 54, 81, 98, 103, 104, 130, 143, 160? (b) What personal value do the Scriptures have for you?

6. (a) Do you treat your Bible as Holy? (b) How can we encourage others, especially the young, to see the Bible as God's Holy Word? (c) Why is it imperative that children be instructed in the Bible more than any other book?

7. Do you treasure God's Word? Come with a prayer request asking the Lord to give you a deeper love and deeper desire for His Holy Word.

# The Gracious Gift of the Word of God!

*2 Timothy 3:16-17*

EVERY week, before each time I teach the ladies who come to our church's Bible Study, we prepare our hearts by singing a song of worship. The song which was selected for our study in 2 Timothy was "Show Us Christ" by Sovereign Grace; I encourage you to listen to it and read the lyrics.

The lyrics of this song are a good reflection of what Paul writes as he ends chapter three of 2 Timothy. Paul writes,

> All Scripture is given by inspiration of God, and is profitable for doctrine, for reproof, for correction, for instruction in righteousness, that the man of God may be complete, thoroughly equipped for every good work. (2 Timothy 3:16-17)

Did you notice the similarities? *All Scripture is given by inspiration of God* is reflected in "Your Word is living light," "speak to us today," and "preaching of Your Word." All Scripture *is profitable for doctrine, for reproof, for correction, for instruction in righteousness* is reflected in "break the hard and stony ground," "cause it to bear fruit," and "Your Word is living light upon our darkened eyes." And, in verse 17, where Paul writes *that the man of God may be complete, thoroughly equipped for every good work*, this song reflects those truths in words like "plant Your Word down deep in us, cause it to bear fruit" and "makes the simple wise."

God has given us a gracious gift—His Word. Abraham Lincoln once said, "I believe the Bible is the best gift God has given to man."[46] As we

46 Abraham Lincoln, quoted in Mark Water, *The New Encyclopedia of Christian Quotations*, (Grand Rapids: Baker Book House, 2000), 115. Reproduced with permission of the Licensor through PLSclear.

consider the gracious gift of the Word of God, our outline will include the following: *How Did We Get the Bible?* (v 16a); *What Do We Gain from the Bible?* (v 16b); and *What Is the Goal of the Bible?* (v 17). In our last chapter, we considered the importance of the Holy Scriptures. We learned that if we reject the Scriptures we run the risk of becoming worse and worse, deceiving others, and being deceived ourselves. However, if we receive the Scriptures, we have the joy of hopefully continuing in them, learning more of them, being more assured of them, and, most important, being saved by them. Now, Paul continues on with why the Holy Bible is so important, and as he does he answers the question, "How did we get the Bible?" in verse 16a.

## How Did We Get the Bible? *2 Timothy 3:16*

> All Scripture is given by inspiration of God, (2 Timothy 3:16a)

Paul begins by writing that *all Scripture is given by inspiration of God.* The word *all* means just that: all, or the whole. At the time of Paul's writing of 2 Timothy, the Scriptures were not yet completely written and collected together as we know them today; they would have included all of the Old Testament books and many of the New Testament books—2 Timothy was one of the last books of the New Testament to be written. Yet, all 66 books of the Bible we have today, 39 in the Old Testament and 27 in the New Testament, are inspired by God and in the canon of Scripture.

The Greek word for *Scripture* is *graphe.* This is the only place this term is used in the New Testament, and it is a reference to the sacred Scriptures, referring to any and all revelation from God, including both the Old and New Testaments. These are holy writings or documents. The Scriptures are about God and are meant to lead us to God. They were given *by inspiration of God. By inspiration* means they were divinely breathed. What was in the mind of God was breathed out by God and men, led by the Holy Spirit, wrote down what God breathed out. This means that every word in the Scriptures was inspired. This same idea, inspired, or God-breathed, is used in Genesis 2:7 (LSB), where it is written, "Then Yahweh God formed man of dust from the ground and breathed into his nostrils the breath of life; and so the man became a living being." God breathed life into Adam. God has breathed out His words to men, who then wrote those words down. In Genesis 2:7, the Greek translation of the Old Testament uses the word *emphusao* to translate the word *breathe*. In John 20:22, John uses the same word when he writes, "And when He had said this, He breathed on them, and said to them, 'Receive the Holy Spirit.'" Now, ladies, this should give us great assurance that we can trust the Word of God, because God Himself wrote it. God is truth, and what He breathes out is truth. John Stott said it well, "Our claim is that God has revealed himself by speaking; that this divine (or God-breathed) speech has been written down and preserved in Scripture; and that Scripture is, in fact, God's word written, which therefore is true and reliable and has divine authority over men."[47]

Paul's spiritual brother (and ours), Peter, confirms this same truth in 2 Peter 1:19-21. He writes,

> And we have as more sure the prophetic word, to which you do well to pay attention as to a lamp shining in a dark place, until the day dawns and the morning star arises in your hearts. Know this first of all, that no prophecy of Scripture comes by one's own interpretation. For no prophecy was ever made by the will of man, but men being moved by the Holy Spirit spoke from God.

What Peter and Paul are both emphasizing is that God's Word, breathed out by Him, was as if God Himself were audibly speaking what He wanted us to know. Pastor John MacArthur helps us as he writes,

> It is both remarkable and significant that, although most, if not all, of the human writers were aware they were recording Scripture and sometimes were overwhelmed by the truths God revealed to them, they exhibit a total lack of self-consciousness or apology, in the common sense of the word. Together, the biblical writers make some 4000 claims to be writing God's Word, yet they offer no defense for being employed by God in such an elevated function. Despite

47 John R. W. Stott, quoted in Mark Water, *New Encyclopedia*, 117. Reproduced with permission of the Licensor through PLSclear.

> their realization of their own sinfulness and fallibility, they wrote with the utter confidence that they spoke infallibly for God and that His revelation itself is its own best and irrefutable defense.[48]

The Holy Spirit did not restrain the personality of the writers. They were not robotic. John Stott helps us here:

> The dual authorship of Scripture is an important truth to be carefully guarded. On the one hand, God spoke, revealing the truth and preserving the human authors from error, yet without violating their personality. On the other hand, men spoke, using their own faculties freely, yet without distorting the divine message. Their words were truly their own words. But they were (and still are) also God's words, so that what Scripture says, God says.[49]

When you read the Bible, you can't help but notice the different writing styles of the human authors. Paul is very different from Peter, who is different from John, who is different from James, and so on. And yet they do not contradict each other, but each writes the same truths. I've noticed through the years how different the Gospel accounts are, and yet they are the same. When you read Luke, you see how often he emphasizes the compassion of Christ. Luke was a doctor and, more than likely, as a doctor, he had compassion on those who were hurting and sick, and therefore he emphasizes those qualities of our Lord. When you read the Gospel of John, you notice that John often focuses on the love of Christ. John, we know, was the apostle of love. Mark's Gospel is short but to the point. He must have been that kind of guy—gets right to the point of the matter, using the words "straightaway" and "immediately." And yet his Gospel does not differ from Matthew's, who is definitely more detailed in the accounts and events of Christ and who emphasizes Christ as King. You know, we see some of this variety even today within the church, not in the giving of new revelation, because that is no longer happening, but as each of us who belong to Christ have been given a variety of spiritual gifts. Even in this diversity, we are

---

48 John MacArthur, *New Testament Commentary: 2 Timothy*, 147.

49 John R. W. Stott, quoted in Mark Water, *New Encyclopedia*, 118. Reproduced with permission of the Licensor through PLSclear

not robotic in how we use the gifts we've been given. Our personalities and passions and talents are different and how we each use our gifts is different, but, hopefully, we all are proclaiming the truth or serving the church in a manner that is consistent with Scripture.

Before we go on, it's important to clarify that it is the Scripture that is God-breathed, or inspired, not the men who wrote it. If God were speaking audibly today—which He is not—His words to us today would be no different than what He has already written to us in the Old and New Testaments. I am concerned—and, frankly, appalled—at those today who say they themselves have been given divine revelation, as though God Himself has inspired these words. It is the Scriptures alone that are inspired by God, not the words these people have supposedly received from Him, words which often contradict what He has already written. J.C. Ryle, one of my favorite authors, wrote, "Let us receive nothing, believe nothing, follow nothing which is not in the Bible, nor can be proved by the Bible."[50]

*So, how did we get the Bible? We got it from God; it was His gracious gift to us!* John Calvin said, "We cannot rely on the doctrine of Scripture until we are absolutely convinced that God is its author."[51] The next question to consider is: "What do we gain from the Bible?"

## What Do We Gain from the Bible? *2 Timothy 3:16*

> and is profitable for doctrine, for reproof, for correction, for instruction in righteousness, (2 Timothy 3:16b)

Paul answers that question by telling us the Scripture *is profitable for doctrine, for reproof, for correction, for instruction in righteousness.* Paul says it is profitable for four things, according to the text here. The word *profitable* means helpful, beneficial, advantageous, useful, and sufficient. Now, we must be careful that we don't put in the text what

50 J. C. Ryle, quoted in Mark Water, *New Encyclopedia*, 117. Reproduced with permission of the Licensor through PLSclear

51 John Calvin, quoted in Mark Water, *New Encyclopedia*, 118. Reproduced with permission of the Licensor through PLSclear

is not there. The Scriptures are not profitable for teaching you how to change a tire, but they are profitable for teaching you how to be patient while you're changing the tire or waiting for roadside service to come. The Scriptures are not profitable for instructing you in how to plan a wedding, but they are profitable in teaching you how to choose a godly man to marry and for preparing your own self to be a godly woman. The Scriptures are not profitable for helping you to know how to build a house from the ground up, but they are profitable for aiding you, once that home has been built, to know how to live in that home as a godly homemaker, wife, and mother. The Bible is an inspired gift of God that we should use for all of life. And, if it is true that God's Word is profitable for all of life (and it is!), we should ask ourselves why we so often run for help to other sources first when we have the inspired, infallible, sufficient, and authoritative Word of God at our fingertips.

*The first thing Paul says we gain from the inspired Word of God is doctrine.* Paul has already written to Timothy about following the doctrine Paul has taught him, in 2 Timothy 3:10: "But you have carefully followed my doctrine, manner of life, purpose, faith, longsuffering, love, perseverance." *Doctrine* is simply instruction in truth; it is truth about God. It includes things like creation, the fall of man, eternal life, and the ministry of the Holy Spirit. To learn doctrine is to learn things that otherwise could not and would not be known apart from the Scriptures. Paul writes about this to the church at Rome, in Romans 15:4 (LSB): "For whatever was written in earlier times was written for our instruction, so that through the perseverance and the encouragement of the Scriptures we might have hope." Luke records a good example of this when the resurrected Christ meets up with a couple of guys on the Emmaus road; it states in Luke 24:27 (LSB), "Then beginning with Moses and with all the prophets, He interpreted to them the things concerning Himself in all the Scriptures." Jesus was teaching doctrine to these two men. In 2 Timothy alone, Paul has instructed Timothy in quite a bit of doctrine. The Scriptures are full of doctrine. And, I don't know about you, but the more doctrine I learn from the Bible, the more I realize I don't know.

*The second thing Paul says we gain from the Holy Bible is reproof. Reproof* is conviction of sin or rebuke regarding sin. This would also include warnings from the Word about any error we are in or any false teaching we have been influenced by. For some of us, we like the doctrine that we gain, but the reproof we get from Scripture is sometimes not so welcomed. Proverbs 15:10 (LSB) reminds us, "Grievous discipline is for him who forsakes the way; he who hates reproof will die." We need to have the attitude mentioned in Proverbs 15:31 (LSB), where it is written, "He whose ear listens to the life-giving reproof will lodge among the wise." We would be wise to receive with meekness both the reproofs of Scripture and the reproofs of those who love us enough to speak such truth to us. The Word of God has the power, as the writer to the Hebrews says in Hebrews 4:12-13 (LSB).

> For the word of God is living and active and sharper than any two-edged sword, and piercing as far as the division of soul and spirit, of both joints and marrow, and able to judge the thoughts and intentions of the heart. And there is no creature hidden from His sight, but all things are uncovered and laid bare to the eyes of Him to whom we have an account to give.

The Scriptures are powerful, they are sharp, they pierce us, they get to our thought-life and the intentions of our heart. We cannot hide from God, the One to Whom we will give an account. What other book besides the Bible has that power? None of them! It is like no other book.

Reproof has a negative connotation, but the next word, *correction*, is the positive counterpart to that. *Correction is the third thing we gain from the Word of God.* Correction means to straighten up again, to restore things to their proper place. Once we have been reproved by the Scriptures, once we have seen how our ways are not straight, we must then correct our path, right? We must change our ways and straighten up, so to speak. Often, this takes discipline as we wrestle and fight and pray. And, often, the good we want to do we end up not doing, and the evil we know we should not do, well, that's what we do (Romans 7:15-23). But, praise God, we have the promises that we are being transformed from glory to glory, even by the Spirit of the Lord, and that He who began that good work in us will perfect it (see 2 Corinthians 3:18 and Philippians 1:6).

*The fourth thing we gain from Scripture is instruction in righteousness. Instruction in righteousness* is teaching regarding what is right. These four things we gain from Scripture are nicely lined up and flow one to the other. Once we have right doctrine, we then are often reproved or rebuked regarding our sin. Then, once we correct our ways and our false ideas, we can do what is right. Having been changed by the Word in all these ways, we can glorify and please God by living in *righteousness.* For example, when I became a Christian, there were many things that had to change. Submission to my husband was one of them. I knew what the Scripture said about this, but now that I was a child of God, the good doctrine of submission had to take root. I was convicted of my sin and knew I needed to straighten up in this area. I became submissive, but in the beginning my husband would often comment that I was being submissive outwardly but not inwardly. I finally progressed to doing what is right. And, by the way, as I began to do the right thing, I also began to see it as freeing and liberating and not a burden. As we've already mentioned, we often run to other sources to figure out how to live right, but all we need for life and godliness is in the Scriptures. Peter writes of this in 2 Peter 1:3-4 (LSB): "His divine power has granted to us everything pertaining to life and godliness, through the full knowledge of Him who called us by His own glory and excellence. For by these He has granted to us His precious and magnificent promises, so that by them you may become partakers of the divine nature." Charles Spurgeon once said, "It is wonderful the effect of a single verse of Scripture when the Spirit of God applies it to the soul. What power would come upon the soul if we would grasp a single line of Scripture and suck the honey out of it till our soul is filled with sweetness."[52]

*What do we gain from the Bible? We gain good, good things like doctrine, reproof, correction, and instruction in righteousness.* Paul now finishes up this portion of his letter by answering our third question, that is, "What is the goal of the Bible?" What effect does the Bible have on believers? Paul answers this question as he ends chapter three.

52 Charles H. Spurgeon, quoted in Mark Water, *New Encyclopedia*, 116. Reproduced with permission of the Licensor through PLSclear.

## What Is the Goal of the Bible? *2 Timothy 3:17*

> that the man of God may be complete, thoroughly equipped for every good work. (2 Timothy 3:17)

The progression here from the previous verse is pretty exciting to consider. As we learn sound doctrine, we are reproved by the Word of God. We then straighten up or are corrected and are instructed in righteousness. And, as we become more disciplined in those righteous things, we grow more like Christ, we are made more complete. *This, then, is the first goal of the Bible, that is, that the man (or woman) of God may be complete.* The word *complete* means to fit or adapt, and it includes the idea of adding nothing to make one complete. The goal is to be holy as He is holy and to be perfect as He is perfect. Paul talks about this when writing to the church at Colossae. He writes in Colossians 1:28, "Him we preach, *warning* every man and *teaching* every man in all *wisdom*, that we may *present every man perfect in Christ Jesus*." It is interesting that in this verse Paul mentions the same things he's mentioned in the verses we're considering in 2 Timothy: teaching (doctrine), warning (reproof), wisdom (correction and instruction in righteousness), and presenting every man perfect in Christ Jesus (that the man of God may be complete). Paul even writes to the carnal church of Corinth regarding this truth, in 2 Corinthians 13:9. "For we are glad when we are weak and you are strong. And this also we pray, that you may be made complete." And the writer to the Hebrews mentions this truth, in Hebrews 13:20-21:

> Now may the God of peace who brought up our Lord Jesus from the dead, that great Shepherd of the sheep, through the blood of the everlasting covenant, make you complete in every good work to do His will, working in you what is well pleasing in His sight, through Jesus Christ, to whom be glory forever and ever. Amen.

Did you notice that those last two passages both mention praying for others to be complete? What a great prayer request for you and me to pray for others and for ourselves—to be complete! And did you know that Jesus even prayed this for us in the High Priestly Prayer before He went to the cross? Listen to John 17:23: "I in them, and You in Me; that they may be made perfect in one, and that the world may know that You have sent Me, and have loved them as You have loved Me." Think about it: if Scripture is not complete, how could it possibly make mere man or woman complete? But Scripture is complete and, therefore, it has the power to make us complete. As one person has put it like this: "It was not given to inform but to transform!"[53]

*The second goal of the Bible is to be thoroughly equipped for every good work.* Again, the progression is simple to see. As we become complete, we are then *thoroughly equipped for every good work.* To be *thoroughly equipped* means that we are thoroughly furnished and ready to *do good works*, which are beneficial deeds. This does not mean that we have to be sinless in order to serve the Lord, but it does mean that we should be striving for that goal. I am always concerned about believers who are content with the status quo and seem to have no desire to grow more into the image of Christ. We should long to be more and more equipped to serve the One who died for us and paid the penalty for our sin and has saved us from the wrath to come.

Remember, Paul has just written, in 2 Timothy 2:20-22, regarding being equipped for good works:

> But in a great house there are not only vessels of gold and silver, but also of wood and clay, some for honor and some for dishonor. Therefore if anyone cleanses himself from the latter, he will be a vessel for honor, sanctified and useful for the Master, prepared for every good work.

In that passage, Paul tells Timothy the necessity of cleaning out God's house of all who are false and not real vessels of God. And, Paul says, as Timothy does this, he will be of use for the Master and prepared for good works. Paul writes to the church at Corinth and says to them, in 2 Corinthians 9:8 (LSB), "And God is able to make every grace abound to you, so that in everything at every time having every sufficiency, you may have an abundance for every good deed." Here we see that concept again, sufficiency, being adequate, being complete to do the work.

53 Unknown author, quoted in Mark Water, *New Encyclopedia*, 112. Reproduced with permission of the Licensor through PLSclear

There is no deficiency in the Scriptures, only sufficiency. Therefore, the Scriptures are able to equip us for all that God has called us to be and to do. We don't read and study the Bible just so that we can have more Bible knowledge; we do it so that we can know more about its Author and be transformed into His image. We read and study to be made complete and to ready ourselves to do His work for His Kingdom. *So, the goal of the Bible is to grow us, that is, to make us complete and thoroughly equipped for every good work.* And, as we do those good works, we must continually go back to those Scriptures as our plum line for ministry.

## Summary

As we consider this gracious gift from God, His Word, we must remember that we got it from God. It is inspired and it is profitable. Do you believe that God's Word is inspired? If you do, then that belief should manifest itself in a longing to know what He has said. The God of the universe has breathed out His words and they are contained in the book we call the Bible. Amazing! Do you believe that God's Word is profitable? What profit have the Scriptures been to you in your life this week?

What do we gain from this gracious gift of God, His Word? We gain good things like doctrine, reproof, correction, and instruction in righteousness. Are you gaining these good things? What about doctrine? Do you know more about God and about the Bible this year than you did last year? Are you increasing in your knowledge of doctrine? What about receiving reproof from God's Word? James tells us we are to be slow to get angry with God's Word, slow to speak back, and we are to receive His Word with meekness (James 1:19-21).[54] When you read something in the Word of God and you become convicted by it, do you receive it and repent of your sin? When others reprove you, do you receive their admonishments with grace? After being convicted by reproof, do you correct the wrong way you are living? Do you straighten up? If it is lack of submission to your husband, do you begin submitting? If it is conviction regarding being negligent in prayer, do you start praying more often? If it is the sin of jealousy, anger, self-righteousness, or pride,

54 For more details, see: Susan J. Heck, *With the Master In the Fiery Furnace* (Irvine, Three Sixteen Publishing), 316Publishing.com.

do you determine to put those off and instead put on love, meekness, righteousness, and humility? This is where the last gain, living a life of righteousness, comes into play: we stop doing those things that are unrighteous, and we start living a life of righteousness.

What is the goal of the Bible? The goal of the Bible is to grow us up in Christ, to make us complete and fully equipped for every good work. Do you look more like Christ today than you did last week, last year, last night? Are you striving with the help of the Holy Spirit to be complete and better equipped to do the work God has called you to do? What good works has He called you to do? Are you excelling more each day in those good works? (Just a reminder: good works do not save us, but they are a sign that we are saved!—see James 2:18). Oh, what a gracious gift of God, His words breathed out to us! Why would we go anywhere else but to the precious Word of God?

There is an interesting portion of Scripture that the writer of our theme song for this study may have had in mind when he wrote "Show Us Christ." The bridge of that song asks and declares, repeatedly, those very truths which are captured in John 6:60-69 (LSB):

> Therefore many of His disciples, when they heard this said, "This is a difficult statement; who can listen to it?" But Jesus, knowing in Himself that His disciples were grumbling at this, said to them, "Does this cause you to stumble? What then if you see the Son of Man ascending to where He was before? The Spirit is the One who gives life; the flesh profits nothing; the words that I have spoken to you are spirit and are life. But there are some of you who do not believe." For Jesus knew from the beginning who they were who did not believe, and who it was that would betray Him. And He was saying, "For this reason I have said to you, that no one can come to Me unless it has been granted him from the Father."
>
> As a result of this many of His disciples went away and were not walking with Him anymore. So Jesus said to the twelve, "Do you also want to go?" Simon Peter answered Him, "Lord, to whom shall we go? You have words of eternal life. And we have believed and have come to know that You are the Holy One of God."

I am interested mainly in Peter's response when the sayings of Christ got so difficult that many disciples left Christ. Jesus asked the twelve disciples if they too were going to leave, to which Peter replied, essentially, "Where else can we go, Lord? You have the words of eternal life!" My friend, do you believe that Jesus has the words of eternal life? Do you believe the Scriptures are God-breathed and sufficient for all of life and godliness? Are you "going" anywhere else but to the One Whose words are sufficient, authoritative, and inerrant?

# QUESTIONS TO CONSIDER

1. (a) What is the value of Scripture, according to 2 Timothy 3:16-17? (b) What is the value of Scripture to you?

2. Memorize 2 Timothy 3:16.

3. (a) Paul refers to the Word of God as Scripture. Read all of Psalm 119 (no moaning!) and write down the other words that are used as synonyms for the Scriptures. (b) Also, what are some of the values of Scripture, according to Psalm 119?

4. Paul says that all Scripture is profitable for doctrine, for reproof, for correction, for instruction in righteousness. Read over 2 Timothy and make note of where each of these occurs in Paul's writings to Timothy. You only need to list a few. (For example: "stir up the gift of God" in 1:6 is a reproof; 1:9-10 would be doctrine; 2:4 would be a correction; 2:22 would be instruction in righteousness.)

5. (a) What book of the Bible has helped you the most in understanding doctrine? (b) What book of the Bible has reproved you the most? (c) What book of the Bible has helped you the most in correcting your wrong thinking? (d) What book of the Bible has helped you the most in instructing you in right living?

6. (a) Considering question number 3, why would we turn to other sources for wisdom, guidance or help? (b) Is Scripture your first go-to when you are in need of help, wisdom, or guidance?

7. Every word of God is inspired, true, sufficient, and authoritative. With those truths in mind, write a prayer request that will reflect *your* personal need for a better relationship with the Holy Scriptures.

# Pertinent Truths Required in a Post-Truth World

*2 Timothy 4:1-5*

OXFORD Dictionary's International Word of the Year for 2016 was "post-truth," defined as "relating to or denoting circumstances in which objective facts are less influential in shaping public opinion than appeals to emotion and personal belief."[55] We certainly are living in a post-truth world. Truth, it seems, is no longer relevant. We see this played out in politics nearly every day to such an extent that it's difficult to know who is telling the truth. We see it in the workplace as businesses fail to tell the truth to their consumers. We see it in the home as children learn the art of lying to their parents and then parents won't correct their children when they lie. And, unfortunately, we see it in the church. The truth of Scripture is no longer important to most professing Christians. They would rather have their ears tickled with fables and nonsense than hear the truth of sound doctrine. This reality is heavy on Paul's heart as he begins chapter four of his second letter to Timothy. Read with me what he writes concerning the pertinent truths that are required in a post-truth world.

> I charge you therefore before God and the Lord Jesus Christ, who will judge the living and the dead at His appearing and His kingdom: Preach the word! Be ready in season and out of season. Convince, rebuke, exhort, with all longsuffering and teaching. For the time will come when they will not endure sound doctrine, but according to their own desires, because they have itching ears, they will heap up for themselves teachers; and they will turn their ears away from the truth, and be turned aside to fables. But you be watchful in all things, endure afflictions, do the work of an evangelist, fulfill your ministry. (2 Timothy 4:1-5)

---

55 Jason Altmire. "The importance of fact-checking in a post-truth world." *The Hill*, https://thehill.com/opinion/technology/405429-the-importance-of-fact-checking-in-a-post-truth-world. Accessed February 15, 2024.

Our outline, as we consider these pertinent truths, will include *Motivations for Obeying These Truths* (vv 1, 3-4), and we will see two of them, and *Mentioning of These Truths* (vv 2, 5), and there will be *nine* of them—the first *five* have to do with others and the last *four* have to do with ourselves. In our last chapter, we considered the gracious gift from God, which is His Word. It is God-breathed and it is profitable. We also saw that we gain good things from this precious book. We gain doctrine, reproof, correction, and instruction in righteousness. And we learned that the goal of the Bible is to grow us, to make us complete and fully equipped for every good work. This gracious gift from God, the Bible, is to be used. We aren't to let it sit on a coffee table and collect dust. The Word has great benefits for us, as we have learned, but with those benefits come great responsibilities, and one of the responsibilities is to preach the Word, as Paul mentions in this chapter's passage. Let's consider the first motivation for heeding the truths Paul mentions in these verses.

## Motivations for Obeying These Truths *2 Timothy 4:1, 3-4*

> I charge you therefore before God and the Lord Jesus Christ, who will judge the living and the dead at His appearing and His kingdom: (2 Timothy 4:1)

Paul begins with the words *I charge you. Charge* means to attest earnestly or to solemnly witness. Paul is serious about what he is writing to Timothy. Paul uses the word *therefore*, which points back, most likely, to the fact that Paul is facing imminent death and he knows his time is short. More than likely, Paul's death will occur in the next few weeks, or even days, from the writing of this letter. He knows his time is short, as mentioned in verse 6, and this is a serious time for him as he writes his final words to his son in the faith. The term therefore can also refer to what Paul has just written in the previous verses. That is, the Word of God is inspired, Timothy, so preach it! Don't preach fables; preach God-breathed words!

Paul writes that he is solemnly testifying to Timothy *before God and the Lord Jesus Christ*. The words *before God* mean that Paul is making a vow or an oath. What he is saying is true, unlike the false teachers he has written about. In Paul's time, an oath was serious and must not be broken. It was sacred and binding, unlike in our day. To break an oath would bring judgment. James writes in his epistle: "But above all, my brothers, do not swear, either by heaven or by earth or with any other oath. But let your yes be yes, and your no, no, so that you may not fall under judgment" (James 5:12, LSB). And Jesus says in His Sermon on the Mount, in Matthew 5:37 (LSB), "But let your statement be, 'Yes, yes' or 'No, no'; anything beyond these is of the evil one."

Paul reminds Timothy that this oath is before God and the Lord Jesus Christ *who will judge the living and the dead.* Paul was very aware that it is appointed once for men to die, but after this comes the judgment. He says this judgment is *at [Christ's] appearing and His kingdom.* This simply means that the Lord's return will be the beginning of the setting up of His Kingdom. *The number one motivator to heed these commands is the Lord's return.* The Lord's appearing is a great motivator to be diligent in the work of the Lord and to be obedient to His commands. Paul writes to the church at Corinth regarding this same truth, in 2 Corinthians 5:9-10 (LSB): "Therefore we also have as our ambition, whether at home or absent, to be pleasing to Him. For we must all appear before the judgment seat of Christ, so that each one may be recompensed for his deeds in the body, according to what he has done, whether good or bad." The judgment to come should be a motivator for us to give heed to these words of Paul regarding our responsibilities. It's possible that Paul is thinking of the judgment to come because he knows that he will soon be facing the Lord.

So, what are some of the commands we would do well to heed? Paul mentions the first five of these truths in verse 2.

## Mentioning of These Truths *2 Timothy 4:2, 5*

> Preach the word! Be ready in season and out of season. Convince, rebuke, exhort, with all longsuffering and teaching. (2 Timothy 4:2)

*The first truth we must heed in a post-truth world is to preach the Word.* I cannot think of anything more needed, can you? We have vacated the Word of God, much to our shame. *Preach the Word* means to herald divine truth. This truth that is the very Word of God is to be heralded—the truth that is breathed out by God Himself and is all-authoritative and all-sufficient is to be preached! This *Word* is the one that gives us sound doctrine; rebukes our sin; corrects our wrong thinking; instructs us in righteousness; grows us by making us complete and fully equipped for every good work. Why would we not preach this Word? Why would we not preach the gospel and all that is contained in this truth? Why would we not preach this rich book? No other book or person has such depth and wisdom. We must preach the Word of God and nothing else! We must not preach ourselves or cute stories we've dreamed up. In fact, do you know that you are in a heap of trouble if you preach anything else? Consider what Paul writes to the church at Galatia, in Galatians 1:8-9 (LSB): "But even if we, or an angel from heaven, should proclaim to you a gospel contrary to the gospel we have proclaimed to you, let him be accursed! As we have said before, so I say again now, if any man is proclaiming to you a gospel contrary to what you received, let him be accursed!" Also, Revelation 22:18-19 warns that adding or taking away from the Word of God has serious implications.

*The second truth that is important to heed is to be ready in season and out of season.* We should be ready in a moment's notice to preach the truth. We should see the urgency of it and buy up the opportunities which come our way. We should be eager and alert to those divine appointments. We don't know who we will see or who will call us, even this day, and yet we are to be ready. We are not to waste opportunities or waste our life. We are not to be lazy. *In season and out of season* means when it's convenient and when it's not convenient. Paul took opportunities whether it was convenient or it was inconvenient. Times which were convenient included meetings, like those in synagogues or by the river, where he knew people would be praying (Acts 18:4 and 16:13). But he also preached when it wasn't so convenient, like in prison, when it was late at night and even on into the morning, and after suffering shipwreck (Acts 16:23-34; 20:7-12; 27:39-28:31). Peter mentions this same truth in 1 Peter 3:15: "But sanctify the Lord God in your hearts, and always be ready to give a defense to everyone who asks you a reason for the hope that is in you, with meekness and fear." Isn't it interesting that Peter says this is to be done in meekness and Paul says in this verse that it is to be done with patience?!

*The third pertinent truth we must observe is to convince,* or reprove, as your translation might read. To *convince* means to convict others of their sin. Instead of diminishing sin and justifying it, like the false teachers do, a genuine believer will love others enough to point out the truth of their sin. Included in this would be the act of convincing others of the error they may be following, which is the context of the next few verses. And, remember, we reprove others from the Word of God. We preach the Word! The inspired Word of God holds up a mirror to our sin and our error.

*Fourthly, we must rebuke.* This command to *rebuke* is a call to admonish those who will not let go of their sin. Once we have reproved them and shown them from the Word of God that what they are doing is sinful or that they are in some sort of doctrinal error, then we must also forbid them to continue in that sin or error. They have to let go of it or it will master them! We don't minimize their sin but, instead, we tell them the danger of their sin. I remember, several years ago, I was working with a gal who came in for counseling. She told me she had been to several "Christian counselors" before coming to me, and yet I was the first one who told her she was in sin. What a blight on the Christian counselors of our day! But, even more so, a disregard for God and His Word, which have the only real power to change lives! With sin, there is always hope, because God has a remedy. When you psychologize or minimize sin, you remove all hope. 1 Thessalonians 5:14 commands us to warn, or rebuke or admonish, the unruly!

*The fifth command or truth needed in a post-truth world is to exhort others.* To *exhort* means to comfort, especially those who are feeble. Again, in 1 Thessalonians 5:14, we are called to comfort the fainthearted. We should never leave one discouraged after a reproof and a rebuke, but we should always leave them with the hope that comes through the Word of God. It's exciting to see that the Word of God has answers to our sins, which are often binding. We have so many passages that help us to put off sin, but we are equally blessed to have as many passages that help us with the virtues we are to put on instead.

An important fact that Paul adds to these five pertinent truths is that we do all of this with *all longsuffering and teaching*, or doctrine, as your translation might read. Paul has already admonished Timothy regarding this important truth, in 2 Timothy 2:24-26. "And a servant of the Lord must not quarrel but be gentle to all, able to teach, patient, in humility correcting those who are in opposition, if God perhaps will grant them repentance, so that they may know the truth, and that they may come to their senses and escape the snare of the devil, having been taken captive by him to do his will." It is worth noting that, in this passage, Paul couples teaching and patience just like he does in chapter four. In fact, the LSB translates this phrase in 2 Timothy 4:2 as "with great patience and teaching." Also Paul writes a similar idea in 1 Thessalonians 5:14. "Now we exhort you, brethren, warn those who are unruly, comfort the fainthearted, uphold the weak, be patient with all." The idea here is that as we warn the unruly, comfort those who are fainthearted, and support the weak, we are to treat all of them with patience. And, yes, we are to be patient with all, but that does not mean that we are ever to compromise doctrine. Paul says we do these things with *longsuffering*, which is forbearance or patience. When we are trying to correct sin or error, there is no need to be brash or rude. I remember vividly a time in the recent past when speaking at a retreat that a lady came up to me during a break. I could tell she was angry and she was shaking and said she wanted to speak to me outside. I hesitated because my practice is to not speak to others without a witness. But I saw that everyone was busy chatting or at the book table, so I agreed. She had this very verse in hand and pointed her finger at it and then at me and declared, "I am going to rebuke you!" I won't go into the details, but she was out of control and began to take me by the shoulders and physically shake me. It was one of those "I can't believe this is happening to me" moments. I was able to diffuse the situation—thanks be to God—and get back inside. Thinking back on the situation now, I wish I had recalled the part of this verse she forgot—with all longsuffering and doctrine. (She practiced neither!)

The wonderful thing about following the principles here in this verse is that the Holy Spirit is a great convincer and convicter of sin. We have a responsibility to deliver the truth, and then we are to let Him do the work. Now, this does not mean that we never rebuke people sharply when it is needed. There are times, especially when dealing with false teachers, that we are to reject them, avoid them, and rebuke them sharply. But this would be after several warnings. Also, a part of the longsuffering we are to exhibit would be to exercise patience with the changing process. People don't change overnight. Paul puts it beautifully in 2 Corinthians 3:18 (LSB): "But we all, with unveiled face, beholding as in a mirror the glory of the Lord, are being transformed into the same image from glory to glory, just as from the Lord, the Spirit." As we exercise patience in this waiting process, it must always be with reminding those we're endeavoring to help of what the Scriptures say regarding their sin or error. And, while Paul doesn't say this in this text, we should always pray while we're waiting! Pray for their hearts to be softened to the truth, and pray that they will thoroughly repent of their sin.

We not only do this with patience but also with *teaching*, or doctrine, which could also be translated as pure doctrine. We tell those we're calling to repentance what God says about their sin or error. We don't minimize it or rationalize it, but we give them the truth in love. It's interesting that Paul starts this verse with the command to preach the word and he ends it with doctrine; it's interesting because everything we do in between in this process must have the inspired Word as its basis. The two slices of bread, so to speak, are preaching the Word and the doctrines of the Word. The inner makings of this sandwich are being diligent to do this when it's convenient and when it's not, and being willing to convince, to rebuke, and to exhort with all longsuffering.

Now, there is one more motivation for heeding these truths, in the next two verses. We've seen one already in verse 1.

## Motivations for Obeying These Truths *2 Timothy 4:1, 3-4*

For the time will come when they will not endure sound doctrine, but

> according to their own desires, because they have itching ears, they will heap up for themselves teachers; (2 Timothy 4:3)

The main reason we try to help others out of their sin and error is because we love them and we don't want them to be enslaved in sin or swept away by false teachers. *Paul gives us a second motivator for why we lovingly help others by preaching the Word to them at all times and in all contexts: It is because there will come a time when they will not endure sound doctrine.* In fact, they will turn away from it, as Paul mentions in the next verse. People who are not confronted with error only tend toward more error. People who don't leave their sin are susceptible to false teachers, as we saw in chapter three, just like the gullible women loaded down with sins. When a person opens the door to the evil one and is taken captive by him, all kinds of sin and error engulfs that person. Paul says this season *will come* upon them and, *when* it does, *they will not endure sound doctrine. Sound doctrine* is doctrine that is uncorrupted or healthy. To *endure* means to put up with. So, the time will come when people will not put up with sound doctrine. Instead, they will, *according to their own desires*, or lusts, *have itching ears.* Because of their selfish, lustful *desires*, they desire their own will and not the will of God. There is a physical condition called "itching ears," but these people have a spiritual condition called itching ears. People in sin or error want their ears scratched. But people who are repenting want that itch to be completely removed with the truth of God's Word, which is the prescribed medicine for such a condition.

When you have an itch, what do you do? You scratch it! And an itch in the ear is the worst in the sense of trying to get relief. Paul is saying that those who have itching ears, spiritually speaking, have chosen to scratch their itch by *heaping up for themselves* false *teachers.* To *heap* means to accumulate, or to seek something in addition. In other words, it's one *teacher* after another after another. And false teachers will gladly scratch that itch! They love to tell fabricated stories that relieve the itches of their followers. It is soothing to the hearer—until the next itch needs to be scratched. So, they run from one bad teacher to another because they don't like the message of the cross of the Lordship of Christ and death to sin. The false teachers of Paul's days were known as sophists, and they would go from city to city with their false teachings. And that's still going on in our day too; false teachers still go from city to city teaching their erroneous ideas. It was going on in Jeremiah's day too, as Jeremiah 5:31 demonstrates: "The prophets prophesy falsely, and the priests rule by their own power; and My people love to have it so. But what will you do in the end?" Just like Jeremiah had a responsibility to the people of his day, we also have a responsibility to heed what Paul has written in these verses so that false teachers will be exposed. We must preach the truth; we cannot be silent as false teachers are sending people to hell with their false gospel. Paul continues on with the tragedy of this turning to false teachers:

> and they will turn their ears away from the truth, and be turned aside to fables. (2 Timothy 4:4)

Not only will they not put up with sound doctrine, but they now *turn their ears away from the truth*. They will listen to all the lies out there about a life of ease and comfort and sin and error, but they will turn their ears from *truth*. They won't even listen to it, but instead they will listen to *fables*, or what is fiction. Paul wrote of this in his first letter to Timothy. 1 Timothy 1:4 (LSB) says, "nor to pay attention to myths and endless genealogies, which give rise to mere speculation rather than furthering the stewardship from God which is by faith." Back when he wrote 1 Timothy, Paul warned Timothy not to give an ear to these foolish ideas, and here, in 2 Timothy, Paul writes that this is exactly what some will do. This was going on in Isaiah's day, as well; he writes, in Isaiah 30:10 (LSB), "Who say to the seers, 'You must not see,' and to those who have visions, 'You must not behold visions for us of what is right, speak to us pleasant words, behold visions of illusions.'" Those who will not allow their sin and error to be dealt with fall prey to nonsense like fables and tales. But why would anyone want to turn to a fable? Warren Wiersbe helps us here:

> Once people have rejected the truth, they turn to fables (myths). It is not likely that man-made fables will convict them of sin or make them want to repent! The result is a congregation of comfortable, professing Christians, listening to a comfortable, religious talk

> that contains no Bible doctrine. These people become the prey of every false cult because their lives lack a foundation in the Word of God. It is a recognized fact that most cultists were formerly members of churches.[56]

My friend, this should motivate us to take heed to what we hear and to be willing to love others enough to warn them of their sin and error.

There are four more pertinent truths to heed in a post-truth world, all mentioned in verse 5. Paul writes,

## Mentioning of These Truths *2 Timothy 4:2, 5*

> But you be watchful in all things, endure afflictions, do the work of an evangelist, fulfill your ministry. (2 Timothy 4:5)

*But you*, Timothy, in contrast to those who are heaping up for themselves teachers to scratch their ears, who are turning their ear away from truth to fables, *you be watchful in all things. This is the sixth truth we must heed in a world where truth is irrelevant.* To be *watchful* means to be alert as to what is going on, to be sober. Paul is telling Timothy—and us—to be sober, to make sure we don't swerve off the beaten path by listening to these false messages. Be a Berean who checks what they hear against the Word of God. Make sure what you hear matches up with healthy doctrine. In recent years, I have listened less and less to the links people send me because I don't want to be influenced by the garbage these false teachers are putting out. I will listen just long enough to discern error, but that's it. We must be watchful over our souls.

*The seventh truth we must obey is to endure afflictions.* This is not a new thought in 2 Timothy. In 2 Timothy 2:3, Paul wrote, "You therefore must endure hardship as a good soldier of Jesus Christ." And in 2 Timothy 3:12, Paul reminded Timothy, "Yes, and all who desire to live godly in Christ Jesus will suffer persecution." Instead of preaching that

56 Excerpted from *The Bible Exposition Commentary on the New Testament* © 1989 Warren W. Wiersbe. Used by permission of David C Cook. May not be further reproduced. All rights reserved. 254.

this is your best life, Timothy, you go preach the message of eternal life through Christ alone. You preach the truth which says no soldier entangles himself in the affairs of this life. You preach that we must *endure afflictions*, or hardships, and that that is part of taking up our cross daily. Don't preach a cushy and crafty message, but preach the message of Christ and Him crucified.

*Doing the work of an evangelist is the eighth truth we must heed in a post-truth world.* To *do the work of an evangelist* means to do the hard work of sharing the gospel. In other words: don't neglect your duty to share the good news. The word *evangelist* is only mentioned three times in the New Testament and one of those times is here in this verse. The other two are in Acts 21:8, where Philip is called an evangelist, and in Ephesians 4:11, where it is mentioned as one of the spiritual gifts. Some have tried to use this as a proof text that Timothy had the gift of evangelism, but that would be hard to prove. Paul is not saying that Timothy has the gift of evangelism; rather, Paul is telling Timothy to evangelize. We may not have the gift of evangelism, but we are commanded to share the gospel. In Matthew 28:18-20, Jesus makes this very clear. If you don't have the gift of mercy, it doesn't exempt you from needing to be merciful. If you don't have the gift of giving, it doesn't exempt you from giving to your local church or to those in need.

*The last truth to heed that Paul mentions here is fulfill your ministry. This is number nine. Fulfill* means to carry out. We are to carry out the ministry or service to which God has called us. In Colossians, Paul reminded someone else to do the same. He writes, in Colossians 4:17 (LSB), "And say to Archippus, 'Take heed to the ministry which you have received in the Lord, that you may fulfill it.'" If both Timothy and Archippus needed to be reminded of this responsibility, how much more do you and I need to be reminded to carry out what God has called us to be and do?! Too often, we allow the cares of this world to distract us from what God has ordained for us to do in this life. But, remember, a true soldier does not entangle himself in those things but, rather, runs the race by the rules like an athlete and works hard like a farmer.

## Summary

The nine truths required for us to heed in a post-truth world are: preach the Word and be ready at all times to do so, convince, rebuke, exhort, be watchful in all things, endure affliction, share the gospel, and carry out what God has called us to do.

The two motivations Paul gives for us to be faithful to heed these pertinent truths are: First, remember the Lord is coming; we will give an account for all we have done—good or bad. And, second, there is coming a time when some will refuse to put up with sound doctrine and will turn their ears away from truth and toward fables.

Are you ready to preach the Word at all times and in all places? Or, do you shy away from opportunities to speak the truth? (In order to herald the truth, you must rightly divide it, as we learned in a previous chapter.) Is your knowledge of the Word increasing so that you are more and more prepared to speak the truth to others when the opportunity arises?

Do you love others enough to point out their sin or error, encouraging them to repent, or have you become calloused about others' sin? Do you give others biblical help and hope for the changes that need to be made in their lives, or do you direct them to worldly, psychologized material?

Are you personally alert to what is going on around you as it pertains to what is being taught among professing Christians? If I were to ask you who the top 10 false teachers of our day are, could you name them? How do you know they are false? Do you check things out to see if they are true biblically?

Are you willing to suffer hardship for Christ or do you secretly desire a life of ease and comfort? What hardships have you encountered this year?

Are you doing the work of an evangelist? Have you shared the gospel recently? How are you fulfilling the work God has called you to do?

My friend, we do these things not for self-righteous works or to be seen by others but because we have an Accounting Day with the One who saved us. Are you ready to give your account? We also do these things because we love those who are captured by the evil one and have fallen prey to sin and false teachers. We grieve that they are turning their ears from incorrupt doctrine to corrupt doctrine, from healthy doctrine to unhealthy.

I will say, as a teacher of the Word of God to women, that it can become discouraging when so many false female teachers are scratching the itch of multitudes of people. But, no matter what God has called each of us to do, we must be faithful to fulfill it. We must be steadfast, immovable, always abounding in the work of the Lord. Our labor is not in vain in the Lord, and we know from the lips of our Lord that only a few will actually find eternal life. Do not let the multitudes of false churches and false teachers discourage you. But you, my sister, in contrast to all of them, be faithful to the end when we will stand before Him to hear, "Well done, good and faithful servant. Enter into the joy of the Lord."

# QUESTIONS TO CONSIDER

1. (a) What are the commands that you observe in 2 Timothy 4:1-5? (b) What do you see that is similar in 2 Timothy 4:1-5 and 2 Timothy 3:16-17?

2. Memorize 2 Timothy 4:1, *or* 2, *or* 3, *or* 4, *or* 5, *or* all of them!

3. (a) Why is it essential that we reprove those who are in sin or error, according to Leviticus 19:17; Proverbs 9:8; 15:32; 29:15; Luke 17:3-4; 2 Timothy 2:24-26? (b) What have you found to be helpful when needing to rebuke or correct another individual? (c) What attitudes should we have when being corrected by others, either for our sin or doctrinal error?

4. (a) What does Jesus say in Mark 4:24-25 about what we hear? (b) In the following passages, what were some doing with the truth of what they heard? Psalm 50:17; Zechariah 7:11; and Acts 7:57. (c) What might happen if we turn our ears away from truth, according to Deuteronomy 30:17-20 and Proverbs 28:9? (d) Why is it essential that we take heed to what we hear, especially in light what Paul says in 2 Timothy 4:3-4? (e) Do you take heed to what you hear?

5. (a) Why it is essential that we heed the command to be watchful, especially in light of the Lord's return, according to Luke 12:35-40 and 1 Thessalonians 5:6-10? (b) Why do you think Paul gave this commandment to be watchful to Timothy at this particular time (2 Timothy 4:5) ? (c) In what ways should we as God's children be watchful in an age which is becoming more evil and more abundant with false teaching?

6. (a) Evaluate your past week and estimate how much time you spent either hearing or reading the truth of God's Word or other forms of truth in comparison to hearing or reading things of no eternal value or things you know to be false (this would include false teachers). (b) Write down anything you discovered from the evaluation of your time from the past week. (c) Did *you* take heed to what you heard this week? (d) How can you better turn your ears away from fables to more truth?

7. Looking over each of Paul's nine commands in this passage, honestly evaluate where you are weak. Bring a request to share in light of your spiritual needs in these areas.

# The Delights of a Dedicated Servant

*2 Timothy 4:6-8*

MANY of you have heard my testimony of how I came to faith in Christ. Suffice it to say, by way of introduction, that before I committed my life to the Lordship of Christ, I was enslaved to much sin. One of those heinous sins was a lack of submission to my husband. He often would say, jokingly, I am sure, "When you die, I am going to put on your tombstone, 'She did it her way!'" What an awful indictment on my life before Christ! After the Lord saved me, many things changed, and one of those was my submission to my husband. When I memorized 2 Timothy years ago, I was struck by Paul's words as he faces death, in 2 Timothy 4:7, "I have fought the good fight, I have finished the race, I have kept the faith." I thought to myself, "That is what I would like written on my tombstone when I die!" That's quite a contrast from "she did it her way!" What else do you think is on Paul's mind as he faces his impending death? Much, I'm sure, but for our task in this chapter, we will consider what Paul writes regarding the delights of being a dedicated servant. As Paul thinks over his life as a believer, he thinks as all of us should, that it has been a delight—and not a drudgery—to be a dedicated servant of Christ. He writes,

> For I am already being poured out as a drink offering, and the time of my departure is at hand. I have fought the good fight, I have finished the race, I have kept the faith. Finally, there is laid up for me the crown of righteousness, which the Lord, the righteous Judge, will give to me on that Day, and not to me only but also to all who have loved His appearing. (2 Timothy 4:6-8)

In our last chapter, we considered nine pertinent truths that we need to heed in this post-truth world in which we live. Five of those truths had to do with others, and four of them had to do with ourselves. We also considered two motivations for obeying those truths. In the verses we'll consider in this chapter, we will discover seven delights of being a dedicated servant, and they will all begin with the letter D. Let's look at the first two, in verse 6. In this verse, Paul continues on with his final writings by saying,

> For I am already being poured out as a drink offering, and the time of my departure is at hand. (2 Timothy 4:6)

The word *for* indicates to us that what follows is being written in response to and because of what Paul has just written to Timothy. Paul is saying, "Timothy, because I am getting ready to die and I am passing the baton to you, then you be watchful, endure afflictions, share the gospel, complete your ministry. I have finished my race, Timothy; you finish your race. I have fought a good fight; you fight the good fight of faith. I have kept the faith; make sure you keep the faith, and don't be like those who have defected." I understand the apostle's heart here because, as I age, I long to pass on the baton to other women who will also be faithful to teach women the truth of God's Word.

Paul goes on to write that he is *already being poured out as a drink offering*. The word *already* communicates that he is even now being poured out. Paul looked at his entire life as a sacrifice or offering to the Lord; that's what he's referring to when he says he is *being poured out*. He writes about this in Philippians 2:17-18 (LSB): "But even if I am being poured out as a drink offering upon the sacrifice and service of your faith, I rejoice and share my joy with you all. And you also, rejoice in the same way and share your joy with me." And, my friend, we also should consider our entire lives as drink offerings unto the Lord. In Luke 9:23-24 (LSB), Jesus is clear about our lives being offerings: "And He was saying to them all, 'If anyone wishes to come after Me, let him deny himself, and take up his cross daily and follow Me. For whoever wishes to save his life will lose it, but whoever loses his life for My sake, he is the one who will save it.'" And, further, He says in Luke 14:27 (LSB), "Whoever does not carry his own cross and come after Me cannot be My disciple." And, again, in Luke 14:33 (LSB), "So then, none of you can be My disciple who does not give up all his own possessions." When you and I committed our lives to the Lordship of Jesus Christ, we gave up all of our rights in order to become His slaves—and it is a delight to serve the One who saved us from death and hell! *This is the first delight of a dedicated servant that Paul recounts as he faces death, that is, denial of self.* He describes this denial of himself as him being poured out as a drink offering. My friend, we must examine whether it is a delight or a dread to us to die to ourselves to live for Him and for others? If it is not a delight to us, then some self-examination of our souls is in need. Even Jesus, the Son of God, denied Himself. He says in John 6:38 (LSB), "For I have come down from heaven, not to do My own will, but the will of Him who sent Me."

When Paul says that he is already being poured out as a drink offering, he not only is referring to the fact that his whole life has been an offering to God, but that there is coming a final offering. He refers to it as a *drink offering*, which is a reference to the drink offering mentioned in Genesis 35:14, Leviticus 23:13, and Numbers 28:14 and 24, among other places. A drink offering was not a literal drink. Rather, when one offered up a drink offering, they would pour oil and wine on the head of the lamb which they were going to sacrifice. Paul is saying that he has, throughout his life as a servant of Christ, had the oil and the wine already poured on his head. He has already been poured out as a drink offering and he is now awaiting the final blow to his head, just like the lamb who was to have its throat slit. Paul's final offering would soon be given in his beheading by Nero.

There is a second delight Paul mentions in this verse. He puts it like this: *and the time of my departure is at hand. The second delight of a dedicated servant is our departure to Heaven.* When Paul says the time is *at hand*, he means that it is present, at this instant. He knows that he is very soon leaving this world, and he calls it a departure. The Greek word *analusis*, *departure*, has two parts to it, and when those two parts are put together, they form a beautiful picture. The word means to loosen or undo, and it is used of a ship that is getting ready to undo its moorings and set sail. The idea being conveyed here is that when a believer dies, they are let loose from the confines of this world and are set free to cross the ocean into eternity. It is as though we set sail into eternity. It is much like Luke 16:22 (LSB), where Jesus is giving the parable of the rich man who dies and goes to hell and the poor man who dies and goes to Heaven. Jesus says there, "Now it happened that the poor man died and was carried away by the angels to Abraham's bosom, and the rich man also died and was buried." The beggar was carried away into eternity. It is also like what Jesus talks about in the upper room when He was encouraging His disciples; He says to them, "In My Father's house are many dwelling places; if it were not so, I would have told you; for I go to prepare a place for you. And if I go and prepare a place for you, I will come again and receive you to Myself, that where I am, there you may be also." (John 14:2-3, LSB). Jesus says He will come again and receive us into Heaven.

The word *analusis* also is used to describe the act of taking down a tent. This would be pictured in what Paul says in 2 Corinthians 5:1-8:

> For we know that if our earthly house, this tent, is destroyed, we have a building from God, a house not made with hands, eternal in the heavens. For in this we groan, earnestly desiring to be clothed with our habitation which is from heaven, if indeed, having been clothed, we shall not be found naked. For we who are in this tent groan, being burdened, not because we want to be unclothed, but further clothed, that mortality may be swallowed up by life. Now He who has prepared us for this very thing is God, who also has given us the Spirit as a guarantee. So we are always confident, knowing that while we are at home in the body we are absent from the Lord. For we walk by faith, not by sight. We are confident, yes, well pleased rather to be absent from the body and to be present with the Lord.

Peter even writes of this, in 2 Peter 1:14 (LSB), when speaking of his own death, which is soon to come: "knowing that the laying aside of my earthly dwelling is imminent, as also our Lord Jesus Christ has indicated to me." So, when we put these two concepts together, the taking down of this dwelling and setting sail into eternity, we're given a glorious picture of leaving this life to enter the next. We are taking down our earthly house, and we are setting sail to receive our heavenly house. Why should any believer fear death when we consider this glorious truth? We are not dying; we are simply departing. Death has no sting for us, and it certainly has no hold on us. Paul moves on to give three more delights of being one of God's servants, in verse 7.

> I have fought the good fight, I have finished the race, I have kept the faith. (2 Timothy 4:7)

Paul used similar terminology in 2 Timothy 2:3-5, when he wrote, "You therefore must endure hardship as a good soldier of Jesus Christ. No one engaged in warfare entangles himself with the affairs of this life, that he may please him who enlisted him as a soldier. And also if anyone competes in athletics, he is not crowned unless he competes according to the rules." Paul compared the Christian to a soldier, an athlete, and a farmer, and he uses two of those terms here in this verse. *The third delight Paul has experienced is that of being a devoted warrior.* He puts it like this: *I have fought the good fight*. In his first letter to Timothy, Paul admonished Timothy to, "Fight the good fight of faith. Take hold of the eternal life to which you were called, and you made the good confession in the presence of many witnesses." (1 Timothy 6:12, LSB). What does it mean that Paul has *fought the good fight*? Well, this statement literally reads: the grand fight I have fought. Most of us look at the Christian life as a battle that is wearisome and dreadful, but not Paul. He embraced it as the grand fight. *Fight* means to labor fervently. It is like wrestling or boxing, which is serious stuff. Paul writes in 1 Corinthians 9:26 (LSB), "Therefore I run in such a way, as not without aim; I box in such a way, as not beating the air." This is serious battle with the world, the flesh, and the devil, with false teachers, with principalities, and with powers. This fight is most certainly not for the fainthearted! And notice that Paul calls it the *good* fight. This means it is an honest or worthy contest. Paul has competed by the rules. He hasn't cheated in order to win.

*The fourth delight of being a devoted follower of Christ is that of being a disciplined runner.* Paul says *I have finished the race*. To have *finished* his race means to have accomplished or concluded it. And when Paul speaks of his *race*, he is referring to the course he's run. You know, it's easy to start things, isn't it? We start a diet; we start projects like cleaning out a closet or a drawer; we start a college course; we start an exercise program; we start saving money; we start a ladies' Bible study. We start many things in this life, but often we do not finish them. Paul started the race at salvation on the Damascus Road and he has now finished it. In 1 Corinthians 9:24-27 (LSB), Paul talks about his life being a race:

> Do you not know that those who run in a race all run, but only one receives the prize? Run in such a way that you may win. Now everyone who competes in the games exercises self-control in all things. They then do it to receive a corruptible crown, but we an incorruptible. Therefore I run in such a way, as not without aim; I box in such a way, as not beating the air; but I discipline my body and make it my slave, so that, after I have preached to others, I myself will not be disqualified.

Paul also mentions this idea in Acts 20:24 (LSB): "But I do not make my life of any account nor dear to myself, so that I may finish my course and the ministry which I received from the Lord Jesus, to testify solemnly of the gospel of the grace of God." Even our Lord finished what He started. Consider John 4:34 (LSB), "Jesus said to them, 'My food is to do the will of Him who sent Me and to finish His work.'" And one of the things Jesus said from the cross was, "It is finished" (John 19:30).

When we studied 2 Timothy 2, we considered the reality that an athlete must compete by the rules. Running the race, as believers, requires that we run according to the rules set forth in the Word of God. Now, perhaps some of you have not even begun the race; you aren't even in the game yet, so to speak. I must tell you, my friend, that it is never too late to repent of your sins and start running the race to eternal life.

*The fifth delight Paul mentions here is being diligent to keep the faith.* Paul says *I have kept the faith.* This phrase is better rendered: I have held fast to the faith. Paul has not defected from the faith, like some of the people he mentioned back in 2 Timothy 1:15 and others he will mention soon in verses 10 and 14. But also included in the meaning of keeping the faith is the idea of guarding it as sacred. Paul made sure that the faith to which he held fast was the faith that is mentioned in the Scriptures, the faith that comes by grace alone through faith alone in Christ alone. Paul did not alter the gospel to make his hearers comfortable. He made people mad, he was stoned for the faith, he went to prison for the faith, and now he's getting ready to die for the faith. Ladies, we must preach the true gospel of Christ being crucified for sinners. Our listeners will have nothing to hold on to if we give them a watered-down gospel; such a distortion of the faith will not give them a strong foundation to lay hold on.

Because Paul has run his race well, competing by the rules, there is a prize awaiting him. He mentions this prize in verse 8 as another of the delights of being a servant of Christ.

> Finally, there is laid up for me the crown of righteousness, which the Lord, the righteous Judge, will give to me on that Day, and not to me only but also to all who have loved His appearing. (2 Timothy 4:8)

It's interesting that Paul has been faithful in the past to wrestle, to fight, to run the race, to keep the faith, and because he has been a good and faithful servant, he can look forward to the future. Paul says it this way: *there is laid up for me the crown of righteousness. This is the sixth delight of a dedicated servant: they are delivered a crown.* The words *laid up for me* mean reserved for me. There is waiting for me *a crown of righteousness.* A *crown* is a symbol of honor. In the biblical world, when the Olympic Games were going on, there would be a judge or an umpire that would declare the winners and give out the crowns. The Olympic crowns were made of things like leaves, wild olives, and parsley. In 1 Corinthians 9:25, Paul writes of this very thing; he reminds us that the crowns earned by the Olympians will perish, but the crowns earned by dedicated servants of Christ will not. He says, "And everyone who competes for the prize is temperate in all things. Now they do it to obtain a perishable crown, but we for an imperishable crown." Earthly crowns are perishable, but eternal crowns are not.

The crown *of righteousness*, or, as it is better translated, the crown which is righteousness, means that this crown is a holy crown. In

James 1:12, James talks about a crown of life being given to those who love the Lord. In 1 Peter 5:4, Peter writes of a crown of glory that doesn't fade away. And in Revelation 2:10, John also mentions the crown of life. Like the earthly crowns earned by the Olympians, Paul says these crowns also come from a judge, but not an earthly judge; instead, they come from *the righteous Judge. The Lord*, who is righteous, is the *Judge* who passes out the righteous crowns. He is the One who is going to judge the living and the dead. He is the One of whom the writer to the Hebrews says, "And there is no creature hidden from His sight, but all things are uncovered and laid bare to the eyes of Him to whom we have an account to give." (Hebrews 4:13, LSB).

Paul says of this crown that it will be given to him *on that Day*. He must have *that Day* much on his mind as he writes this final letter. He mentions it in 2 Timothy 1:12: "For this reason I also suffer these things; nevertheless I am not ashamed, for I know whom I have believed and am persuaded that He is able to keep what I have committed to Him until that Day." Then again, in 2 Timothy 1:18, "The Lord grant to him that he may find mercy from the Lord in that Day—and you know very well how many ways he ministered to me at Ephesus." Also, in 2 Timothy 4:1, he writes, "I charge you therefore before God and the Lord Jesus Christ, who will judge the living and the dead at His appearing and His kingdom." This coming day of judgment would naturally be on Paul's mind because his death is just around the corner.

Notice that this crown of righteousness isn't only for the apostle Paul, as evidenced by his final words in verse 8. He says *and not to me only but also to all who have loved His appearing*. Those who run the race and have fought the good fight and have kept the faith have also looked forward to *His appearing*. They have *loved* the thought of His appearing, and it has been in their hearts throughout their pilgrimages. And the closer they get to the finish line, the more they should look forward to His appearing. They should look forward to seeing the righteous Judge! They love his appearing, and they are waiting for it with anticipatory joy, as a bride waits for her groom.

In my opinion, one of the biggest indicators of love for the Lord and genuine salvation is a longing and love for His return. I remember as a child coming out of church one evening and standing next to one of the older ladies in our church. She was looking up into the sky and said to me, "Wouldn't it be great if it were tonight?" I knew what she was referring to because my dad preached often on the Lord's return. But, rather than agreeing with her, I got weak in my knees and was terrified when she asked me that question. I knew I did not want Him to come; I had too much I wanted to do yet. But when the Lord saved me, I remember reading 1 John and coming to 1 John 4:17-18 (LSB), which says, "By this, love has been perfected with us, so that we may have confidence in the day of judgment, because as He is, so also are we in this world. There is no fear in love; but perfect love casts out fear, because fear involves punishment, and the one who fears is not perfected in love." It struck me why I had been terrified all those years ago about the Lord's return: I had not been made perfect in love.[57] I had not known the One who was coming. Those who know Him have no fear of the Day of Judgment; instead, they have boldness.

*The seventh—and best—of all the delights of a dedicated servant is our greatest prize of all—our Dear Lord!* Paul says we love *His* appearing! Why do we love our Lord's appearing? Because we get to see Him face to face! John writes of this in 1 John 3:1-3 (LSB):

> See how great a love the Father has given to us, that we would be called children of God; and we are. For this reason the world does not know us, because it did not know Him. Beloved, now we are children of God, and it has not been manifested as yet what we will be. We know that when He is manifested, we will be like Him, because we will see Him just as He is. And everyone who has this hope fixed on Him purifies himself, just as He is pure.

Job encourages us with these words, in Job 19:26 (LSB), "Even after my skin is destroyed, yet from my flesh I shall behold God."

57 For more details, see: Susan J. Heck, *With the Master Before the Mirror of God's Word* (Irvine, Three Sixteen Publishing), 316Publishing.com.

## Summary

The seven delights of a dedicated servant are: denial of self, departure to Heaven, being a devoted warrior, being a disciplined runner, being diligent to keep the faith, a delivered crown, and our Dear Lord. What is on your mind when you think of your departure from this life to the next? When you think of the delights that the Christian life brings, do you think of these seven things that Paul has mentioned?

◊ Has it been a delight to you to deny yourself and be poured out for God and for others, or do you hold tightly to your time and your schedule for your selfish desires?

◊ Is departing to Heaven a delightful thought to you, or do you fear the thought of dying?

◊ And what about being a devoted warrior? Is it a delight to you to wage war with the spiritual enemies out there? Are you fighting the good fight of faith, or have you given up the fight?

◊ Does the thought of finishing the race as a disciple bring joy to your heart, or are you thinking about bailing out of the race, finding it too difficult?

◊ In the age in which we live, in which many are departing from the faith, do you delight in being diligent to keep the faith? Does it make you more determined to draw near to God and His Word? Have you toyed with the idea of denying your faith?

◊ What about the joy of having a crown delivered to you by the righteous Judge? Does that bring delight to your heart?

◊ And, last, but not least, our Dear Lord. Are you excited beyond measure to meet Him face to face? Does it thrill your soul to think of His coming, or are you as I was before I knew Christ, terrified to think of the Lord's return and facing Him in judgment?

While we are on the subject of departing from this life: for what do you want to be remembered? What would you like to have written on your tombstone? I have fought the good fight, or I gave up the fight? I have finished the race, or I gave up on the race? I have kept the faith, or I have denied the faith? I did it my way, or I did it His way?

The morning I was writing this chapter, I learned that a woman I had poured my life into for many years was on life support in one of our local hospitals. In all the years I spent discipling her, she had never really changed, and, eventually, she was disciplined out of our church for a variety of reasons. It was a sobering time when that took place, and I immediately saw the truth of what Paul means when he says that they are given over to Satan for the destruction of their flesh (1 Corinthians 5:5). I took a break from my studies to go say my goodbyes to this woman, hoping she might hear my voice and consider Christ. She did arouse, and the friend who came with me and I made the most of the few minutes we had with her. I left that hospital room sobered because I had on my mind the joy of being loosed from my earthly tent and sailing into eternity to see Jesus. And I thought of her. Unless she repented, she did not have the joy of sailing into eternity to see Jesus. To my knowledge, she never ran the race, she did not fight the good fight, she did not finish the course. It's too late for her, but it's not too late for others. My friend, the righteous Judge will come, and now is the time to be ever so delighted with what He has called us to do as His servants. Deny yourself; be a devoted warrior, a disciplined runner, and diligent to keep the faith. Then, and only then, will you depart to Heaven and be delivered a crown by your dear Lord!

# QUESTIONS TO CONSIDER

1. (a) Read 2 Timothy 4:6-8. What is your favorite part of this passage, and why? (b) Can you honestly echo these words with the apostle Paul? (c) Why or why not?

2. Memorize 2 Timothy 4:7.

3. (a) In 2 Timothy 4:7, Paul recalls that he has finished his race. According to 1 Corinthians 9:24-27 and Hebrews 12:1-2, what things are essential when running the Christian race? (b) Which one of these things seems most essential to you, and why?

4. (a) In 2 Timothy 4:7, Paul tells Timothy that he has fought the good fight. What were some ways in which Paul fought the good fight? (Demonstrate your answers from Scripture.) (b) In what ways are you fighting the good fight of faith? (c) How can you improve your strategic plans in your spiritual battle?

5. (a) 2 Timothy is Paul's last letter before his death, and 2 Peter is Peter's last letter before his death. Read 2 Timothy 3:16-4:22 and 2 Peter 1:1-21, and write down the things you see which are similar in these chapters. (b) If you wrote a final letter before your death, what would you want to include in it, and why?

6. (a) What is essential to keeping the faith? (Again, demonstrate your answers from Scripture.) (b) How do you make sure you are keeping the faith?

7. (a) Are you running the race, fighting the battles, and keeping the faith? (b) What are your needs in these areas? (c) Put them in a form of prayer request to share with your group.

# What is Needed in the Face of Death?

*2 Timothy 4:9-13*

"IT IS better to wear out than to rust out." These words were often spoken by Henry Lyte, a pastor who lived from 1795 to 1847. Lyte struggled with tuberculosis all of his life, but it never seemed to cause his faith to waver. Toward the end of his life, it was said that Lyte would almost crawl to his pulpit to preach. His final words from the pulpit were, "It is my desire to induce you to prepare for the solemn hour which must come to all, by a timely appreciation and dependence on the death of Christ." Lyte's hymn, "Abide with Me," was written prior to that final sermon. Its first stanza reads, "Abide with me, fast falls the eventide. The darkness deepens, Lord with me abide; when other helps fail and comforts flee, help of the helpless, O abide with me!"[58] Well could the apostle Paul have echoed with Lyte, "when other helps fail and comforts flee," as Paul neared the day of his own death. The helps and comforts of people and possessions are on Paul's mind in the portion of his letter to Timothy which we will consider in this chapter. Let's look at it together.

> Be diligent to come to me quickly; for Demas has forsaken me, having loved this present world, and has departed for Thessalonica—Crescens for Galatia, Titus for Dalmatia. Only Luke is with me. Get Mark and bring him with you, for he is useful to me for ministry. And Tychicus I have sent to Ephesus. Bring the cloak that I left with Carpus at Troas when you come—and the books, especially the parchments. (2 Timothy 4:9-13)

As we look to these verses and consider the question, "What is needed in the face of death?" we will find the answer in three kinds of needs, and these will form our outline for this text. Paul will write of his

58 Kenneth W. Osbeck, "Abide With Me", *Amazing Grace: 366 Inspiring Hymn Stories for Daily Devotions* (Grand Rapids: Kregel Publications, 1990), paraphrase, 130.

*Emotional Needs* (vv 9-12), which are filled by his friends, Timothy, Luke, and Mark; his *Physical Needs* (v 13a), which are met in items like a coat; and his *Spiritual Needs* (v 13b), which are met in valuable resources like parchments and books. In our last chapter, we saw Paul recount the delights of being a dedicated servant of the Lord Jesus. Those delights include: denial of oneself, being a devoted warrior, being a disciplined runner, being diligent to keep the faith, departure to Heaven, being delivered a crown, and—best of all—our Dear Lord. As Paul nears the close of his final letter to Timothy, Paul is wrapping up his thoughts. As he awaits his trial and death there in prison, there are some needs that he has, and so he asks his spiritual son Timothy for certain things and certain people. Let's look at the first emotional need Paul communicates here: the need for people. He mentions the first person he needs, in verse 9.

## Emotional Needs *2 Timothy 4:9-12*

> Be diligent to come to me quickly; (2 Timothy 4:9)

The first emotional need Paul mentions is the need for Timothy to come and be with him. As he faces death, Paul wants to be with his spiritual son Timothy. Back in 2 Timothy 1:4, Paul began this letter to Timothy with similar words, saying that he was "greatly desiring to see you, being mindful of your tears, that I may be filled with joy." Here, in chapter four, verse 9, Paul tells Timothy to *be diligent to come to me quickly. Be diligent* means to be prompt, to make every effort. The word *quickly* means speedily or rapidly. "Hurry up and get here," we might say. Paul's departure is at hand, as we learned in our last chapter, and, more than likely, Paul would want Timothy to come so that he could provide comfort and strength to Paul. Even Jesus, the very Son of God, had emotional needs. I know some may think of Christ as a stoic robot, but even He had needs, even though He was God in the flesh. Recall that Jesus desired his closest companions to be with Him in His final hour. Mark 14:32-42 (LSB) tells us,

> Then they came to a place named Gethsemane; and He said to His disciples, "Sit here until I have prayed." And He took with Him

> Peter and James and John, and began to be very distressed and troubled. And He said to them, "My soul is deeply grieved to the point of death; remain here and keep watch." And He went a little beyond them, and fell to the ground and began to pray that if it were possible, the hour might pass from Him. And He was saying, "Abba! Father! All things are possible for You; remove this cup from Me; yet not what I will, but what You will." And He came and found them sleeping, and said to Peter, "Simon, are you sleeping? Could you not keep watch for one hour? Keep watching and praying that you may not come into temptation; the spirit is willing, but the flesh is weak." And again He went away and prayed, saying the same words. And again He came and found them sleeping, for their eyes were very heavy; and they did not know what to answer Him. And He came the third time, and said to them, "Are you still sleeping and resting? It is enough; the hour has come; behold, the Son of Man is being betrayed into the hands of sinners. Get up, let us go; behold, the one who betrays Me is at hand!"

(Just a side note, for fun: Jesus had three companions whom He desired to be with Him when He was facing death, and Paul mentions three companions in the text we're considering, as well.)

It is possible that Paul wanted to remind Timothy of his need to be faithful to pass on the baton of truth; to warn of false teachers; to not be fearful of using his gifts. No doubt, there were many things on Paul's mind that warranted his desire for Timothy to come quickly. But it is also true that, in the biblical world, when a father died, the sons would receive the body of their deceased father and were then responsible for burying it. So, it's possible that when Paul was beheaded his body was given to Timothy for a proper burial. Paul did not have any children of his own, but Timothy was his son in the faith; Philippians 2:20-22 (LSB) shows us clearly that Paul thought of Timothy as a son. There, Paul writes, "For I have no one else of kindred spirit who will genuinely be concerned about your circumstances. For they all seek after their own interests, not those of Christ Jesus. But you know of his proven worth, that he served with me in the furtherance of the gospel like a child serving his father."

There is perhaps another reason that Paul wants Timothy to come quickly, and it is found in the next verse.

> for Demas has forsaken me, having loved this present world, and has departed for Thessalonica—Crescens for Galatia, Titus for Dalmatia. (2 Timothy 4:10)

Why does Paul want Timothy to come quickly? Because, he says, only Luke is with him, which we see in verse 11, and, as Paul says, *Demas has forsaken me. Demas*, if you recall, was with Paul in his first imprisonment and actually joins in the greetings Paul sends to the Colossians. Colossians 4:14 (LSB) states, "Luke, the beloved physician, sends you his greetings, and also Demas." And, in Philemon 1:23-24 (LSB), Paul writes, "Epaphras, my fellow prisoner in Christ Jesus, greets you, as do Mark, Aristarchus, Demas, Luke, my fellow workers." So, Demas once served alongside Paul in ministry. But now Demas has *forsaken* Paul, deserted him. The reason Demas did this is that he *loved this present world*. What a contrast to loving Christ's appearing, which we saw when we looked at verse 8! People who love the world will not love Christ's appearing. People who love His appearing will not love the world. People who love the world cannot be believers. You might be thinking, "Susan, that is a bit far-fetched!" Well, not according to what God says! Listen to James 4:4 (LSB): "You adulteresses, do you not know that friendship with the world is enmity toward God? Therefore, whoever wishes to be a friend of the world sets himself as an enemy of God." Or, perhaps a more familiar passage, 1 John 2:15-17 (LSB):

> Do not love the world nor the things in the world. If anyone loves the world, the love of the Father is not in him. For all that is in the world, the lust of the flesh and the lust of the eyes and the boastful pride of life, is not from the Father, but is from the world. And the world is passing away, and also its lusts, but the one who does the will of God abides forever.

There isn't a lot of wiggle room in these passages (or numerous others!), even though some of you might find yourself wiggling as you read them! These clear statements beg us to ponder the unmistakable reality that loving the world means we do not belong to God—it is an impossibility!

Now, some have tried to soften this and say that Demas forsook only Paul and that Demas actually left for Thessalonica for an easier ministry or something; some even assert that it was Demas' hometown. But even if you want to take that weak view, you still have to deal with passages like Matthew 25:31-46 (LSB):

> But when the Son of Man comes in His glory, and all the angels with Him, then He will sit on His glorious throne. And all the nations will be gathered before Him; and He will separate them from one another, as the shepherd separates the sheep from the goats; and He will put the sheep on His right, and the goats on the left.
>
> Then the King will say to those on His right, "Come, you who are blessed of My Father, inherit the kingdom, which has been prepared for you from the foundation of the world. For I was hungry, and you gave Me something to eat; I was thirsty, and you gave Me something to drink; I was a stranger, and you invited Me in; naked, and you clothed Me; I was sick, and you visited Me; I was in prison, and you came to Me." Then the righteous will answer Him, saying, "Lord, when did we see You hungry, and feed You, or thirsty, and give You something to drink? And when did we see You a stranger, and invite You in, or naked, and clothe You? And when did we see You sick, or in prison, and come to You?" And the King will answer and say to them, "Truly I say to you, to the extent that you did it to one of these brothers of Mine, even the least of them, you did it to Me."
>
> Then He will also say to those on His left, "Depart from Me, accursed ones, into the eternal fire which has been prepared for the devil and his angels; for I was hungry, and you gave Me nothing to eat; I was thirsty, and you gave Me nothing to drink; I was a stranger, and you did not invite Me in; naked, and you did not clothe Me; sick, and in prison, and you did not visit Me." Then they themselves also will answer, saying, "Lord, when did we see You hungry, or thirsty, or a stranger, or naked, or sick, or in prison, and did not take care of You?" Then He will answer them, saying, "Truly I say to you, to the

> extent that you did not do it to one of the least of these, you did not do it to Me." And these will go away into eternal punishment, but the righteous into eternal life.

Even here, Jesus makes it clear that those who go to hell are those who do not live in active concern for the needs of others, and Jesus specifically points out the need to visit those in prison. Paul is in prison, close to death, and Demas has chosen to leave Paul rather than visit him. We also have to deal with passages like 1 John 3:16-17 (LSB), which states, "By this we have known love, that He laid down His life for us; and we ought to lay down our lives for the brothers. But whoever has the world's goods, and sees his brother in need and closes his heart against him, how does the love of God abide in him?" In other words, the love of God does not abide in a person when he is calloused toward the needs of his brother. Paul was in need and Demas shut up his heart to Paul, and John says very plainly that the love of God cannot dwell in such a person. The cross and its demands were too much for Demas and the world and its temptations overcame him. Demas departed to Thessalonica, but Paul has just reminded us in verse 6 that he is departing to glory.

Paul goes on to mention that *Crescens* is departing *for Galatia*, and *Titus for Dalmatia*. Some believe that Crescens departed in the same way that Demas did, deserting Paul as he left for Galatia. But we don't know that to be a fact. Also, that would not make sense because Paul mentions Titus next, who left for Dalmatia. We know that Titus was Paul's other spiritual son and he was a faithful man (Titus 1:4). Both Crescens and Titus must have been there to see Paul in prison but then needed to leave for Galatia and Dalmatia, more than likely, to do ministry. And there are two more men that Paul mentions in verse 11 who are important to him in terms of his emotional needs.

> Only Luke is with me. Get Mark and bring him with you, for he is useful to me for ministry. (2 Timothy 4:11)

Paul says *only Luke is with me.* In contrast to Demas, who forsook Paul, and the others who had gone on to serve in other places, we have *Luke*. He is the *only* one with Paul at this time. Perhaps you're wondering why Luke is there? As you might recall, Luke is a doctor, and so perhaps he is there to help Paul with any physical problems he might have. No doubt, with all of Paul's sufferings and beatings, especially the stoning that left him half-dead, Paul would be weak and worn. His body was, more than likely, abounding with the effects of wounds and bruises and injuries, not to mention just being plain ole sore! I haven't been through physical sufferings quite like Paul's, but I have had injuries to my body and there are times when my body decides to remind me of them!

We know that Luke was a physician, but we also know that he wrote the Gospel of Luke and the book of Acts. Paul mentions Luke in Colossians 4:14 (LSB): "Luke, the beloved physician, sends you his greetings, and also Demas." Paul also mentions Luke in Philemon 1:23-24 (LSB): "Epaphras, my fellow prisoner in Christ Jesus, greets you, as do Mark, Aristarchus, Demas, Luke, my fellow workers." The first-person accounts in Acts, as well as the times he is mentioned in Paul's epistles, tell us that Luke was with Paul often on his missionary journeys, and here we find Luke with Paul in his final imprisonment as he awaited his death.

Paul also mentions a third man he needs. Paul says *get Mark and bring him with you, for he is useful to me for ministry.* Now, it might seem strange that Paul asks Timothy, on his way to come to see Paul, to pick up Mark and bring him along. The reason we might think this odd is because of what is mentioned in Acts 15:36-41 (LSB).

> Now after some days Paul said to Barnabas, "Let us return and visit the brothers in every city in which we proclaimed the word of the Lord, and see how they are." And Barnabas wanted to take John, called Mark, along with them also. But Paul kept insisting that they should not take him along who had deserted them in Pamphylia and had not gone with them to the work. And there was such a sharp disagreement that they separated from one another, and Barnabas took Mark with him and sailed away to Cyprus. But Paul chose Silas and left, being committed by the brothers to the

> grace of the Lord. And he was traveling through Syria and Cilicia, strengthening the churches.

According to this passage, Paul and Mark had a parting of the ways, but now Paul wants Timothy to pick Mark up and bring him to visit Paul in prison because, as Paul says of Mark here, *he is useful to me for ministry.* The one Paul said, in Acts 15, did not do the work of the ministry in Pamphylia is the one Paul now wants to come do that work. I do appreciate knowing this about Paul and Mark because, as someone who works in women's ministry, I have found that caution with some is better than casualty. Paul was wise to wait. Mark had obviously grown in his walk with the Lord, so much so that Paul is now in need of Mark. What an encouragement this is for all of us, not only for ourselves and our own spiritual growth, but also for those we look at now and wonder whether they will ever amount to any use for the Lord. We sometimes forget what Paul wrote to the church at Philippi, in Philippians 1:6 (LSB), "For I am confident of this very thing, that He who began a good work in you will perfect it until the day of Christ Jesus." You and I are not now what we were, and we are not now what we will be! Praise God for His promise and His work in us! Mark had changed, and Paul needed him.

Paul now says of Mark that *he is useful*, which means that he is profitable. In fact, it is the same word that was used back in 2:21, which referred to being fit for the Master's use. The one who was once unprofitable and un-useful, back in Acts 15, is now profitable and useful. Timothy would have known of the dissension between Paul and Mark, so these words from Paul would help Timothy to receive Mark and to bring him along with confidence. Without Paul's commendation of Mark, Timothy might have been hesitant to pick Mark up and might have thought Paul to be delusional or something. Why Paul needed Mark at this time we do not know. Perhaps it was to confirm Paul's approval of Mark's ministry or to encourage him to keep on in his ministry. Perhaps Paul wanted to affirm his love for Mark. We really are not told why. But Paul goes on to write in verse 12,

> And Tychicus I have sent to Ephesus. (2 Timothy 4:12)

Who is *Tychicus*, and why was he *sent* by Paul *to Ephesus*? Tychicus was a traveling companion of Paul, and he must have been a great blessing because Paul mentions him in Ephesians 6:21-22 (LSB), and says, "But that you also may know about all my affairs, how I am doing, Tychicus, the beloved brother and faithful servant in the Lord, will make everything known to you. I have sent him to you for this very purpose, so that you may know our circumstances, and that he may encourage your hearts." So, Tychicus was a beloved and faithful brother who ministered to and who comforted others. When Paul says that he sent Tychicus to Ephesus, we are not told the exact reason why Tychicus was sent, but it was probably to take this letter to the church there.

We have considered Paul's emotional needs for friends Timothy, Luke, and Mark. Paul now mentions some other needs he has: physical and spiritual. Let's look at verse 13, as we draw this chapter to a close.

## Physical Needs *2 Timothy 4:13*

> Bring the cloak that I left with Carpus at Troas when you come (2 Timothy 4:13a)

The physical need Paul mentions here is the cloak that he left with a guy named Carpus in Troas. A *cloak* would be a mantle that was used as an outer garment. This was a type of coat that was equipped with a hood and would be used for rainy or cold weather. There are some scholars who believe this cloak was more like a satchel, called a cloak bag, that one would use to carry books; it would be similar to what is known today as a backpack. I wouldn't split hairs over which of these Paul is referring to, as this would be yet another one of those issues you would not want to get in an argument about. Personally, I think Paul is referring to a coat because he says to Timothy, in verse 21, to do his best to get to Paul before winter; it seems Paul would need a coat for the coming cold weather. But, there are some who argue (hopefully, not literally) that the cloak here is a satchel because Paul mentions books in his sentence, as well. Either interpretation is possible.

Paul does mention, however, that he left this cloak *with Carpas in Troas*. To understand how this may have happened, let's read Acts 16:1-11 (LSB).

> Now Paul also arrived at Derbe and at Lystra. And behold, a disciple was there, named Timothy, the son of a Jewish woman who was a believer, but his father was a Greek, and he was well spoken of by the brothers who were in Lystra and Iconium. Paul wanted this man to go with him, and he took him and circumcised him because of the Jews who were in those parts, for they all knew that his father was a Greek. Now while they were passing through the cities, they were delivering the decrees which had been decided upon by the apostles and elders who were in Jerusalem, for them to keep. So the churches were being strengthened in the faith, and were abounding in number daily.
>
> And they passed through the Phrygian and Galatian region, having been forbidden by the Holy Spirit to speak the word in Asia; and after they came to Mysia, they were trying to go into Bithynia, and the Spirit of Jesus did not permit them; and passing by Mysia, they came down to Troas. And a vision appeared to Paul in the night: a man of Macedonia was standing and appealing to him, and saying, "Come over to Macedonia and help us." And when he had seen the vision, immediately we sought to go into Macedonia, concluding that God had called us to proclaim the gospel to them.
>
> So setting sail from Troas, we ran a straight course to Samothrace, and on the day following to Neapolis

*Carpus* was probably the man with whom Paul was staying while he was in *Troas*. As you can see from this passage in Acts, Paul received a vision in the night and was strongly urged to go to Macedonia to help. Luke says here in Acts that they immediately left Troas and sailed to Samothrace. It was midnight when Paul received this vision, and the text says that they left immediately. Being the selfless guy that he was, Paul likely didn't want to wake Carpus so he could get his coat. Carpus isn't mentioned anywhere else in Scripture, but now Paul is asking Timothy to not only get Mark on his way to be with Paul, but also to pick up Paul's coat from Carpus as well.

## Spiritual Needs *2 Timothy 4:13*

—and the books, especially the parchments. (2 Timothy 4:13b)

Paul also has some spiritual needs. He writes to Timothy to bring *the books, especially the parchments.* In the biblical world, *books* were made out of the inner bark of trees. We don't know what kinds of books these were, but perhaps some of them were books that Paul had written or books he especially enjoyed. We all have our favorite books, for sure. But Paul also says *especially the parchments. Parchments* were different from books in that they were fashioned out of paper made from sheepskin. The parchments would have been the most important to Paul, as evidenced by Paul's use of the word *especially,* which means chiefly. These were the most important to him. More than likely, these parchments would have been parts of the Old Testament and perhaps even some of the New Testament letters. Paul did not have a cell phone Bible app, and most people were quite fortunate to have access to any portion of Scripture. Copies of Scripture were rare and expensive. Paul was hungry spiritually to have his books and to have God's Word. One man says of this, "One can only guess what rolls the old preacher longs to have with him, probably copies of the Old Testament books, possibly copies of his own letters, and other books used and loved. The old preacher can be happy with his books."[59] It's likely that when Paul passed to glory, these beloved books and parchments were passed on to Timothy so that he could use them and then someday pass them on to others.

## Summary

What did Paul need in the face of death? He had emotional needs that were fulfilled in his good friends, Timothy, Luke, and Mark. It's encouraging that these men weren't all the same. Timothy was a spiritual son to Paul, someone Paul poured his life into. Paul needed Timothy. Luke was a traveling companion as well as a physician. Paul needed Luke. And Mark, well, he was formerly not useful, but now is

---

59 A. T. Robertson, *Word Pictures*, Biblesoft.

useful. Paul needed Mark. All three of these men were Paul's spiritual brothers. Paul wanted godly people with him at the time of his death. In your final hour, whom would you desire to be with you to meet your emotional needs, and why?

Paul also had a physical need: a coat. Now, ladies, this is an actual, physical need. I remember hearing a missionary say once that all we really need is a bowl, a spoon, and a Bible. Often, we allow our wants to be redefined as needs. What physical needs might you desire to have filled if you were facing death? One thing is for sure: if we need it, God will provide it, because He has promised to supply all of our needs. It's likely that we will not know what those needs are until that time comes, and some of us may not even have the opportunity to ask for anything because we may be ushered into eternity in a flash.

Lastly, and perhaps most importantly, Paul had spiritual needs as he faced death: books and parchments. What a wonderful example for all of us even in the face of death! Paul isn't going to waste precious time, even in prison. We are never without the need to study the most important book, God's Holy Word. Didn't Paul just write that we are to preach the Word, both when it's convenient and when it's not (2 Timothy 4:2)?! I'm afraid that some believers would wonder why they'd even need the Word at the time they're getting ready to meet the Author of the Word. But this was not Paul's heart—he was going to read and study all the way into Heaven. What spiritual need do you think you would have if you were facing your final days? I hear often of people who want the Word read to them or Christian music played or sung. What a wonderful spiritual blessing! Especially in comparison to some who would rather binge watch their favorite show or eat their favorite meal. Paul wanted to learn more about his favorite Person, his Dear Lord, the One he was getting ready to meet.

Just as Paul could echo in the face of his death the first stanza of the hymn, "Abide with Me," he could also echo the last two stanzas.

> I need Thy presence every passing hour:
> What but Thy grace can foil the tempter's power?

Who like Thyself my guide and stay can be?
Through cloud and sunshine, oh, abide with me.

I fear no foe, with Thee at hand to bless:
Ills have no weight, and tears no bitterness:
Where is death's sting? Where, grave, thy victory?
I triumph still, if Thou abide with me.[60]

60 Henry Francis Lyte, "Abide with Me", Public Domain, 1847.

# QUESTIONS TO CONSIDER

1. Read 2 Timothy 4:9-13. (a) Who is with Paul at this time? (b) Who else does Paul want to come to him? (c) Why do you think Paul desires to have these individuals come at this time? (d) If you were in prison and facing death for the gospel's sake, who would you want to come, and why?

2. Memorize 2 Timothy 4:10.

3. (a) What things does Paul want brought to him, according to 2 Timothy 4:13? (b) Why do you think Paul wants these things at this time? (c) Again, if you were in prison and facing death for the gospel's sake, what things would you want brought to you, and why?

4. (a) Paul writes that Demas forsook him because he loved the present world. What might have been some of the "worldly things" that caused Demas to leave the Christian faith, according to Luke 9:57-62; 14:16-27; 16:13; 1 Timothy 6:10; 1 John 2:15-16. (b) According to 1 John 2:15-16 and 1 John 5:4-5, is it possible to love the world and be a believer?

5. (a) What do you learn about Tychicus from Acts 20:1-6; Ephesians 6:21-22; Colossians 4:7-9; Titus 3:12? (b) What contrast do you observe between Tychicus and Demas?

6. (a) Looking over your answers from question 4, would you say that you are a lover of the world or a lover of God? (b) According to Romans 12:1-2, how can believers fight against the pull of the world?

7. (a) In what ways can we as believers be an encouragement to those who are aging and/or dying?

8. (a) What has God taught you through this chapter? (b) What changes need to be made in your life? Please bring a prayer request to share with your group.

# A Godly Wish and a Godly Warning Regarding Wicked Men

*2 Timothy 4:14-15*

THERE have been certain occasions in my life when either myself or close family members have had evil things done to them by wicked people. One of my first recollections is when my daughter was threatened by a young man in the Christian school she was attending. She had reported his drug use to the principal of their school, and the young man went on to write a song about how he was going to kill her. I remember pleading with my husband to do something, and he responded that the Lord would take care of it and we would wait upon Him. There also have been numerous times when my husband was threatened by those in our church whom he had either confronted over their sin or with whom he had followed the steps of church discipline set forth in Matthew 18. There were also occasions in which evil people involved themselves in slandering his good name. I can recall, in almost every instance, that Doug would say the same thing to me: "Susan we will not defend ourselves. We will not take vengeance. We will wait upon the Lord and trust Him." Now, I admit to you that some of those times I wasn't so thrilled about waiting on the Lord to see what would happen. I certainly did not want my daughter murdered, and I did not like my husband's life being threatened or his good name being tarnished either. But my husband was right; we are not to take vengeance on those who do us evil.

The apostle Paul had many enemies, and in the text we'll study in this chapter, he mentions one of the many who did evil toward him. What was Paul's wish and what was his warning regarding this man? Let's read what Paul says in these two verses, which will, Lord willing, aid us in determining what we are to do when others attempt to harm us in some way.

> Alexander the coppersmith did me much harm. May the Lord repay

> him according to his works. You also must beware of him, for he has greatly resisted our words. (2 Timothy 4:14-15)

Our outline for these verses will include the following: *What Did this Man Do to Paul?* (vv 14a, 15b); *What Is Paul's Wish for this Man?* (v 14b); and *What Is Paul's Warning about this Man?* (v 15a). In our last chapter, we considered what Paul needed in the face of death. We learned that Paul had emotional needs, which were met by his three friends, Timothy, Luke, and Mark. He also had a physical need for a coat. And, lastly, he had spiritual needs, which were met in the books and the parchments he requested of Timothy, likely spiritual books and portions of the Scriptures. Paul now turns his focus to another need, this time the need to tell Timothy about a dangerous man, Alexander. This man was on Paul's mind as he faced death. He is concerned for Timothy because he knows that evil men will, no doubt, seek to devour this young man and his ministry. Timothy's mentor is soon going to glory and it will be up to Timothy to carry the baton of truth and to wage war against not only his own sin but also those who would like to deter him from ministry. Let's take a look at this man, Alexander, and the first thing he did to Paul.

## What Did this Man Do to Paul? *2 Timothy 4:14-15*

> Alexander the coppersmith did me much harm. (2 Timothy 4:14a)

Paul mentions this man by name. I think this is an important fact to bring out because, in our day, we allow the fear of man to keep us from naming dangerous people who are lurking behind the scenes in an effort to destroy the church and the lives of godly men and women. We are fearful to name false teachers, but we should not be. There is ample precedent in Scripture for doing so. Paul names people in his epistles. Jesus called out the false teachers by name in His day. We must get over our fears and realize that this is done to protect both the flock and the name of our Lord. The particular man Paul names here is *Alexander*. Alexander was a common name during Paul's time, but we know from this verse that this particular Alexander was a *coppersmith*, which would refer to someone who works with any type of metal. It is very possible that this is the man mentioned in Acts 19, especially when we consider his trade. In Acts 19:21-41 (LSB), we read,

> Now after these things were finished, Paul purposed in the Spirit to go to Jerusalem after he had passed through Macedonia and Achaia, saying, "After I have been there, I must also see Rome." And having sent into Macedonia two of those who ministered to him, Timothy and Erastus, he himself stayed in Asia for a while. Now about that time there occurred no small disturbance concerning the Way. For a man named Demetrius, a silversmith, who made silver shrines of Artemis, was bringing no little business to the craftsmen; these he gathered together with the workers of similar trades, and said, "Men, you know that our prosperity is from this business. And you see and hear that not only in Ephesus, but in almost all of Asia, this Paul has persuaded and turned away a considerable crowd, saying that things made with hands are not gods. And not only is there danger that this trade of ours fall into disrepute, but also that the temple of the great goddess Artemis be considered as worthless and that she, whom all of Asia and the world worship, is even about to be brought down from her majesty."
>
> When they heard this and were filled with rage, they began crying out, saying, "Great is Artemis of the Ephesians!" And the city was filled with the confusion, and they rushed with one accord into the theater, dragging along Gaius and Aristarchus, Paul's traveling companions from Macedonia. And when Paul wanted to go into the assembly, the disciples would not let him. Also some of the Asiarchs who were friends of his sent to him and repeatedly urged him not to venture into the theater. So then, some were shouting one thing and some another, for the meeting was in confusion and the majority did not know for what reason they had come together. And some of the crowd concluded it was Alexander, since the Jews had put him forward; and having motioned with his hand, Alexander was intending to make a defense to the assembly. But when they recognized that he was a Jew, a single cry arose from them all as they shouted for about two hours, "Great is Artemis of the Ephesians!" Now after calming the crowd, the city clerk said, "Men of Ephesus, what man is there after all who does not know that the city of the Ephesians is guardian of the temple of the great Artemis and of the image which fell down from heaven? So, since

> these are undeniable facts, you ought to keep calm and to do nothing rash. For you have brought these men here who are neither robbers of temples nor blasphemers of our goddess. So then, if Demetrius and the craftsmen who are with him have a complaint against anyone, the courts are in session and proconsuls are available; let them bring charges against one another. But if you want anything beyond this, it shall be settled in the lawful meeting. For indeed we are in danger of being accused of a riot in connection with today's events, since there is no cause for which we can give as an account for this disorderly gathering." After saying this he dismissed the meeting.

When Paul went to Ephesus, he was grieved at the idolatry he encountered, and, of course, he spoke out against it. But the craftsmen, whose trade was the making of idols like that of Diana, were upset because their very livelihood appeared to be put in jeopardy by Paul's preaching. Because of this, the city was in an uproar and in confusion, and Alexander was put forth to say something about this mess. He was likely chosen because he had some skill in public speaking and may even have been one of their religious leaders. He never got a chance to speak, though, so we are not sure what he would have said, other than that he was the spokesman called upon to speak against Paul and his companions. More than likely, Alexander, being a Jew himself, would have defended the Jews' uproar as they were known by the Romans to cause religious disturbances. So, if this is the same Alexander mentioned in 2 Timothy, it may be that the harm Paul is referring to was that Alexander spoke out against Paul or failed to come to his defense. We do not know what other interactions Paul may have had with this Alexander after this incident.

There is also the possibility that this Alexander is also the man mentioned in Paul's first letter to Timothy. Consider what Paul says in 1 Timothy 1:18-20 (LSB):

> This command I entrust to you, Timothy, my child, in accordance with the prophecies previously made concerning you, that by them you may fight the good fight, keeping faith and a good conscience, which some, having rejected, suffered shipwreck in regard to their

> faith. Among these are Hymenaeus and Alexander, whom I have handed over to Satan, so that they will be taught not to blaspheme.

This passage, of course, is more concerning because the harm Alexander did here, along with Hymenaeus, was to reject the faith. Paul delivered Alexander over to Satan so that Alexander would learn not to blaspheme. While this may sound extreme to us, this is really just part of the church discipline process. Paul mentions this very thing in 1 Corinthians 5:5 when speaking of a man who was committing incest. He tells the church at Corinth, "Deliver such a one to Satan for the destruction of the flesh, that his spirit may be saved in the day of the Lord Jesus." And, I must say that the destruction of the flesh is a real thing; I have personally witnessed it with those I have known who have been put out of the church. I recall one person who was disciplined who the next day was never able to walk again. I recall people who have died mysteriously after being church disciplined and some who have gotten dreadful illnesses. This is not something we should think will not happen. It does happen, and it should sober each of us. Acts 5 tells us of Ananias and Sapphira, husband and wife, who agreed together to lie to Peter and to the Holy Spirit; both were struck dead, their bodies taken immediately out of the church and buried.

Now, if this Alexander in 1 Timothy is the same Alexander mentioned in 2 Timothy, some believe that he may have repented of his sins, been restored to the church, but then gone back to his sin. This would be like what Peter says, in 2 Peter 2:20-22 (LSB),

> For if they are overcome, having both escaped the defilements of the world by the knowledge of the Lord and Savior Jesus Christ and having again been entangled in them, then the last state has become worse for them than the first. For it would be better for them not to have known the way of righteousness, than having known it, to turn away from the holy commandment handed on to them. The message of the true proverb has happened to them, "A dog returns to its own vomit," and, "A sow, after washing, returns to wallowing in the mire."

The latter end of that man is worse than the beginning.

Some scholars believe that after Alexander's church discipline, mentioned in 1 Timothy, Alexander had a vendetta against Paul and was out to ruin him. This could be true, as well, and it certainly is a possibility to consider. Alexander may have turned Paul in to the Roman authorities, or may have been a witness against Paul at his trial. We cannot be dogmatic about any of these possibilities, but we do know that Alexander did Paul *much harm*. This would mean that Alexander did an abundance of evil to Paul. So, this is the first thing Alexander did to Paul—he harmed him.

## What Is Paul's Wish for this Man? *2 Timothy 4:14*

> May the Lord repay him according to his works. (2 Timothy 4:14b)

What is Paul's wish for Alexander? Hang him high!? Off with his head!? Gouge out his eyes!? None of these things are on Paul's mind, though that would have been the thing to do in Paul's day—and in our day too! In the Greco-Roman world in which Paul lived, it was normal to retaliate for personal insults or injuries. In fact, it was considered a virtue to do so. But Paul was not taken up with culture and what culture dictated he should do. Paul was taken up with his God and what He would have Paul do. Paul's wish was: *may the Lord repay him according to his works*. Paul was content to let the Lord deal with Alexander. Even in verse 16, Paul writes, "At my first defense no one stood with me, but all forsook me. May it not be charged against them." Paul knew very well that what he wrote to the church at Rome was a principle for all of God's children. Romans 12:17-21 (LSB) clearly tells us,

> Never paying back evil for evil to anyone, respecting what is good in the sight of all men, if possible, so far as it depends on you, being at peace with all men, never taking your own revenge, beloved—instead leave room for the wrath of God. For it is written, "Vengeance is Mine, I will repay," says the Lord. "But if your enemy is hungry, feed him, and if he is thirsty, give him a drink; for in so doing you will heap burning coals on his head." Do not be overcome by evil, but overcome evil with good.

There are times when we need to leave evil people in the hands of our Lord. I am not saying that we do not confront when there is an offense and we don't try to make peace. I have no doubt, knowing what I do about the apostle Paul, that he did confront Alexander when Alexander resisted his words. But as we all well know, not all will receive our admonitions, and sometimes doing the right thing means we will incur more persecution. This is the probable case here. Paul may have feared that Alexander would go on to do even worse evil to his son in the faith, Timothy. That may very well be part of Paul's reasoning as he goes on to give Timothy a warning about Alexander, in verse 15.

## What Is Paul's Warning about this Man? *2 Timothy 4:15*

> You also must beware of him, (2 Timothy 4:15a)

What is Paul's warning about Alexander? Beware of him, Timothy. Paul says *you also must beware of him. You*, along with myself and others, must *beware of him*. This is a necessity, not an option. This is a dangerous man, Timothy. *Beware* means to be on watch, to guard yourself. Where Alexander is at this time, we do not know, but, evidently, Paul knew that Alexander was around. More than likely, as it would for so many others, the news of Paul's coming death would soon reach Alexander, and he may already even be aware of Timothy's timidity and fear and like nothing more than to try to influence Timothy. This would certainly be one way Alexander could do Paul more harm even after his death. At this point in Timothy's ministry, Timothy is not as strong as Paul, and Paul knew that evil men like Alexander like to prey on unsuspecting victims. So Paul tells Timothy in this verse to beware of Alexander.

In what ways could Timothy be ready spiritually to deal with Alexander and others like him? Thankfully, Timothy has already been given some instructions on how to arm himself against evil and false men right here in this last letter from his spiritual father. From the beginning of 2 Timothy, Paul has instructed Timothy in these things. He wrote in, 2 Timothy 1:8, to not be ashamed of the testimony of the Lord. It's as though Paul has said to Timothy, "Timothy, when Alexander comes to harm you, be brave regarding your faith in Christ." Paul has also admonished Timothy, in 2 Timothy 1:12 to be convinced of his commitment: "Remember, Timothy, when confronted by Alexander, remember your commitment to Christ. You belong to Him alone! Also, Timothy, hold fast to sound teaching." Paul says, in 2 Timothy 1:13, "Don't listen to Alexander; remember, he made a shipwreck of his faith. You know the truth, hold tight to it." Paul also commanded Timothy, in 2 Timothy 2:1, to "be strong in the grace that it is Christ Jesus" In 2 Timothy 2:2, "Timothy, don't go back to being fearful and timid when Alexander and men like him come against you. And, by all means, start discipling other men so that they, in the future, will be able to disciple other faithful men to be strong." In 2 Timothy 2:3, "There will always be Alexanders lurking, Timothy. Be strong in Christ by committing yourself to disciple faithful men. Also, remember, Timothy, when you're tempted by Alexander, that you must endure hardship like a good soldier." This Christian life is not one of peaches and cream. In 2 Timothy 2:9, "When Alexander or men like him intimidate you, remember that the Word is not bound. You speak truth to these men and God will use his Word, Timothy. God is not frustrated about the Alexander's who are out there." In 2 Timothy 2:10, "Also, my son, endure to the end for the elect's sake. Don't be like Alexander who left the faith." In 2 Timothy 2:12, "Beware of him, Timothy, and do not forget that if you deny the Lord, the Lord will deny you." In 2 Timothy 2:14, "Timothy, often I have warned you in this letter to not get involved in foolish arguments and striving about unprofitable words. Alexander and his companions will want to do that. Don't do it!" In 2 Timothy 2:15, "My son, I have admonished you to study the Word to show yourself approved. There are men out there like Alexander who know the Scriptures; they have a form of godliness but deny its power. You, my son, study the Scriptures; hide them in your heart." In 2 Timothy 2:19-21, "I have made it clear that there are vessels in the church made of wood and clay and they are not to be in the church. Depart from them, Timothy. Alexander is one of them." In 2 Timothy 2:22, "Alexander may lure you into his camp and promise you power or prestige. Timothy, flee these youthful lusts!" Also in 2 Timothy 2:22, "You pursue the right things; you be faithful, love others, and follow peace." In 2 Timothy 2:25, "Don't let Alexander persuade you in the things of unrighteousness. Having said these things, if his heart is open, Timothy, correct Alexander's error with humility and perhaps he will repent." In 2 Timothy 3:8, "I have warned you of Jannes and Jambres, who resisted Moses, and Alexander has resisted me. Beware, my son." In 2 Timothy 3:12, "You have seen my sufferings for doing the right thing. Remember that you too will suffer persecution for doing the right thing. Do the right thing with Alexander." In 2 Timothy 4:5, "Finally, my son, be watchful, endure afflictions, do evangelism, fulfill your ministry. Don't let men like Alexander deter you from what God has gifted and called you to do."

I bring these points out from 2 Timothy because, often, when facing difficult people, we run everywhere but to the Word. God has given us everything we need for life and godliness in His Word, which is infallible and sufficient and authoritative. The Word is replete with helps on what to do with difficult people.

I would also encourage you to remember, when facing difficult people, that God is sovereign over every person, even the difficult ones. He has a plan that we do not always understand. Our responsibility is to trust Him and do the right thing. One of my favorite verses in the Word of God is 1 Peter 2:23, which speaks of our Lord's response to those who did Him harm. Peter writes, "Who, when He was reviled, did not revile in return; when He suffered, He did not threaten, but committed Himself to Him who judges righteously."

## What Did this Man Do to Paul? *2 Timothy 4:14, 15*

> for he has greatly resisted our words. (2 Timothy 4:15b)

Paul finishes writing about Alexander by listing the second harm he did: *he has greatly resisted our words. Greatly* means mega, so this wasn't just a small resistance; it was a great resistance to the words of Paul. *Resisted* means to stand against, to oppose. The *words* here would be the words of our faith; more than likely, it would refer to the public preaching of the Word, which was done by Paul. But it also could include Alexander standing against Paul as a witness at his trial. It is like those two men we saw back in 2 Timothy 3:8 (KJV), where Paul writes, "Now as Jannes and Jambres withstood Moses, so do these also resist the truth: men of corrupt minds, reprobate concerning the faith." When someone resists our words, if those words are God's words, then we must remember that it is not us they are resisting, but it is God they are resisting. Stephen makes this clear after his sermon which led to his death by stoning; he says, in Acts 7:51 (LSB), "You men—stiff-necked and uncircumcised in heart and ears—are always resisting the Holy Spirit. As your fathers did, so do you."

## Summary

What did this man, Alexander, do to Paul? He did much harm to Paul and greatly resisted Paul's words. Is there someone in your life who is trying to harm your reputation? Is there someone who is resistant to the truth that you are endeavoring to share with them from God's Word? Do not be discouraged, but take courage that the Lord knows and He promises that all will work together for your good. Take heart that what others mean for evil, God means for good. Remember that you have some wonderful resources when dealing with those who resist you: you have the Lord, you have His Word, you have full access to His throne of grace to find help in your time of need. You also have the body of Christ, many of whom have gone through the same sufferings you have gone through, which can be a source of great consolation to you.

What was Paul's wish for Alexander? May the Lord repay him according to his works. Do you desire to take vengeance on those who have hurt you or who have hurt those you love? Do you pray the imprecatory Psalms in hopes that God will "give them their due"? (These are Psalms that invoke judgment or curses on one's enemies.) Leave them in the hands of the Lord, dear one. Let the Lord repay them according to their deeds. And don't harbor resentment and bitterness in your heart—that will destroy you and those around you. Leave those who have harmed you to the Lord. I have lived long enough to see this flesh out, and it is a fearful thing to fall into the hands of a living

God. God has a way of dealing with evil men and women in this life, and it is sobering, to say the least. Some will not receive their just punishment until the judgment seat of Christ, after which all the wicked will be cast into the lake of fire. King David pens it, oh, so well, when recounting the evil done to him by Ahithophel. David writes these encouraging words, in Psalm 55:22-23 (LSB), "Cast your burden upon Yahweh and He will sustain you; He will never allow the righteous to be shaken. But You, O God, will bring them down to the pit of corruption; men of bloodshed and deceit will not live out half their days. But I will trust in You."

What was Paul's warning regarding Alexander? Beware of him. Are you fearful of warning others of dangerous men or women who are resisting the truth of God's Word? While it is true that we should not be going around blabbing about all the evil of everyone who has ever harmed us, we are to name those who are endeavoring to harm the truth of God's Word. Who knows? In our faithfulness to do so, we might save someone from the harm done by those who are intent on deceiving others or maligning the name of Christ.

For some of you, the idea of anyone resisting the truth of God's Word or the thought of anyone wanting to harm you because you are a Christian may be a foreign thought. May I remind you of what Paul has already written: that all who desire to live godly lives will suffer persecution (2 Timothy 3:12)? I would like to leave you with a poem from Amy Carmichael that should stir each of us. Miss Carmichael served as a missionary in India for 55 years—without a furlough. She endured suffering, persecution, and numerous enemies while endeavoring to help young girls who were unwanted and given to the temple to serve as temple prostitutes. Miss Carmichael's most often told story is of a girl named Preena, who one day ran away from the temple and arrived at Miss Carmichael's front door. She knew she could not send this little girl back; she'd be beaten, even killed, if she were returned, and Miss Carmichael could have been charged with kidnapping and thrown into prison. But it was a chance she was willing to take. In the many years she was in India, Amy Carmichael took in hundreds of unwanted children. She became known as "Amma," or mother, to them. While she was serving in India, Miss Carmichael received a letter from a young lady who was considering life as a missionary; she asked, "What is missionary life like?" Miss Carmichael wrote back, saying simply, "Missionary life is simply a chance to die."[61] (If you haven't read it, Elisabeth's book, *A Chance to Die*, is well worth reading.)

Hast thou no scar?
No hidden scar on foot, or side, or hand?
I hear thee sung as mighty in the land;
I hear them hail thy bright, ascendant star.
Hast thou no scar?
Hast thou no wound?

Yet I was wounded by the archers; spent,
Leaned Me against a tree to die; and rent
By ravening beasts that compassed Me, I swooned.
Hast thou no wound?
No wound? No scar?

Yet, as the Master shall the servant be,
And pierced are the feet that follow Me.
But thine are whole; can he have followed far
Who hast no wound or scar?[62]

61 Elisabeth Elliot, *A Chance to Die: The Life and Legacy of Amy Carmichael* (Ada: Revell 1987).

62 Amy Carmichael, "Hast Thou No Scar." *Toward Jerusalem* (Fort Washington: Christian Literature Crusade, 1936), 85.

# QUESTIONS TO CONSIDER

1. (a) What do you learn about Alexander in 2 Timothy 4:14-15? (b) Write a summary statement about Alexander from what you have learned of him.

2. Memorize 2 Timothy 4:14.

3. (a) Paul is content to let the Lord repay Alexander for his evil deeds. Who else in Scripture desired the same thing? See 1 Samuel 24:8-15; 2 Samuel 3:27-39; Psalm 28:1-4; Jeremiah 15:15. (b) Why do you think it's a good idea to let the Lord repay those who have done evil instead of taking matters in our own hands?

4. (a) How is Psalm 109:1-5 similar to what Paul recounts in 2 Timothy 4:14-15? (b) How is Paul's attitude different about Alexander compared to the Psalmist's attitude toward his enemies in Psalm 109:6-20? (c) How do we reconcile these two seemingly different attitudes?

5. (a) Name an individual (besides Paul) in Scripture who had wrong done to them and who responded righteously. (b) What do you learn from their example? (c) Name an individual who did not respond well to the evil done to them and what you learn from their example. (d) What are some of the things we can and should do when others do evil toward us?

6. (a) Why do you think Paul warned Timothy regarding Alexander? (b) When do you think it is right to warn others regarding those who may wrongly influence them?

7. Is there someone who has caused you great harm or resisted the truth of God's Word? What is your prayer for them? (Please be discreet.)

# Paul's Defender, Deliverer, and Doxology

*2 Timothy 4:16-18*

CHARLES Haddon Spurgeon once said, "I have a great need for Christ and I have a great Christ for my need." Let me repeat that: "I have a great need for Christ: I have a great Christ for my need." Just as these words rang true for Charles Spurgeon, so they rang true for the apostle Paul as he came to the end of his life and recounted both his great need for Christ and the great Christ he has for his need. In the verses we'll consider in this chapter, we see Paul express these very thoughts. Let's listen to what he says in 2 Timothy 4:16-18:

> At my first defense no one stood with me, but all forsook me. May it not be charged against them. But the Lord stood with me and strengthened me, so that the message might be preached fully through me, and that all the Gentiles might hear. Also I was delivered out of the mouth of the lion. And the Lord will deliver me from every evil work and preserve me for His heavenly kingdom. To Him be glory forever and ever. Amen!

In these verses, we'll learn of *Paul's Defender* (vv 16-17a); *Paul's Deliverer* (vv 17b-18a); and *Paul's Doxology* (v 18b). In our last chapter, we learned that a man named Alexander had done much harm to Paul by greatly resisting his words. Paul did not take vengeance but, rather, asked the Lord to repay Alexander according to his works. Paul also warned Timothy to beware of Alexander. Now, Paul continues to write regarding those in his life, this time recalling those who did not stand with him in his trial. Let's read verse 16 together.

## Paul's Defender *2 Timothy 4:16-17*

> At my first defense no one stood with me, but all forsook me. May it not be charged against them. (2 Timothy 4:16)

*At my first defense no one stood with me, but all forsook me.* The question might come to mind, "When was Paul's first defense?" *Defense* is a legal term which describes a verbal defense. Paul mentions it as the *first* defense, which would indicate that there had been more than one. The legal system in the Roman world had a process that often included more than one trial. If at the first defense there was a doubt about the charges, then the accused would be offered a second defense. Evidently, at Paul's first trial there was not enough evidence to convict him, so a second trial followed. We are not sure when this first defense was, but, as we can tell here, it was a trial that took place before he wrote 2 Timothy. We also know that because Paul is now in his final imprisonment.

About his first defense, *no one stood with me*, Paul writes, *but all forsook me*. This might prompt a question in your mind about Onesiphorus, since Paul mentions him in 2 Timothy 1:16-18: "The Lord grant mercy to the household of Onesiphorus, for he often refreshed me, and was not ashamed of my chain; but when he arrived in Rome, he sought me out very zealously and found me. The Lord grant to him that he may find mercy from the Lord in that Day—and you know very well how many ways he ministered to me at Ephesus." We might wonder where Onesiphorus was during this first defense Paul writes about, especially since Onesiphorus didn't seem to be ashamed of Paul's imprisonment. We really don't know where Onesiphorus was at that time, as Paul doesn't fill us in on those details. But because Paul says that no one was there at this first defense, we can assume that Onesiphorus couldn't have been present at the time. It was normal in a trial for the accused to have others with him who would come to his defense, so it would seem that, if Onesiphorus had been around, he would have come to Paul's first defense. To have *stood with him* would mean they would have been present there at his side defending him, but no one did.

Instead of standing with him, Paul says they *all forsook* him. This means they all deserted him and left. Now, we must consider the time in which Paul is writing this letter. Nero was in power, and he was viciously killing Christians. Terrible persecution was happening to believers. Many were being burned at the stake; many lost their homes and jobs; many were being falsely accused of things they did not do. So, any potential defenders of Paul would likely have been fearful of identifying with Paul because they too might have been taken to prison. If they stood with Paul, they too would be subject to imprisonment and possibly even death.

So, no one stood with Paul. I am certain that Paul must have recounted to himself the words of His Lord because this, too, happened to Him. Matthew records for us, in Matthew 26:55-56 (LSB), "At that time Jesus said to the crowds, 'Have you come out with swords and clubs to arrest Me as you would against a robber? Every day I used to sit in the temple teaching and you did not seize Me. But all this has taken place in order that the Scriptures of the prophets would be fulfilled.' Then all the disciples left Him and fled." We also know that, in the Garden of Gethsemane, when Jesus was praying, Peter, James, and John did not stay awake with the Lord during His dark trial (Luke 22:39-46).

But Paul, like his Lord, has an amazing attitude about being forsaken by his friends and asks that it might *not be charged against them*. Paul is asking the Lord to not take inventory of this failure and count it against them. Paul definitely practices what he preaches; he wrote, in 1 Corinthians 13:5, that if you love someone, you do not keep a record of the wrongs they have done to you. Paul understood the danger they would be in and doesn't hold it against them. It is interesting that, while they did not come to Paul's defense, Paul does come to their defense. He thinks well of them, just as he commanded us to do in Philippians 4:8-9 (LSB):

> Finally, brothers, whatever is true, whatever is dignified, whatever is right, whatever is pure, whatever is lovely, whatever is commendable, if there is any excellence and if anything worthy of praise, consider these things. The things you have learned and received and heard and seen in me, practice these things, and the God of peace will be with you.

This is certainly one of those instances in which we can see that Paul thought well of others. Once again, Paul is emulating his Lord. He, too, was forgiving at a time when He was deserted. He asked His Father from the cross to forgive those who nailed Him there because they did not know what they were doing (Luke 23:34). When Stephen was being stoned, in Acts 7, after his masterful sermon, it says in verse 60 (LSB), "Then falling on his knees, he cried out with a loud voice, 'Lord, do not hold this sin against them!' And having said this, he fell asleep." Charles Spurgeon once said, "Forgive, as you hope to be forgiven."[63] The Lord's prayer teaches us that we should pray, "forgive us our debts, as we also have forgiven our debtors" (Matthew 6:12, LSB). And the Golden Rule, which we all know so well, but live so little, is: do unto others as you would have them do unto you (Matthew 7:12). This is how Paul lived.

Now, I do want to bring out that often fear will easily keep us from doing the right and sacrificial thing. Paul knew Timothy struggled with fear in the use of his gifts, and Paul has already reminded Timothy, in 2 Timothy 1:7, "For God has not given us a spirit of fear, but of power and of love and of a sound mind." Even though Paul did not speak evil of those who had deserted him, and he asked the Lord to not hold it against them, there is inherent in this verse a reminder that we are prone to let fear rule our hearts. The worst that can happen to us is death and yet that's the best for a believer. Jesus reminds His disciples of the danger of fear, in Matthew 10:28-31 (LSB). He says,

> And do not fear those who kill the body but are unable to kill the soul; but rather fear Him who is able to destroy both soul and body in hell. Are not two sparrows sold for an assarion? And yet not one of them will fall to the ground apart from your Father. But the very hairs of your head are all numbered. So do not fear; you are more valuable than many sparrows.

You might be wondering why Paul asked the Lord to repay Alexander

63 Charles H. Spurgeon, "Morning by Morning-February 11," *The Spurgeon Center*, https://www.spurgeon.org/resource-library/books/morning-by-morning-february/#flipbook/. Accessed 4/5/2024.

for the evil he had done to Paul but not those who refused to come to his defense. Alexander was an evil man who was put out of the church and delivered over to Satan, as is made clear in 1 Timothy 1:20. Alexander apostatized and took others down the road with him. However, these other men Paul mentions here, more than likely, allowed fear to cripple them. Alexander was a false teacher energized by Satan; these men were fearful and weak at the moment Paul needed them. Peter is a good example of this very thing; he denied the Lord three times in a moment of fear and weakness (Luke 22:54-62). Fear can be crippling at times, but we should learn to put it off and put on trusting in the Lord. And while no one defended Paul in his first trial, there was one who stood with Paul and helped him. Paul mentions his defender in 17a.

> But the Lord stood with me and strengthened me, so that the message might be preached fully through me, and that all the Gentiles might hear. (2 Timothy 4:17a)

*But*, in contrast to those who did not stand with Paul, we have *the Lord* who, Paul says, *stood with me*. What does it mean that the Lord *stood* with Paul? It means that the Lord assisted him. This is a different Greek word than the one in verse 16, which meant to defend. It is of great comfort to know that when all forsake us, the Lord is with us. In fact, the following verses should be an amazing comfort during times like what Paul was experiencing. Hebrews 13:5-6 (LSB) says, "Make sure that your way of life is free from the love of money, being content with what you have; for He Himself has said, 'I will never desert you, nor will I ever forsake you,' so that we confidently say, 'The Lord is my helper, I will not be afraid. What will man do to me?'" And, as Paul wrote in Romans 8:31-35 (LSB),

> What then shall we say to these things? If God is for us, who is against us? He who indeed did not spare His own Son, but delivered Him over for us all, how will He not also with Him graciously give us all things? Who will bring a charge against God's elect? God is the one who justifies; who is the one who condemns? Christ Jesus is He who died, yes, rather who was raised, who is at the right hand of God, who

> also intercedes for us. Who will separate us from the love of Christ? Will affliction, or turmoil, or persecution, or famine, or nakedness, or peril, or sword?

When all forsake us, we have the Lord and, my friend, He is enough. Even the Psalmist writes, in Psalm 27:10, "When my father and my mother forsake me, then the Lord will take care of me." Even Jesus knew this truth; He says, in John 16:31-32 (LSB), "Jesus answered them, 'Do you now believe? Behold, an hour is coming, and has already come, for you to be scattered, each to his own home, and to leave Me alone; and yet I am not alone, because the Father is with Me.'" When we feel like no one understands, when no one comes to our defense, the Lord understands and He is our great defender. We are never alone.

The Lord not only came to Paul's defense, but Paul goes on to write that the Lord *strengthened me*. When the Lord stands with us, He gives us strength. And, my friend, His strength is amazing and limitless. For the Lord to *strengthen* Paul means that the Lord empowered Paul by infusing strength into him or, we might say, pouring power into Him. We see a beautiful example of this when Jesus was wrestling in prayer before going to the cross, pleading with His Father to take the cup from Him. Jesus was agonizing, sweating great drops of blood. Luke tells us, in Luke 22:43 (LSB), "Now an angel from heaven appeared to Him, strengthening Him." The Lord was alone, the three disciples He'd taken with Him having fallen asleep on Him, and yet His Father sent an angel to strengthen Him in His hour of need.

Paul experienced this strengthening from the Lord at other times, as well. A familiar example is found in 2 Corinthians 12, where he begs the Lord to remove the thorn in his flesh. But God told Paul no, and Paul records for us, in 2 Corinthians 12:9 (LSB), God's reason for doing so: "My grace is sufficient for you, for power is perfected in weakness" And Paul's response is, in the rest of that verse and in 2 Corinthians 12:10 (LSB): "Most gladly, therefore, I will rather boast in my weaknesses, so that the power of Christ may dwell in me. Therefore I am well content with weaknesses, with insults, with distresses, with persecutions and hardships, for the sake of Christ, for when I am weak, then I am strong." In Philippians 4:13, Paul writes, from much experience, that he can do all things through Christ who strengthens him. The context for that verse, of course, is contentment and the ability to be content in all circumstances and with all people—not because Paul is able, in and of himself, but because Christ infuses Paul with the strength to do so. And, my friend, you and I have the same Christ and the same power that can strengthen us in our time of trouble and need. We may not be able to imagine that kind of power in our comfy, American Christianity, but our brothers and sisters in difficult places can attest to it. And if God calls us to that same difficulty, He will also give us that same power, infusing us with His strength. We must remember that we cannot borrow grace for something that has not happened yet.

The strength that was given to Paul wasn't only for Paul himself but for a greater purpose. He puts it like this: *so that the message might be preached fully through me, and that all the Gentiles might hear.* God infused strength in Paul so that he could preach the gospel at his trial. The strength infused in Paul was for the eternal purpose of preaching the gospel. Often, in our troubles, we think it's about us, but it's really about Him and His Kingdom and the lost who are going to a Christless eternity. There are greater purposes at work than sometimes we can even imagine. We often get caught up in our own sorrows and discomforts and don't stop to think of what God is doing with our troubles. When the angel came to Jesus in the Garden of Gethsemane and strengthened Him, it was for a bigger reason than just helping our Lord get through that moment. The angel strengthened Jesus to go on and face the beatings, the mocking, the crucifixion, the death on the cross for a sinful world, the separation from His Father, and the wrath of God.

Notice that Paul says *so that the message might be fully preached through me*. Paul is saying that he was strengthened so that the gospel might be made known, might be accomplished and carried out. And note that it is *fully preached*, which means it was preached in all its fullness. Paul gave the whole gospel, not a partial gospel. Oh, how

I wish we had men today (and women) who would proclaim a clear and complete gospel, not a cheap gospel! I recently emailed a friend who had asked me to pray about a funeral she was attending. I asked her how it went, and she answered, "Baaaad! No gospel, no sin, no repentance, no cross!" Paul is clear, in 1 Corinthians 1:23 (LSB), "but we preach Christ crucified, to Jews a stumbling block and to Gentiles foolishness." Paul would not preach the watered-down gospel that is so often preached today. Instead, he says, he preached the gospel *so that all the Gentiles might hear.* Remember, Paul was sent to take the true gospel to *the Gentiles*, as Jesus told him on the Damascus Road, in Acts 9:15.

## Paul's Deliverer *2 Timothy 4:17-18*

Also I was delivered out of the mouth of the lion. (2 Timothy 4:17b)

The Lord was not only Paul's defender but his deliverer, as well, as we can see in the rest of this verse and in verse 18a. Paul writes *also I was delivered out of the mouth of the lion.* Paul states that he was *delivered*, or rescued, out of *the mouth of the lion.* Is Paul being literal or figurative here? We cannot be dogmatic, but it appears to me to be figurative because we have no record of Paul encountering and being delivered from a real lion, though he does talk about perils in the wilderness, in 2 Corinthians 11:26. Often, travelers in the biblical world would be subject to wild animals attacking them, and Paul certainly endured some dangerous travels. It is also true that Nero fed Christians to lions, and while we don't have any indication that Paul was threatened with that kind of torture, it certainly was going on in Paul's day. It's possible that Paul is referring to either of these things and means that he was literally delivered from the mouth of the lion.

But Paul could also be using figurative language here, referring to those at his trial as though they were like wild animals. We know that his accusers hated him and wanted to tear him to pieces like a lion would. In fact, the mouth of *the lion* would indicate the most tumultuous danger. Nero himself would have been the king of the lions, in that he regularly killed Christians. This could also be a reference to Satan; Peter writes of Satan this way, in 1 Peter 5:8 (LSB): "Be of sober spirit, be watchful. Your adversary, the devil, prowls around like a roaring lion, seeking someone to devour." If Paul is speaking figuratively of Satan, the idea would be that Satan had wanted Paul to fail in his trial and because no one was willing to stand with Paul, Satan may have been wanting Paul to question whether this Christianity was worth death! Paul may have even feared that he would apostatize, just as others had done. Paul writes of this fear in 1 Corinthians 9:27 (LSB): "but I discipline my body and make it my slave, so that, after I have preached to others, I myself will not be disqualified." Paul knew that he must lose his life in order to save it; that he must take up his cross and follow the Lord; that if he denied the Lord, the Lord would deny him. I am sure that many martyrs, upon facing their own death, have had thoughts of turning back. Satan is real, and we must never think that, in our hour of trial, he would not like to steal, kill, and destroy us. Satan wants us to deny our faith! Jesus warns Peter of this, in Luke 22:31-34 (LSB):

> "Simon, Simon, behold, Satan has demanded to sift all of you like wheat. But I have prayed earnestly for you, that your faith may not fail; and you, once you have returned, strengthen your brothers." But he said to Him, "Lord, with You I am ready to go both to prison and to death!" And He said, "I say to you, Peter, the rooster will not crow today until you have denied three times that you know Me."

Paul would have known of this account. He would have known that Peter faced prison and even death with the Lord. But Paul also knew how the story continued, that what Jesus said came to pass—Peter did deny the Lord.

When Paul says he was delivered from the mouth of the lion, it could be literal, it could refer to Paul's accusers or to Nero, or it could refer to Satan or to something else. We can't be certain of any of these possibilities, but we can be certain that it was *the Lord* who delivered Paul out of the mouth of this lion. And that is Paul's focus as he continues to write of his Lord, his deliverer, in the first part of verse 18.

> And the Lord will deliver me from every evil work and preserve me for His heavenly kingdom. (2 Timothy 4:18a)

What does it mean when Paul says that the Lord *will deliver me from every evil work*? More than likely, Paul is referring to what he just said about being delivered out of the mouth of the lion, that is, that he was convinced that the Lord would help him not to shrink from death when the hour came, that the Lord would help him not apostatize, that the Lord would keep him from this great evil. The Greek word *poneros*, translated as *evil*, here refers to that which is grievous, harmful, or hurtful. Remember, Paul said Alexander did him much evil. Alexander's evil is what led him to apostatize. The Psalmist feared this, as well, and writes, in Psalm 19:13, "Keep back Your servant also from presumptuous sins; let them not have dominion over me. Then I shall be blameless, and I shall be innocent of great transgression." The great transgression the Psalmist speaks of would be denying the Lord. I have known many who, during a dark trial, left the faith. It is a fact that should sober all of us and prompt us to be armed with the Word of God and prayer and an intimate relationship with our Lord, which cannot be severed. Proverbs 24:10 puts it well: "If you faint in the day of adversity, your strength is small." Paul's strength was not small; it was great because it came from the Lord. The Lord had infused Paul with strength.

The Lord was not only Paul's defender and deliverer, but Paul also says of the Lord that *he will preserve me for His heavenly kingdom. He* will *preserve*, or keep, Paul from apostasy in the hour of trial so that he will enter into *His heavenly kingdom*. Paul was assured, as he writes this to Timothy in prison, that the Lord would deliver him, not out of death, but into Heaven, into glory. Paul knew this would be his final deliverance; he's already written that the time of his departure was at hand. He knew he was going to die soon at the hands of Nero. Being well versed in the Old Testament, Paul might have been thinking back to Psalm 73:24-26: "You will guide me with Your counsel, and afterward receive me to glory. Whom have I in heaven but You? And there is none upon earth that I desire besides You. My flesh and my heart fail; but God is the strength of my heart and my portion forever."

What is Paul's response to the fact that the Lord was his defender and deliverer? His response was not, "Woe is me!" but praise to God, which is what we call a doxology! And, my friend, this should be our response, as well, when we're going through dark times. Paul ends this verse with the following doxology:

## Paul's Doxology *2 Timothy 4:18*

> To Him be glory forever and ever. Amen! (2 Timothy 4:18b)

*To Him be glory forever and ever. Amen!* To God alone be *glory*, which is dignity and honor. And this glory will be eternal because God is eternal, *forever and ever*! *Amen*—so be it! Paul was fully convinced that he would be going to glory and this was thrilling to him—as it should be to us. Paul wrote and knew first-hand the truth of Romans 8:38-39 (LSB): "For I am convinced that neither death, nor life, nor angels, nor rulers, nor things present, nor things to come, nor powers, nor height, nor depth, nor any other created thing, will be able to separate us from the love of God, which is in Christ Jesus our Lord." There are many truths that should cause us to break out in an anthem of praise to our God. Once again, Charles Spurgeon writes,

> I, the preacher of this hour, beg to bear my little witness that the worst days I have ever had have turned out to be my best days, and when God has seemed most cruel to me he has then been most kind. If there is anything in this world for which I would bless him more than for anything else it is for pain and affliction. I am sure that in these things the richest, tenderest love has been manifested towards me. ... Our Father's wagons rumble most heavily when they are bringing us the richest freight of the bullion of his grace. Love letters from heaven are often sent in black-edged envelopes. The cloud that is black with horror is big with mercy. ... Fear not the storm, it brings healing in its wings, and when Jesus is with you in the vessel the tempest only hastens the ship to its desired haven.[64]

64 Charles H. Spurgeon. "Ziklag; or, David Encouraging Himself in God," *The Spurgeon Center*, https://www.spurgeon.org/resource-library/sermons/ziklag-or-david-encouraging-himself-in-god/. Accessed 4/22/2024.

## Summary

What a blessed portion of Scripture that should encourage all of us! The Lord is Paul's defender. The Lord defended Paul when no one else did. Is the Lord your defender? Have you had times in your life in which you felt all alone, with no one on your side? Have you had moments where it seemed like everyone had forsaken you? Have you experienced the Lord assisting you in time of great trouble or darkness? How has He assisted you and strengthened you? Have you praised Him and thanked Him for His defense of you?

The Lord is also Paul's deliverer. The Lord delivered Paul out of the mouth of the lion and from every evil work. I doubt any of us have been delivered out of a mouth of a real lion, but, perhaps, some of you have. Have you ever been in a difficult situation where your life was threatened because of the gospel? Are there times when others have wanted to tear you to pieces with their mocking words because of your faith in Christ? Have you ever wanted to shrink back from your faith because of their evil? Don't do it! It's not worth it! Trust the Lord, lean on Him, and let Him deliver you. Often, we need to get out of the way and let Him fight our battles for us. He is the great deliverer!

Finally, all of this causes Paul to break out in a doxology. He knew His God would ultimately deliver him to Heaven. He knew Jesus was preparing a place for him. He knew the Lord would receive him at the time of his death into His heavenly Kingdom. Does the reality of Heaven make the trials of this life seem trivial to you? It should. Paul writes of this truth in Romans 8:18 (LSB): "For I consider that the sufferings of this present time are not worthy to be compared with the glory that is to be revealed to us." When the Lord has delivered you from evil, do you praise and thank Him? Do you break out in a hymn or words of praise? You should!

The next time you feel forsaken, remember that you have a defender and a deliverer and His name is Jesus Christ. Remember what our brother Charles Spurgeon said: "I have a great need for Christ and I have a great Christ for my need."

# QUESTIONS TO CONSIDER

1. (a) Read 2 Timothy 4:16-18. What are the difficult things Paul went through or will go through, according to these verses? (b) What are the encouraging things Paul went through or will go through, according to these verses? (c) How do these verses encourage you?

2. Memorize 2 Timothy 4:18.

3. (a) What similarities do you observe in Psalm 22 and 2 Timothy 4:16-18? (b) What have the Psalms meant to you during times of distress? (c) What has been your favorite Psalm during times of trouble, and why?

4. (a) What things are similar in Daniel 6:1-28 and 2 Timothy 4:16-18? (b) Do you think Paul was delivered from a literal lion?

5. (a) What prompts Paul to break out in a doxology (praise to God) in 2 Timothy 4:18? (b) What prompted Paul to break out in a doxology in Romans 11:33-36; 16:25-27; Galatians 1:3-5; Ephesians 3:20-21; Philippians 4:18-20; 1 Timothy 1:15-17; 6:13-16; Hebrews 13:20-21? (c) What prompts Peter to break out in a doxology in 1 Peter 5:10-11 and 2 Peter 3:17-18? (d) What prompts Jude to break out in a doxology in Jude 24-25? (e) What prompts *YOU* to break out in a doxology?

6. (a) Has there been a time in your life when you felt forsaken by others? (b) What did you learn about yourself and about God during that time? (c) In what ways has God been your defender and deliverer?

7. Read Psalm 27, which was written during a time of distress in David's life. What verses from this Psalm would you like to pray for either yourself or for another who is going through a distressing time? Please write it down to share with your group.

# Paul's Final Words Before His Death

*2 Timothy 4:19-22*

DIETRICH Bonhoeffer (1906-1945), was a pastor and theologian who lived in Germany. The last two years of his life were spent in prison and concentration camps, and he was eventually put to death by hanging. His final words were, "This is the end, but for me it is the beginning of life."[65]

Justin Martyr, who was born in A.D. 100 and died in A.D. 165, was scourged and beheaded for his faith. His final words were, "If we are punished for the sake of our Lord Jesus Christ we hope to be saved, for this shall be our salvation and confidence before the more terrible judgment-seat of our Lord and Saviour who shall judge the whole world."[66]

The apostle Paul, who was born in A.D. 5 and died in A.D. 67, suffered much in life for the gospel. He was a church planter and wrote many of the books in the New Testament. Twenty-five percent of his life was spent in prison because of the gospel, including the last of his days on earth. Beheaded for his faith by Nero, Paul's final written words are found in 2 Timothy 4:19-22, the verses we'll consider in this chapter. They are:

> Greet Prisca and Aquila, and the household of Onesiphorus. Erastus stayed in Corinth, but Trophimus I have left in Miletus sick.
>
> Do your utmost to come before winter.
>
> Eubulus greets you, as well as Pudens, Linus, Claudia, and all the brethren.
>
> The Lord Jesus Christ be with your spirit. Grace be with you. Amen.

---

65 Dietrich Bonhoeffer, quoted in Duane W. H. Arnold, *Prayers of the Martyrs* (Grand Rapids: Zondervan, 1991), 102.

66 Justin Martyr, quoted in E. C. E. Owen, *Some Authentic Acts of the Early Martyrs*, https://archive.org/details/owen-earlymartyrs/page/n49/mode/2up?view=theater. Accessed March 15, 2024.

As we consider Paul's final words before his death, we will see: *The Final Individuals* (vv 19-20, 21b-22a), and there will be ten of these; *The Final Instruction* (v 21a); and *The Final Intercession* (v 22), and there will be two parts to that. In our last chapter, we learned that the Lord was Paul's defender. The Lord defended Paul when no one else did. The Lord was also Paul's deliverer. The Lord delivered Paul out of the mouth of the lion and from every evil work. These facts about God caused Paul to break out in a doxology: "To Him be glory forever and ever. Amen!" As Paul ends this letter to Timothy, Paul turns his thoughts briefly away from His Lord to those who have been a blessing to him on his journey. Let's consider the first few individuals he mentions, in verse 19.

## The Final Individuals *2 Timothy 4:19-20, 21-22*

> Greet Prisca and Aquila, and the household of Onesiphorus. (2 Timothy 4:19)

Before we consider the first three individuals mentioned in verse 19, we should bring out that even though Paul's death is around the corner, he is not thinking of himself; instead, he is thinking of others. This makes me think of Jesus, who also thought of others in the face of His own death. Jesus thought of His disciples, as evidenced by His time with them in the upper room, and He was concerned for His mother, making sure that she had a caregiver after His death (John 13-17 and John 19:25-27). This is a reminder to us that even in dark trials and, yes, even in the face of death, we ought to be thinking of others and how we might encourage them.

The first people Paul mentions are made known to us in Paul's instruction to Timothy to *greet Prisca and Aquila*. The word *greet* means to enfold in the arms; we might say, "Give them a hug for me!" *Prisca and Aquila* are two individuals, wife and husband, who are mentioned six times in the Scriptures. I mention *Prisca*, or Priscilla, as she is also called, first because here and in 4 of the 6 times she's mentioned in Scripture she is mentioned first. She is mentioned first, more than likely, because she was a strong woman in spiritual matters and perhaps even more so than her husband. By the way, ladies, it is good to have a husband who is more knowledgeable and mature than you are spiritually, but often that does not happen. Do not let that hinder your spiritual growth. I married a very knowledgeable man and often found that to be very intimidating, but God freed me from that bondage and helped me to realize that I needed to have my own personal walk with God and press on to know Him more. When we get to glory, none of us will be holding our husbands' hands when we stand before God; we will each individually give an account to Him.

Now, who is this husband and wife team, and what do we know about them? Let's see what Scripture has to say about them. The first place they are mentioned is in Acts 18:1-4 (LSB).

> After these things he departed Athens and went to Corinth. And he found a Jew named Aquila, a native of Pontus, and his wife Priscilla, who recently came from Italy because Claudius had commanded all the Jews to depart from Rome. He came to them, and because he was of the same trade, he was staying with them and they were working, for by trade they were tent-makers. And he was reasoning in the synagogue every Sabbath and trying to persuade both Jews and Greeks.

From these verses, we learn that Paul met Aquila and Priscilla in Corinth, that they were Jews who had been expelled from Rome, and that they had the same occupation as Paul, that of being tent-makers. It is interesting to note that these two believers had an occupation but that their occupation did not keep them from ministering to Paul and to others. I often hear people using their work or career as an excuse for why they can't attend church or minister to others, and it is troubling to me. Many who have gone before us worked very long hours, and in hard physical labor, I might add, but that did not deter them from serving others and from assembling regularly with fellow believers. This is more an issue of the heart than it is of time or opportunity, because we will find time to do what is most important to us.

The second place these two are mentioned is in Act 18:18-19 (LSB): "And Paul, having remained many days longer, took leave of the brothers and put out to sea for Syria, and with him were Priscilla and Aquila. In Cenchreae he had his hair cut, for he was keeping a vow. And they arrived at Ephesus, and he left them there." From these verses, we learn that Priscilla and Aquila ministered alongside Paul, even traveling with him and settling in a new city to minister there.

The third placed Priscilla and Aquila are named is in Acts 18:24-28 (LSB):

> Now a Jew named Apollos, an Alexandrian by birth, an eloquent man, arrived at Ephesus; and he was mighty in the Scriptures. This man had been instructed in the way of the Lord; and being fervent in spirit, he was speaking and teaching accurately the things concerning Jesus, being acquainted only with the baptism of John; and he began to speak out boldly in the synagogue. But when Priscilla and Aquila heard him, they took him aside and explained to him the way of God more accurately. And when he wanted to go across to Achaia, the brothers encouraged him and wrote to the disciples to welcome him; and when he had arrived, he greatly helped those who had believed through grace, for he powerfully refuted the Jews in public, demonstrating by the Scriptures that Jesus is the Christ.

We learn from this passage that Priscilla and Aquila were educated enough in the Scriptures that they were able to take Apollos aside and explain the way of God more accurately to him. It's important to note that the Greek order of the names in this passage lists Priscilla first, which would indicate that she did most of the instructing. In fact, in the LSB and in a number of other translations, Priscilla is correctly named first. Now, before you think I'm advocating for women preaching in the pulpit to men, I am not! But men can learn from women, and here we have a biblical example of that.

The fourth mention of Priscilla and Aquila in the Scriptures is found in Romans 16:3-5 (LSB), "Greet Prisca and Aquila, my fellow workers in Christ Jesus, who for my life risked their own necks, to whom not only do I give thanks, but also all the churches of the Gentiles; also greet the church that is in their house." We learn from this passage that Priscilla and Aquila were fellow workers of Paul, that they had a church in their house (in Corinth, where Paul was when he wrote to the Romans), that all the churches of the Gentiles were thankful for them, and that they risked their lives for Paul. We don't know when this took place, but they certainly practiced genuine love; in John 15:13 (LSB), Jesus says, "Greater love has no one than this, that one lay down his life for his friends."

The fifth place we find Priscilla and Aquila mentioned is in 1 Corinthians 16:19 (LSB): "The churches of Asia greet you. Aquila and Prisca greet you heartily in the Lord, with the church that is in their house." Once again, we are told about the church that was in their house, this time in Ephesus, where Paul was when he wrote 1 Corinthians. Having "been there, done that" on more than one occasion, I know the sacrifice and energy it takes for such a task.

The sixth and last mention of Priscilla and Aquila is in the verse we're now considering, 2 Timothy 4:19. From this verse, we see that Paul wants Timothy to greet them, to embrace them for Paul. From what we've learned of this couple from all the other places they're mentioned in Scriptures, we know them to be a married couple who were sold out for service to the Lord and ministry to the saints. I am always encouraged to see married couples who are serving the Lord together and using their gifts for His glory and the benefit of others.

There is a third individual Paul mentions in this verse and that is *Onesiphorus*, and Paul sends a greeting to his *household*. We learned of Onesiphorus back in 2 Timothy 1:16-18: "The Lord grant mercy to the household of Onesiphorus, for he often refreshed me, and was not ashamed of my chain; but when he arrived in Rome, he sought me out very zealously and found me. The Lord grant to him that he may find mercy from the Lord in that Day—and you know very well how many ways he ministered to me at Ephesus." Onesiphorus' name means profit-bearer, and we learned that it is possible that he was a deacon in the church at Ephesus. We also learned that Onesiphorus refreshed Paul in prison and was not ashamed of Paul, as so many others were. In fact, Onesiphorus had to search diligently just to find the prison in which Paul was being held. Onesiphorus was a determined guy! So Paul sends greetings to Onesiphorus and his household. He must have been a special friend and a sacrificial friend to Paul. And Paul wanted to make sure—before his death—to send these three greetings.

Two more individuals are mentioned by Paul, in verse 20.

> Erastus stayed in Corinth, but Trophimus I have left in Miletus sick. (2 Timothy 4:20)

The fourth individual Paul mentions is *Erastus*. His name means beloved, and we find him mentioned in a few places in the New Testament. Paul speaks of him in Romans 16:23 (LSB), where he writes, "Gaius, host to me and to the whole church, greets you. Erastus, the city treasurer greets you, and Quartus, the brother." So, we know Erastus was the city treasurer in Corinth, where Paul was writing Romans from. And then, in Acts 19:21-22 (LSB), Luke writes, "Now after these things were finished, Paul purposed in the Spirit to go to Jerusalem after he had passed through Macedonia and Achaia, saying, 'After I have been there, I must also see Rome.' And having sent into Macedonia two of those who ministered to him, Timothy and Erastus, he himself stayed in Asia for a while." We learn from this that Erastus ministered to Paul alongside Timothy. So, now, Paul sends greetings to Erastus also and mentions that he is staying at Corinth, which was Erastus' hometown. Perhaps, for some reason, he couldn't get away to see Paul.

Paul next mentions a fifth individual, *Trophimus*, and writes that he *left* Trophimus *in Miletus sick*. Trophimus is mentioned two other times in Scripture. In Acts 20:4-6 (LSB), it says, "And he was accompanied by Sopater of Berea, the son of Pyrrhus, and by Aristarchus and Secundus of the Thessalonians, and Gaius of Derbe, and Timothy, and Tychicus and Trophimus of Asia. But these had gone on ahead and were waiting for us at Troas. And we sailed from Philippi after the days of Unleavened Bread, and came to them at Troas within five days; and there we stayed seven days." We can see from this passage that Trophimus also traveled with and ministered alongside Paul. We see this fact also in Acts 21:26-29 (LSB), where we see Trophimus in Jerusalem with Paul and a number of other disciples:

> Then Paul took the men, and the next day, purifying himself along with them, went into the temple giving notice of the completion of the days of purification, until the sacrifice was offered for each one of them.
>
> Now when the seven days were almost over, the Jews from Asia, upon noticing him in the temple, began to throw all the crowd into confusion and laid hands on him, crying out, "Men of Israel, help! This is the man who teaches to everyone everywhere against our people and the Law and this place; and besides, he has even brought Greeks into the temple and has defiled this holy place." For they had previously seen Trophimus the Ephesian in the city with him, and they supposed that Paul had brought him into the temple.

Because Paul mentions here in 2 Timothy, his final letter, that he had to leave Trophimus in Miletus sick, we can surmise that Trophimus must have gotten sick on the last of Paul's missionary journeys. We are not told what kind of sickness Trophimus had, but it needs to be said that being in ministry does not exempt one from becoming ill. Believers get sick, and believers die. The sign gifts of healing, tongues, and miracles were given to authenticate the gospel, and, as the apostolic age was winding down the sign gifts were ceasing. For some reason, Paul was not able to heal Trophimus, and this is a reminder to us that not all were healed in Paul's day and not all receive healing in our day. Paul told Timothy, in 1 Timothy 5:23, to drink some wine for his stomach problems and other infirmities. Paul also mentions, in Philippians 2:25-27, a man named Epaphroditus and the fact that he almost died because he had been so sick. It is also supposed, from several comments in Paul's letters, that Paul may have had an eye condition that never got healed (see Galatians 4:14-15; 6:11). John MacArthur has a few words on this which I think are helpful:

> [In] Second Timothy 4:20, Paul mentioned he left Trophimus sick at Miletus. Now why leave a good friend sick? Why did he leave his

> Christian friend sick? Why didn't he heal him? Well, maybe he didn't have that ability as the time passed on out of the apostolic era, but for sure he recognized that healing was not something you run around doing for your Christian friends. It was never intended as a permanent way to keep the church healthy. Yet today, charismatics teach that God wants every Christian well all the time. If that's true, then why did he let him get sick to start with? Seems a basic question. God didn't give you an HMO in your salvation, a sort of supernatural HMO that works automatically. God heals when He wants and when He wishes, but that's up to Him. Has God promised to heal everybody who has faith? He doesn't promise He'll always heal, but I think a Christian can look to heaven for healing.[67]

As we move on to verse 21, we see that Paul mentions four more individuals, along with his final instruction for Timothy. He begins with the final instruction.

## The Final Instruction *2 Timothy 4:21*

> Do your utmost to come before winter. (2 Timothy 4:21a)

*Do you utmost to come before winter* means make every effort, be prompt, to come before winter. The word for *winter* here means a storm or pouring rain. Remember, Paul had already asked for a coat, back in verse 13. Winter was coming, and Paul needed extra clothing for the cold weather, which is perhaps one reason why he wants Timothy to come sooner rather than later. But the bigger reason Paul wanted Timothy to come was, more than likely, that he wanted to see Timothy one last time before he died. If I was facing death, there would be many people I would like to see and some of those people would be women I have poured my life into, those who are my spiritual daughters.

Another reason that Paul would want Timothy to come before winter is because winter was not conducive to sailing. One man helps us here:

---

67 John MacArthur. "Does God Still Heal?" *Grace to You*, https://www.gty.org/library/sermons-library/90-60/does-god-still-heal. Accessed February 22, 2024.

> The seas were closed down to traffic in winter; shipping was completely closed down from around November 10 to as late as March 10, but the periods from about September 15 to November 10 and March 11 to May 26 were risky periods as well. Timothy thus could not sail from Ephesus in winter, but even if he took the overland route north of Greece, as Paul seems to expect (4:13), he would still need to sail across the Adriatic, which was also closed. If Timothy delayed, he would not be able to come until spring—and Paul might not still be alive then. Paul may have sent this letter by Tychicus in summer, leaving Timothy little time to set matters in order and come to him.[68]

## The Final Individuals *2 Timothy 4:19-20, 21-22*

> Eubulus greets you, as well as Pudens, Linus, Claudia, and all the brethren. (2 Timothy 4:21b)

Paul now mentions four more individuals. First, he mentions *Eubulus*, who sends his greeting to Timothy. Eubulus must have been with Paul at this time, and yet little is known about him. Next, Paul mentions *Pudens, Linus, Claudia and all the brethren*. Eubulus, Pudens, and Linus are all men, and Claudia is a woman. Little, if anything, is known of these three men, at least from a historical context, but God knows who they are. The last individual mentioned here, Claudia, is thought to have been Pudens' wife, been converted by Paul, and later brought the gospel to Britain. You may have noticed that there are two women mentioned here in Paul's closing remarks: Prisca and Claudia. Paul also mentions *all the brethren*, who are, more than likely, the believers at Rome.

Paul has one more individual he mentions, in verse 22. He saved the best for last! He also has one last intercession to pray, also in verse 22.

> The Lord Jesus Christ be with your spirit. (2 Timothy 4:22a)

---

68 Craig S. Keener, *Bible Background Commentary*, Biblesoft.

The last individual Paul mentions is his defender and his deliverer, *the Lord Jesus Christ.* Paul started his letter by speaking of Jesus Christ, and he ends it by speaking of Him. Second Timothy 1:1 says, "Paul, an apostle of Jesus Christ by the will of God, according to the promise of life which is in Christ Jesus." Here, in the final verse of his final letter, Paul uses the words *the Lord* when speaking of *Jesus Christ.* In the LSB, as well as the ESV and the NIV, the words Jesus Christ are not included because they do not appear in the Greek; Paul simply refers to Jesus as the Lord. Perhaps this is intended to serve as a reminder to Timothy—and to us—that Paul will soon be standing before the Lord. Paul was clear, in Philippians 2:10-11 (LSB), "so that at the name of Jesus every knee will bow, of those who are in heaven and on earth and under the earth, and that every tongue will confess that Jesus Christ is Lord, to the glory of God the Father." Soon, Paul will be standing before his Lord and that may be what is on his mind as he ends this letter.

## The Final Intercession *2 Timothy 4:22*

> The Lord Jesus Christ be with your spirit. Grace be with you. Amen. (2 Timothy 4:22)

In mentioning the Lord Jesus Christ, Paul also ends with a twofold intercession for Timothy. The first part of Paul's intercession is his prayer that the Lord Jesus Christ would be *with* Timothy's spirit. The word *your* is in the singular, and we know that this letter is addressed to Timothy, so this is Paul ending his letter with a prayer for his dear son in the faith, Timothy. Timothy's *spirit* will need to be strengthened when his spiritual father dies; it won't be easy taking the apostle Paul's baton and carrying the torch of truth and passing it on to others. Timothy knows that truth isn't popular and that many false teachers are luring others into their unhealthy doctrine. Timothy knows that carrying the torch of truth will include pain and suffering and hatred from many. Timothy knows that he will probably land in prison for preaching the gospel. Timothy sees all this, and his spirit needs to be strong. It's also possible that Paul is thinking of the time in his own life when he longed to be relieved of his thorn in the flesh and the Lord was unwilling to remove it (2 Corinthians 12). The Lord reminded Paul that, in his weakness, he would be strong by the power of Christ that would be infused into him. So, Paul prays this now for his son, "Oh, that your spirit will be strong, Timothy, by the One who is able to give strength. He has given me strength in my weakness—to the point that I can glory in my infirmities—and He will give you that same strength, my son!"

Timothy did carry the torch of truth, and tradition tells us that it cost him his life; he died a martyr, stoned to death for the faith. It is interesting that Paul also tells Philemon something very similar, in Philemon 1:25 (LSB); as he closes that little epistle, Paul says, "The grace of the Lord Jesus Christ be with your spirit." And to the church at Galatia, in Galatians 6:18 (LSB), Paul also writes, under very different circumstances, "The grace of our Lord Jesus Christ be with your spirit, brothers. Amen." Certainly, the Galatians' spirits needed much strength; as a church, they were flirting with going back to Judaism and legalism and denying the grace of God. Much spiritual strength would be needed, indeed, to combat that false gospel.

The second part of Paul's intercession is for all the church; he prays *grace be with you. Amen.* The *you* here is not singular but plural. So, Paul is praying that *grace* would *be with* them all, not just with Timothy. Given that Timothy was pastoring the church at Ephesus, this prayer would be for the church at Ephesus, but it would also be for the church universal, which includes you and me. *Grace* is divine influence upon the heart; it is God's unmerited favor and influence upon us. Grace would be ever so needed, as these are Paul's very last words to the church. He has been a pillar of the church and is soon to be martyred. The New Testament church will need grace, indeed, because Paul will soon be gone. And, knowing this will be their need, Paul ends with a hearty *Amen*, which means so be it!

## Summary

Who are the individuals mentioned in Paul's final words? There are 10 of them, not counting all the brethren he mentions. They are:

Prisca, Aquila, Onesiphorus, Erastus, Trophimus, Eubulus, Pudens, Linus, Claudia, and the Lord Jesus Christ. And, I guess we could say Timothy is mentioned by way of Paul's prayer for him. All of these men and women were helpful to Paul in the ministry. They were his co-laborers. And, of course, Paul mentions his Lord, who saved him on the Damascus road and gave him a new heart and a mission to take the gospel to the Gentiles. Who are the ones who have been by your side on your spiritual journey? Have you thanked them for all they have done for you? We don't have a word from the Lord that we are going to die soon, like Paul did, but we all will die unless we are taken up when the Lord returns. Why not take some time to write a note or to send a text or make a phone call or even to have a meal with those who have poured their lives into you and been an encouragement to you. And, while we are on the topic, please take time to thank the Lord for saving your soul and giving you a purpose in life.

What is the final instruction Paul gives to Timothy? Paul tells Timothy to come before winter. Paul was concerned for Timothy and did not want him sailing in the winter months because it was so dangerous. Paul also wanted to see Timothy one last time. If you had a few days or weeks left on earth, what would be your final instructions to those you love, those you have poured your life into? Woe is me, or how are you? Come see me, or come so I can see you? To the end, Paul was concerned for the welfare of others. Are you?

What is Paul's final intercession? It is twofold: a prayer that the Lord would be with Timothy's spirit and that grace would be extended to all the church. What would be your last prayer for those you have ministered to? Would you ask the Lord to give them strength of heart and mind, or would your prayers be more focused on you? And what about the grace that is needed for others when you leave this life? There are few like Paul in our day, but we all are making a mark on someone. Do we ask the Lord to grant them grace should we suddenly be taken home?

We know that the church will always go on in this life because it is built on Jesus Christ, the pillar and ground of the truth. But men like Paul are hard to find in our day. Where are the Pauls of our day? Where are the men who will teach the truth, fight for the truth, be persecuted for the truth, and die for the truth? Where are the men who will hold fast to the truth? Where are the women who will hold fast to the truth? May God give us those who will hold fast to the truth and fight for the truth and even die for the truth, if need be. My dear friend, will *you* be one of those who will hold fast to the end?

# QUESTIONS TO CONSIDER

1. (a) Read 2 Timothy 4:19-22. Without looking at any other helps, do you know anything about any of the individuals Paul lists? (b) If so, who do you know and what do you know about them?

2. Memorize 2 Timothy 4:22.

3. (a) Paul lists several individuals who have been helpful to him in the Lord's work. Who has been helpful to you in your work for the Lord? (b) These also are Paul's final words that are written down before his death. If you could write down any last words before your death, what do you think you would write? (c) If you could write a final prayer before your death, what do you think you would pray?

4. (a) What does the Bible say about Paul in Acts 19:11-12? (b) What does Paul write in 2 Timothy 4:20? (c) Paul had healing gifts. Why, then, did he not heal Trophimus? (d) Do you think anyone has power to heal today? Why or why not? Use Scripture to demonstrate your answer.

5. (a) This study on 2 Timothy has been given the title *With the Master Holding Fast to the Truth*. What are the reasons we should hold fast to the truth, according to what Paul has written in 2 Timothy? (b) What are some of the other reasons we should hold fast to the truth? (c) In what ways can you hold fast to the truth?

6. (a) What things have you gleaned from our study on 2 Timothy? (b) What changes have you made as a result of the study?

7. In what ways do you need to be more tenacious in holding fast to the truth? Please write a prayer request down for prayer support from your group.

# God's Plan of Salvation

Everyone is destined to die, but life does not end with death. The Bible says that after death there will be a judgment where each person will give an account of his life to God (Hebrews 4:13; 9:27). When God created Adam and Eve in His own image in the garden of Eden, He gave them an abundant life, and the freedom to choose between good and evil (Genesis 2:9). They chose to disobey God and go their own way. As a consequence, death was introduced into the human race; not only physical death, but also spiritual death (Romans 5:12). For this reason, all human beings are separated from God.

Unfortunately, man's sinful nature and his ongoing choices to sin result in men living in continual disobedience to God: *for all have sinned and fall short of the glory of God* (Romans 3:23). This is humanity's problem: because of sin, everyone is separated from God (Isaiah 59:2).

People have tried to overcome this separation in many ways: by doing good, by practicing religion, by creating their own ideas of salvation, or by attempting to live a good moral life. However, none of these things is enough to cross the barrier of separation between God and humanity, because God is holy and human beings are sinful (Isaiah 64:6; Philippians 3:7). Regardless of how good you think you are, every human has lied, stolen, hated, or otherwise disobeyed God's perfect will.

This spiritual separation has become the condition of mankind, and because of this all humanity is condemned: *He who believes in Him is not judged; he who does not believe has been judged already, because he has not believed in the name of the only begotten Son of God* (John 3:18).

## God's Love and Plan

Jesus Christ said:

> *For God so loved the world, that He gave His only begotten Son, that whoever believes in Him shall not perish, but have eternal life* (John 3:16).
>
> *...I came that they may have life, and have it abundantly* (John 10:10).
>
> *He who believes in the Son has eternal life; but he who does not obey the Son will not see life, but the wrath of God abides on him* (John 3:36).
>
> *...I am the way, and the truth, and the life; no one comes to the Father but through Me* (John 14:6).

God's holiness makes it impossible for Him to have a loving relationship with sinful people (Habakkuk 1:13). His justice demands that every sinner be judged and condemned to an eternal separation from God. Because of this, all people have become enemies of God. Although God has every right to condemn every person, because of His love He provided a solution through His Son, Jesus Christ. God sent Jesus, who is truly God and truly man, to bear the sins of the whole world on the cross (1 John 2:2). Jesus' death was the only acceptable sacrifice for sin: *And there is salvation in no one else; for there is no other name under heaven that has been given among men by which we must be saved* (Acts 4:12).

Through Jesus' death for us on the cross, He establishes a loving relationship that unites us with the Father. Because of this sacrifice, every person who is born again can have true fellowship with God both now and forever.

## Jesus Christ Is Alive Today

After Jesus Christ died on the cross at Calvary, where He received the punishment that we deserved, the Bible says that He was buried in a tomb. But He did not remain there: Christ rose from the dead! For all those who believe in Jesus Christ, His resurrection is a guarantee that they will also be resurrected to eternal life in the presence of God forever. This is very good news! *Christ died for our sins...was buried, and...He was raised on the third day according to the Scriptures* (1 Corinthians 15:3-4).

## How to Receive God's Love and Plan

In His mercy, God has determined that salvation is free. To receive it, agree with and believe these four things:
1. Acknowledge the problem: separation from God because of sin (Romans 3:10-12).
2. Admit to being a sinner, and that you need salvation (Ephesians 2:3).
3. Repent by turning from your sins, and put your faith in Christ, who paid the penalty for the forgiveness of your sins (Acts 2:38).
4. Commit yourself to Jesus Christ as your Savior and Lord (2 Peter 3:18).

The Bible says:

> *that if you confess with your mouth Jesus as Lord, and believe in your heart that God raised Him from the dead, you will be saved* (Romans 10:9).
> *for "Whoever will call on the name of the Lord will be saved"* (Romans 10:13).

## A Prayer for Salvation

Lord Jesus, I know that I have sinned against You and that I do not live according to Your plan; therefore, I plead with You to forgive me of my sins. I believe that You love me and died for me, and in doing so, You paid the debt for my sins. I repent of my sin and want to live every day with You and for You. Please come into my life and be my Savior. Help me to follow You and to obey You as Lord. I love you, thank you for loving me and redeeming me.

## Living As a New Creation in Christ

When Jesus makes you born again, several things take place: your sins are forgiven (Colossians 2:13), you become a child of God (John 1:12), and you receive eternal life (John 3:16).

You may feel strong emotions, but don't put your confidence in the way you felt when you prayed to Christ because feelings can change day to day. Daily put your complete confidence for salvation in what Jesus did for us on the cross (1 John 4:10).

You are not saved by a one-time confession, but a lifetime of devotion to Christ as your Lord and Savior (1 Corinthians 15:2). It is important to have daily fellowship with God through prayer and reading the Bible. Also, have fellowship with other Christians, especially the local church, so that you can receive support and Biblical wisdom (Hebrews 10:25).

## This presentation is courtesy of Three Sixteen Publishing